Perspectives on Palliative and End-of-Life Care

Individuals and families face challenges at the end of life that can vary significantly depending on social and cultural contexts, yet more than ever is now known about the needs that cut across the great diversity of experiences in the face of dying and death. A number of behavioural interventions and clinical approaches to addressing these needs have been developed and are available to help providers care for clients and assist them in achieving their goals. *Perspectives on Palliative and End-of-Life Care: Disease, Social and Cultural Context* explores how these interventions can be used to address a range of issues across social and cultural contexts for those in need of end-of-life care.

With perspectives from experienced clinicians, providers and caregivers from around the world, the book offers a strong foundation in contemporary evidence-based practice alongside seasoned practice insights from the field and explores interventions for people as diverse as HIV caregivers in Africa and individuals dying with dementia. In addition, readers will learn about the process of caring for individuals with chronic illnesses, including severe mental illness; weigh the impact of policy regulations on the availability of and access to palliative care and interventions; and be able to compare the different issues experienced by family caregivers and formal caregivers.

As the companion volume to *Perspectives on Behavioural Interventions in Palliative and End-of-Life Care*, this book will be of interest to a wide variety of individuals, such as academics, researchers and postgraduates in the fields of mental health, medicine, psychology and social work. It will also be essential reading for healthcare providers and trainees from psychosocial and palliative medicine, social work and nursing.

Rebecca S. Allen is Professor of Psychology at the Alabama Research Institute on Aging and the Department of Psychology, University of Alabama, USA.

Brian D. Carpenter is Professor of Psychological & Brain Sciences, Washington University, St. Louis, USA.

Morgan K. Eichorst is a clinical psychologist working within the Veterans Affairs Medical Center, USA.

Aging and Mental Health Research
Series Editor: Martin Orrell

In the 21st century, the world's aging population is growing more rapidly than ever before. This is driving the international research agenda to help older people live better for longer and to find the causes and cures for chronic diseases such as dementia. This series provides a forum for the rapidly expanding field by investigating the relationship between the aging process and mental health. It compares and contrasts scientific and service developments across a range of settings, including the mental changes associated with normal and abnormal or pathological aging, as well as the psychological and psychiatric problems of the aging population. The series encourages an integrated approach between biopsychosocial models and etiological factors to promote better strategies, therapies and services for older people. Creating a strong alliance between the theoretical, experimental and applied sciences, the series provides an original and dynamic focus, integrating the normal and abnormal aspects of mental health in aging so that theoretical issues can be set in the context of important new practical developments in this field.

In this series

Cognitive Stimulation Therapy for Dementia
History, Evolution and Internationalism
Edited by Lauren A. Yates, Jen Yates, Martin Orrell, Aimee Spector, and Bob Woods

Perspectives on Behavioural Interventions in Palliative and End-of-Life Care
Edited by Rebecca S. Allen, Brian D. Carpenter and Morgan K. Eichorst

Perspectives on Palliative and End-of-Life Care
Disease, Social and Cultural Context
Edited by Rebecca S. Allen, Brian D. Carpenter and Morgan K. Eichorst

For more information about the series, please visit www.routledge.com/Aging-and-Mental-Health-Research/book-series/AMHR

Perspectives on Palliative and End-of-Life Care

Disease, Social and Cultural Context

Edited by Rebecca S. Allen, Brian D. Carpenter and Morgan K. Eichorst

LONDON AND NEW YORK

First published 2018
by Routledge
2 Park Square, Milton Park, Abingdon, Oxon OX14 4RN

and by Routledge
711 Third Avenue, New York, NY 10017

Routledge is an imprint of the Taylor & Francis Group, an informa business

© 2018 selection and editorial matter, Rebecca S. Allen, Brian D. Carpenter and Morgan K. Eichorst; individual chapters, the contributors

The right of Rebecca S. Allen, Brian D. Carpenter and Morgan K. Eichorst to be identified as the authors of the editorial material, and of the authors for their individual chapters, has been asserted in accordance with sections 77 and 78 of the Copyright, Designs and Patents Act 1988.

All rights reserved. No part of this book may be reprinted or reproduced or utilised in any form or by any electronic, mechanical, or other means, now known or hereafter invented, including photocopying and recording, or in any information storage or retrieval system, without permission in writing from the publishers.

Trademark notice: Product or corporate names may be trademarks or registered trademarks, and are used only for identification and explanation without intent to infringe.

British Library Cataloguing-in-Publication Data
A catalogue record for this book is available from the British Library

Library of Congress Cataloging-in-Publication Data
Names: Allen, Rebecca S., editor.
Title: Perspectives on palliative and end-of-life care : disease,
    social and cultural context / edited by Rebecca S. Allen, Brian D.
    Carpenter and Morgan K. Eichorst.
Description: Milton Park, Abingdon, Oxon ; New York, NY :
    Routledge, 2018. | Series: Aging and mental health research |
    Includes bibliographical references and index.
Identifiers: LCCN 2018004505 (print) | LCCN 2018009086
    (ebook) | ISBN 9780429489259 (E-book) | ISBN
    9781138593817 (hbk : alk. paper) | ISBN 9780429489259 (ebk)
Subjects: LCSH: Palliative treatment—Psychological aspects. |
    Terminally ill—Psychology. | Terminal care—Social aspects. |
    Terminally ill—Family relationships. | Terminal care—Moral and
    ethical aspects.
Classification: LCC R726.8 (ebook) | LCC R726.8 .P472 2018
    (print) | DDC 616.02/9—dc23
LC record available at https://lccn.loc.gov/2018004505

ISBN: 978-1-138-59381-7 (hbk)
ISBN: 978-0-429-48925-9 (ebk)

Typeset in Bembo
by Apex CoVantage, LLC

Contents

List of contributors	vii

1   The international context of behavioural palliative and end-of-life care revisited   1
REBECCA S. ALLEN, BRIAN D. CARPENTER, AND MORGAN K. EICHORST

SECTION I
Specific populations and palliative and EOL care   5

2   Living and dying well with HIV/AIDS   7
CHRISTINA P. PARKER, ELLEN L. CSIKAI, AND PAMELA PAYNE FOSTER

3   Serious mental illness and palliative care   32
JULIA KASL-GODLEY AND KIMBERLY E. HIROTO

4   Person-centred end-of-life care for individuals living with dementia in the United Kingdom   58
JANE CHATTERJEE AND MURNA DOWNS

SECTION 2
Social and cultural contexts, including ethics, bereavement, and policy issues   89

5   Ethical issues in palliative and end-of-life care   91
ANNE HALLI-TIERNEY, AMY ALBRIGHT, DEANNA DRAGAN, MEGAN LIPPE, AND REBECCA S. ALLEN

6   Diversity in family bereavement   119
LEE H. MATTHEWS, JANET R. MATTHEWS, SHIVA AKULA, LAURA PHILLIPS, AND KEISHA D. CARDEN

vi Contents

**7 Policy and practice on psychosocial care in palliative
care programs**   **148**
MAI-BRITT GULDIN AND SHEILA PAYNE

8 Synthesis and the future of end-of-life care   **170**
BRIAN D. CARPENTER, MORGAN K. EICHORST, HILLARY R. DORMAN,
AND REBECCA S. ALLEN

Index   185

Contributors

Shiva Akula (MD, MPH) is President of the non-profit Akula Foundation. He is also President, Canon Hospice, which has programs (both home care and inpatient care) in several locations in Louisiana, as well as Mississippi, USA. He oversees various clinical interventions regarding end-of-life care. For the past two decades, he has been involved in various community bereavement and grief related projects and continuing education workshops. These include a variety of Akula Foundation free activities to the community, such as grief groups in multiple locations in Louisiana, Mississippi and North Carolina; reminiscence groups at local nursing homes and senior centers; in-home outreach programs for those chronically ill; weekend bereavement camps for children ages 7–12; a weekly radio health hour program; and continuing education programs for medical students, physicians, nurses and social workers.

Amy Albright (MSc) is a doctoral student in the Clinical Geropsychology program at the University of Alabama. Her research focuses on health literacy and the end of life, and she has a particular interest in factors that influence seeking medical assistance in dying. This includes both patient and provider attitudes towards physician–assisted death, as well as health and palliative care literacy.

Rebecca S. Allen (Ph.D., ABPP) is Professor of Psychology at the Alabama Research Institute on Aging and the Department of Psychology at the University of Alabama, USA. Her research and clinical interests are: 1) interventions to reduce the stress of individuals, family, and professional caregivers within the context of advanced chronic or terminal illness; 2) the cultural dynamics (race/ethnicity; rural/urban) of healthcare decision making; and 3) clinical training issues, particularly ethics, LGBTQ+ issues, and acceptance and commitment therapy. She has published on translation of end-of-life/dignity interventions, diversity in advance care planning, clinical training, behavioral interventions in long-term care, and mental health among aging prisoners. Dr. Allen is a member of the American Board of Geropsychology, a member of the APA Working Group on End-of-Life Issues and Care, a viii Contributors

Fellow of the Gerontological Society of America and the APA, and is Editor for the Americas of *Aging and Mental Health*.

Keisha D. Carden (MA) is a fourth-year graduate student in Clinical Geropsychology at the University of Alabama, USA, working under the mentorship of Dr. Rebecca S. Allen. Her primary research interests include: family caregiving for older adults (with and without cognitive impairment/Alzheimer's disease and dementia); resilience; existential/death anxiety; intergenerational relationships; and outcomes and treatment mechanisms of non-pharmacological interventions that incorporate aspects of positive affect maximization, empathy, meaning in life optimization, and mindfulness.

Brian D. Carpenter (Ph.D.) is Professor of Psychological & Brain Sciences, Washington University, St. Louis, USA. His research, clinical, and teaching interests focus on family relationships later in life, particularly at the end of life, with an emphasis on effective collaboration and communication among patients, their care partners, and healthcare providers.

Jane Chatterjee (RN) is a UK Registered Nurse with a BSc in Cancer and Palliative Care and MSc in Dementia Care Training from the University of Bradford. She is currently a Lecturer in Palliative Care at St. Gemma's University Teaching Hospice in Leeds, United Kingdom, and is a Visiting Lecturer to the University of Leeds. Having worked in clinical practice in both elderly care and palliative care, her specific area of interest is addressing the end-of-life care needs for people living with dementia.

Ellen L. Csikai (LCSW, MPH, Ph.D.) is Professor in the School of Social Work at the University of Alabama, USA. She has over 11 years of direct social work practice experience, a majority of which was in the hospital and hospice settings. Areas of teaching are: social work practice in health care, end-of-life and palliative care, and gerontology. Dr. Csikai is the founding and ongoing editor of the *Journal of Social Work in End-of-Life and Palliative Care*, encompassing 15 years. Her ongoing research addresses communication and decision making about end-of-life and palliative care with the primary aim of improving communication and quality of life for those with serious and life-limiting illnesses as well as social work practice and education in the field.

Hillary R. Dorman (BA) is a second-year graduate student in Clinical Geropsychology at the University of Alabama, USA, working under the mentorship of Dr. Rebecca S. Allen. Hillary's primary research interest focuses upon the promotion of late life resilience utilizing a biopsychosocial and ecological framework. She is also interested in end-of-life care, underscoring the importance of choice, autonomy, and communication.

Murna Downs (Ph.D.) is Professor in Dementia Studies in the Centre for Applied Dementia Studies at the University of Bradford, United Kingdom, a centre of excellence in research, education, training and consultancy in dementia care. She has published on a range of topics from early diagnosis through end-of-life care, most recently on person-centred care in the community. Murna's current research focuses on improving transitions in dementia care, emphasising the importance of attending to the perspective of people living with dementia and their families; and developing and testing ways to improve health and social care outcomes for home care residents. She co-directs the University's Alzheimer's Society-funded Doctoral Training Centre on dementia care and services research, 'Improving transitions in dementia care'. She is co-editor of the highly commended textbook *Excellence in Dementia Care: Research into Practice* and is series editor of the Jessica Kingsley Good Practice Guides on Dementia Care. Murna is on the editorial board of several journals, a member of the Dementia Expert Advisory Group for Health Education England, the National Institute for Health Research Portfolio Development Group for Dementia and Neurodegenerative Diseases and the Research Strategy Council of the Alzheimer's Society. She is an ambassador for the Alzheimer's Society, social care adviser to Alzheimer Europe and a Fellow of the Gerontological Society of America.

Deanna Dragan (BA) is a third-year graduate student in Clinical Geropsychology at the University of Alabama, USA, working under the mentorship of Dr. Rebecca S. Allen and Dr. Martha R. Crowther. Her primary research interests include religiousness and spirituality as coping strategies; family caregiving for older adults; and clinical treatment mechanisms related to the use of mindfulness.

Morgan K. Eichorst (Ph.D.) is a clinical psychologist working within the Veterans Affairs Medical Center, USA.

Julia Kasl-Godley (Ph.D.) is a clinical psychologist for CHE Psychological Services and adjunct faculty at the Wright Institute, California, USA. Prior to her current position she served for 16 years as a staff psychologist at the VA Palo Alto Hospice and Palliative Care inpatient unit and palliative care consult service and as a faculty member of the Stanford/VA Palliative Care Interprofessional fellowship program. Dr. Kasl-Godley is a member of the American Psychological Association's Working Group on End-of-Life Issues and Care and the VA National Hospice and Palliative Care Employee Education System Planning Committee. She has served as a faculty member and trainer for the Education in Palliative and End-of-Life Care (EPEC) for Veterans project and the Advocating for Clinical Excellence—Transdisciplinary Palliative Care Education (ACE) project as well as working on a NIMH-funded Internet-based education project on end-of-life issues for mental health professionals. Her areas of clinical and research interest include aging and mental illness in advanced serious illness and end of life; palliative care teams; and roles and training of psychologists in palliative care and hospice.

Mai-Britt Guldin (Ph.D.) is a postdoctoral researcher at Aarhus University and clinical psychology specialist, Palliative Care Team, Aarhus University Hospital, Denmark.

x Contributors

Anne Halli-Tierney (MD) is Assistant Professor of Medicine, Alabama Research Institute on Aging and Department of Family and Internal Medicine, University of Alabama, Tuscaloosa, USA.

Kimberly E. Hiroto (Ph.D.) is a Clinical Geropsychologist in the Hospice and Palliative Care Program at the VA Palo Alto Health Care System, USA. She remains involved in the geropsychology community through activities at local and national levels, including working on various task forces and committees within the American Psychological Association. Her interests include palliative and end-of-life care, training in clinical geropsychology and multicultural sensitivity with a focus on social justice.

Megan Lippe (Ph.D., MSN, RN) is a Registered Nurse who is currently an Assistant Professor and Simulation Specialist at the Capstone College of Nursing at the University of Alabama, USA. Her area of research focuses on palliative and end-of-life care education, interprofessional education, simulation, and social justice. She is a core investigator on the End of Life Nursing Education Consortium (ELNEC) undergraduate research team.

Janet R. Matthews (Ph.D., ABPP, ABAP) is a licensed and Board Certified Clinical Psychologist. She is Professor Emerita, Loyola University New Orleans, USA. She is currently Associate Editor for the journal *Professional Psychology: Research & Practice*. She is on the Advisory Committee for the Chicago School of Professional Psychology at Xavier University New Orleans and on the Advisory Board of the Akula Foundation. She has served on the Board of Directors of the American Psychological Association, on the Board of Directors of the American Board of Assessment Psychology, and on the Louisiana State Board of Examiners of Psychologists. She was named 2011 Distinguished Psychologist of the Year by the Louisiana Psychological Association. She is co-editor of four books, and co-author of a book on clinical psychology. She is President and co-owner of a private practice, Psychological Resources, PC, with her husband, Dr. Lee H. Matthews.

Lee H. Matthews (Ph.D., ABPP, ABAP) is a Consulting Psychologist for the Akula Foundation, New Orleans, USA. He is a licensed neuropsychologist. He is Board Certified in Clinical Psychology and in Assessment Psychology. He has been involved with the Foundation for 10 years. He previously served as Director, Grief Resource Center, a program founded following Hurricanes Katrina and Rita in 2006 to provide outpatient services for the community and professional education on clinical treatment for depression, anxiety disorder, PTSD and other emotional difficulties. He has served as Chair, Louisiana State Board of Examiners of Psychologists. He was named 2014 Distinguished Psychologist of the Year by the Louisiana Psychological Association. Since 2000 he has co-authored six book chapters on graduate training, undergraduate training and psychotherapy; and six journal articles on personality assessment and licensing, neuropsychology, professional life after a natural disaster, and adolescence psychology. He is co-owner of a private practice, Psychological Resources, PC, with his wife, Dr. Janet R. Matthews. He is on Clinical Faculty at two university medical centers, and consultant to five area hospitals or treatment centers.

Christina P. Parker (MA) is a fourth-year graduate student in the Clinical Geropsychology doctoral program at the University of Alabama, USA, under the mentorship of Drs. Forrest Scogin and Martha R. Crowther. Her research and clinical work explore the intersection of older adults' physical and psychological health, focusing on the adjustment to and behavioral management of chronic health conditions (e.g., HIV, metabolic syndrome, osteoarthritis).

Sheila Payne (Ph.D.) is Emeritus Professor, International Observatory on End-of-Life Care, Division of Health Research, Faculty of Health and Medicine, Furness College, Lancaster University, United Kingdom.

Pamela Payne Foster (MD, MPH) is a Preventive Medicine/Public Health physician who currently is an Associate Professor in the Department of Community Medicine and Population Health and Deputy Director, Institute for Rural Health Research at the University of Alabama School of Medicine, Tuscaloosa campus, USA. Her overall research area is Rural Health disparities, including academic/community partnerships. Her specific research area is in HIV/AIDS-related stigma in faith-based settings in the rural Deep South of the USA.

Laura Phillips (MSW, LCSW) is a reminiscence group coordinator at a private practice, New Orleans, USA.

Chapter 1

The international context of behavioural palliative and end-of-life care revisited

Rebecca S. Allen, Brian D. Carpenter, and Morgan K. Eichorst

As described in our first book, *Perspectives on Behavioural Interventions in Palliative and End-of-Life Care*, palliative care is defined by the World Health Organization (WHO) as meeting the physical, psychosocial, and religious/spiritual needs of patients with life-limiting, terminal, or advanced chronic or progressive illness, as well as the needs of their families and caregivers, through an interprofessional team (World Health Organization, 2002). Similarly, the 2014 Institute of Medicine (IOM) report on Dying in America defined palliative care as "relief from pain and other symptoms, that supports quality of life, and that supports patients with serious advanced illness and their families". The IOM definition does not specifically mention psychosocial needs and largely omits reference to the potential role of behavioural health professionals.

As described in our first book, behavioural mental health and wellness interventions within the context of palliative and end-of-life care may be defined as directly addressing psychosocial issues that arise and may reflect conflicts of cognition, emotion, and communication both within the individual and within the interpersonal and environmental care context. This chapter briefly revisits the history of hospice and the palliative care movement and the theoretical models relevant to behavioural intervention delivery covered in our first book. Finally, this introductory chapter ends with an overview of content within this book.

History of the hospice and the palliative care movement in brief

The hospice movement is based on a holistic view of human nature and the fundamental idea that not only physical but also psychological, social, spiritual, and existential suffering may impede a satisfactory quality of life for the dying individual and his/her family. The modern hospice concept was developed by Cicely Saunders (Clark, 1998, 1999). In 1963, prior to the establishment of the first hospice, Saunders traveled to the United States to discuss her ideas about hospice care and soon encountered Florence Wald who later aided in the founding of the first United States hospice. Around this same time in the U.S.,

Elisabeth Kübler-Ross published *On Death and Dying* (1969), with interviews of dying patients. Thus, Saunders, Kübler-Ross, and Wald contributed to the development of the modern hospice movement in the United States, Canada, and Europe. The hospice movement spread apace in Westernized cultures (e.g., Australia) but then lagged behind in other countries and cultures (e.g., Asia, Africa) (Milicevic, 2002; Siebold, 1992).

During the 21st century, the term palliative care has emerged as a distinct, complementary model of care in comparison with hospice (Kelly & Morrison, 2015). Palliative care encompasses all phases of advanced chronic illness and may be initiated at the time of diagnosis and provided concurrently with other disease-related or curative treatments. This book emphasizes the context of palliative care internationally with consideration of specific disease contexts including HIV (Chapter 2), serious mental illness (Chapter 3), and dementia (Chapter 4). Importantly, ethical considerations (Chapter 5) and policy and reimbursement issues (Chapter 7) are considered using an international lens.

Unfortunately, direct attention to mental and behavioural health within palliative and hospice care systems has lagged behind its recognition and alleviation of physical, and perhaps even spiritual, symptoms. Kasl-Godley and colleagues (Kasl-Godley, King, & Quill, 2014) describe the work of psychologists practicing in primary care settings wherein palliative care may be provided. These authors provide case illustration to enrich their discussion of needed competencies for work in palliative care. Psychologists may bring unique theoretical knowledge, expertise in program evaluation, and other research skills into intervention design and delivery across wide-ranging disease and treatment contexts. Foundational knowledge in the biopsychosocial model, as well as developmental and stress and coping theories, may guide treatment and facilitate the functioning of and communication within interprofessional teams. These models and theories are described in our first book and will only briefly be reviewed here.

The biopsychosocial-spiritual model and lifespan stress and coping theories revisited

The cornerstone of this model is the premise that individuals are innately spiritual, as many individuals search for transcendent meaning, perhaps particularly near the end of life. Sulmasy (2002) elaborates upon Engel's (1977) original biopsychosocial model by adding spirituality and proposes assessing four domains as necessary in the measurement of healing, including religiosity, spiritual/religious coping, spiritual well-being, and spiritual need. Hence, in addition to addressing biological needs for the relief of suffering in palliative and end-of-life care, psychosocial and spiritual needs require direct attention and possible intervention for healing. As suggested by Sulmasy's expansion of the biopsychosocial model, many interventions targeting behavioural and mental health and wellness near the end of life incorporate elements of meaning-seeking or spirituality into their treatment approach.

Lifespan development theories, including socioemotional selectivity theory (Carstensen, Fung, & Charles, 2003; Carstensen, Isaacowitz, & Charles, 1999) and the strength and vulnerability integration model (Charles, 2010), posit that a foreshortened perspective on time left to live shifts an individual's motivation toward regulating emotions and engaging in meaningful activities. Stress and coping theories also have considered the importance of meaning-making and suggested how these activities sustain the coping process (Folkman, 1997; Lazarus & Folkman, 1984). Clearly, individuals of different ages or developmental "stages" may approach the end of their lives with differing levels of acceptance and proclivities for positive or negative emotional reactions. Thus, behavioural interventions often focus on individuals' development by considering lifetime accomplishments and challenges, relationships, and values.

Scope of this book: disease, social and cultural contexts

The overarching goal of these texts is to offer accessible resources for scientists, practitioners, and trainees with relevant information on the context of behavioural and psychosocial mental health and wellness interventions in palliative and end-of-life care. Hence, the first section of this book describes behavioural interventions within specific disease contexts, including living and dying globally with HIV/AIDS (Chapter 2), individuals with serious mental illness (Chapter 3), and individuals with dementia (Chapter 4). The second section of this book focuses on the social and cultural contexts of behavioural interventions in palliative and end-of-life care. Ethical considerations are reviewed in Chapter 5. Chapter 6 describes the immense variation in bereavement practices across cultures. Finally, policy issues including reimbursement models are covered in Chapter 7.

Across the two books, the editors recruited 11 writing groups of authors who were asked to include in their work certain material in every chapter. Thus, each chapter includes: 1) a review of behavioural interventions, 2) an evaluation of the strength of the evidence base of intervention and topic-based research, 3) identification of gaps within the knowledge base, 4) coverage of cultural and diversity issues, 5) consideration of ethical issues, 6) practice implications, and 7) at least one case example with questions illustrating salient issues. Of necessity, chapter content and emphasis varies by topic in each book. In every chapter, an attempt has been made to address palliative and end-of-life care globally, but each chapter is written by an authorship team from a specific national or regional perspective. While authors are primarily from the United States, Europe, and Canada, perspectives from Africa and Australia are included in certain chapters.

The global growth in palliative care necessitates a renewed focus on behavioural and psychosocial issues. Definitions of palliative care provided by WHO and the IOM within the United States have not traditionally emphasized the potential role of psychologists and other behavioural healthcare providers in addressing these issues in clinical and scientific realms. Our hope is that these books will provide a foundation for collaborative international and interprofessional work by providing state-of-science information on behavioural interventions addressing mental health and wellness in palliative and end-of-life care.

References

Carstensen, L. L., Fung, H. H., & Charles, S. T. (2003). Socioemotional selectivity theory and the regulation of emotions in the second half of life. *Motivation and Emotion, 27*(2), 103–123.

Carstensen, L. L., Isaacowitz, D. M., & Charles, S. T. (1999). Taking time seriously: A theory of socioemotional selectivity theory. *American Psychologist, 54*(3), 165–181.

Charles, S. T. (2010). Strength and vulnerability integration: A model of emotional well-being across adulthood. *Psychological Bulletin, 136*(3), 1068–1091.

Clark, D. (1998). Originating a movement: Cicely Saunders and the development of St. Christopher's hospice, 1957–1967. *Mortality, 3*, 43–63.

Clark, D. (1999). "Total pain", disciplinary power and the body in the work of Cicely Saunders, 1958–1967. *Social Science & Medicine, 49*, 727–736.

Engel, G. L. (1977). The need for a new medical model: A challenge for biomedicine. *Science, 196*(4286), 129–136.

Folkman, S. (1997). Positive psychological states and coping with severe stress. *Social Sciences and Medicine, 45*, 1207–1221.

Institute of Medicine. (2014). *Dying in America: Improving quality and honoring preferences near the end of life*. Washington, DC: The National Academies Press.

Kasl-Godley, J. E., King, D. A., & Quill, T. A. (2014). Opportunities for psycholoists in palliative care: Working with patients and families across the disease continuum. *American Psychologist, 69*(4), 364–376.

Kelly, A. S., & Morrison, R. S. (2015). Palliative care for the seriously ill. *New England Journal of Medicine, 373*(8), 747–755.

Kübler-Ross, E. (1969). *On death and dying*. New York: Scribner.

Lazarus, R. S., & Folkman, S., (1984). *Stress, appraisal, and coping*. New York: Springer.

Milicevic, N. (2002). The hospice movement: History and current worldwide situation. *Archives of Oncology, 10*, 29–32.

Siebold, C. (1992). *The hospice movement: Easing death's pains*. New York: Maxwell Macmillan International.

Sulmasy, D. P. (2002). A biopsychosocial-spiritual model for the care of patients at the end of life. *The Gerontologist, 42*(Spec. no. III), 24–33.

World Health Organization. (2002). *The world health report 2002: Reducing risks, promoting healthy life*. World Health Organization. Retrieved from www.barnesandnoble.com/w/world-health-report-2002-world-health-organization/1119231978?ean=9789241562072

Section 1

Specific populations and palliative and EOL care

Chapter 2

Living and dying well with HIV/AIDS

Christina P. Parker, Ellen L. Csikai, and Pamela Payne Foster

Chapter introduction

Despite the advent and accessibility of highly active antiretroviral therapies (HAARTs), HIV disease still presents numerous palliative care challenges and opportunities related to aging, multimorbidity, managing psychological symptoms, pain, and medication adherence. This chapter presents an overview of the behavioral (psychological, social, and spiritual) interventions related to palliative and hospice care for individuals diagnosed with human immunodeficiency virus (HIV). Additionally, we describe and evaluate the state of palliative and hospice care for people with HIV/AIDS diagnoses, as well as identify emerging cultural, diversity, and ethical issues in treatment provision. Authors also discuss implications for future research and treatment both from a "Deep South" (U.S.) as well as global perspective.

Overview of HIV/AIDS and palliative care

HIV/AIDS

Few can dispute that, early in the epidemic, receiving an HIV/AIDS diagnosis was terminal and required many practitioners to quickly become experts in palliative care. Patients dying with AIDS-related illness required the interdisciplinary approach of palliative care to assuage the pain and other (incurable) symptoms experienced during the dying process, including those related to primitive, toxic antiretroviral medications (e.g., AZT) of the early treatment era. Because of poor prognoses – combined with limited knowledge about how to treat and cure HIV/AIDS – palliative care was necessary.

Since the start of the epidemic, much has changed and functional cures exist (Justice & Falutz, 2014; Emlet & Hughes, 2016). Today, AIDS-related deaths account for less than one-half of all deaths in patients with HIV disease (Merlin, Tucker, Saag, & Selwyn, 2013). Advances in therapeutics have altered HIV from a terminal, fatal disease to one that can be managed successfully, like diabetes or arthritis (Emlet & Hughes, 2016). HIV does still claim lives, however. By

8 Christina P. Parker et al.

the end of 2015, an estimated 1.1 million people died of AIDS-related illnesses worldwide, and another 36.7 million globally lived with HIV (World Health Organization [WHO] HIV/AIDS Department, 2018). But deaths attributable to AIDS in the time of HAART have shifted from fate to an event that can be linked mostly to late diagnosis (Emlet & Hughes, 2016), failures in treatment adherence, or discontinuance in HIV primary care (Merlin et al., 2013). Deaths related to non-AIDS-defining malignancies (e.g., Hodgkin's lymphoma) or comorbidities are also significant.

The reason for this shift lies, paradoxically, in the effectiveness of HAARTs that have enabled many patients to achieve life expectancies commensurate with those of uninfected cohorts (Nightengale et al., 2014). Consequentially, we have observed a substantial and consistent growth in the number of adults over 50 living with HIV infection, particularly as incidence and long-term survival rates (prevalence) intersect (Emlet & Hughes, 2016). Additionally, in the United States alone, adults over 50 constitute 17% of new HIV infections and are estimated to account for one-half of all persons living with the disease (Emlet & Hughes, 2016). Globally, 13% of the adult population living with HIV is aged 50 or older (UNAIDS, 2013). While individuals living *in spite of* HIV reflects an undoubted triumph of modern medicine, one consequence is that comorbidities like cardiovascular, renal, and liver disease are complicating medical management with and enlarging the application of palliative care to those living with HIV (Emlet & Hughes, 2016; Merlin et al., 2013).

Palliative care

Palliative care describes the combination of measures designed to relieve suffering and improve quality of life for those facing problems associated with life-limiting, progressive, chronic illnesses such as HIV, cancer, or chronic obstructive pulmonary disease. According to the WHO (2015) definition, palliative care:

> improves the *quality of life* of patients and their families facing the problems associated with life-threatening illness through the *prevention and relief of suffering* by means of early identification and impeccable *assessment and treatment of pain and other problems: physical, psychosocial, and spiritual.*

The WHO's definition of palliative care has been adopted and applied in more than 115 countries globally and will be the standard definition assumed in this chapter.

As discussed, palliative care in the context of HIV/AIDS has evolved in tandem with treatment advances. However, for those living (and aging) with HIV/AIDS, issues such as stigma, access to HIV treatment, pain management, and family support present unique challenges and opportunities for the palliative care of those living with HIV/AIDS. Table 2.1 illustrates some of these.

Deciding whether to continue HAART as a palliative measure, for example, illustrates these disease-specific difficulties. Weighing the cost-to-benefit ratio

Living and dying well with HIV/AIDS 9

Table 2.1 Example HIV/AIDS palliative care interventions

General	• Holistic clinical or lay assessment of physical (e.g., neuropathy pain), behavioral (e.g., medication adherence), emotional (e.g., managing depressive symptoms), social, and spiritual needs of the HIV patient and his or her family • System of referrals linking HIV patients to services that can address continuum of HIV care needs and prevention, including to alternative therapies such as Tai Chi and acupuncture • Providing psychoeducation about nature of HIV and its treatment
Behavioral/physical	• Assessment, prevention, and treatment of HIV-related pain (e.g., neuropathy) • Assessment, prevention, and treatment of other behavioral features associated with HIV and its management, including increasing adherence to medication(s) and targeting substance abuse • Assessment and treatment of HAART side effects • Teaching self-care skills for managing HIV symptoms and medication side effects in the home as well as for recognizing danger signs • Attending to physical needs of HIV patients during end of life (e.g., comfort, moistening mouth)
Psychological/ emotional	• General counseling and supportive psychotherapy for HIV patients • Treatment of specific psychiatric problems, including major depression and anxiety, among PLWHA • Care of caregivers to PLWHA (lay and professional providers and family) through counseling or support groups • Bereavement support • Helping families manage future care planning
Social	• Targeting and managing HIV/AIDS related stigma (e.g., internalized, institutionalized) and discrimination • Provide support and guidance on legal issues, such as preparing wills • Provide assistance with financial and other material needs of HIV patients such as nutrition, housing, jobs, and education
Spiritual/religious	• Provide spiritual/religious counseling as appropriate • Facilitate life-review work • Funeral preparation and other life completing tasks

PLWHA = people living with HIV/AIDS.

over time, although complicated, often leads patients to stop these treatments because of their side effects or the burden of taking pills, especially as patients grow sicker. Moreover, HAART is expensive, and if HIV is the primary diagnosis for hospice admission, hospices often need to look for creative ways to pay for it. Additional barriers to providing excellent end-of-life care could include limited patient income and social capital, family support, or viable housing (Ludwig & Chittenden, 2008).

Evolving role of palliative care for HIV/AIDS in the era of HAARTs

History of highly active antiretroviral therapies (HAARTs)

A major factor in the development of HIV treatment and resulting long-term survival with it has been the advent of HAART, which refers to using customized combinations of different classes of physician-prescribed medications that act on different clinical targets, including viral load, virus strain, CD4+ cell count, and disease symptoms (Moore & Chaisson, 1999). HAART, when successful, decreases the patient's total burden of HIV, maintains function of the immune system, and prevents opportunistic infections that accelerate or invite the onset of progression to AIDS, thereby prolonging survival in people infected with HIV.

Distinct from early FDA approved antiretroviral therapies such as zidovudine (AZT) – which alone lacked the potency to prevent HIV replication and suppress the virus – HAART combines earlier drugs with newer classes of antiretrovirals, such as protease inhibitors, which rapidly reduce rates of AIDS, death, and hospitalization, AIDS-related cancers, HIV related cognitive decline, and otherwise improve health outcomes (Moore & Chaisson, 1999).

In an era of functional cures and largely accessible treatments for HIV, the temptation to dismiss the utility of palliative care is unjustified for several reasons. Clinical advances notwithstanding, individuals who are HIV positive continue to die at a higher rate than the uninfected (Harding et al., 2005). For example, treatment medications (i.e., HAARTs) are associated with significant toxicity, general pain, and painful side effects like peripheral neuropathy, and gastrointestinal problems. And as a result of survival prolongation, managing HIV often requires coordinated treatment for comorbidities such as end stage liver disease secondary to Hepatitis C (Merlin et al., 2013).

Pain management

Pain management represents an important consideration in palliative care for HIV. The combination of a maturing, "graying" epidemic with painful diseases such as peripheral neuropathy secondary to HAART contribute to a high burden of pain and other physical symptoms among HIV patients (Parker, Stein, & Jelsma, 2014). Point prevalence estimates, for example, appear to fall between a range of 54% to 83% (Parker et al., 2014). These data are relevant because pain appears to influence treatment retention, adherence, virologic suppression, and physical functioning in HIV-positive patients (Merlin et al., 2012). Pain management, particularly among aging patients presenting with painful HAART-associated diseases, typically requires combined pharmacological and behavioral intervention that fall under the jurisdiction of modern palliative care for the disease.

Challenges and opportunities facing HIV palliative care

Despite significant strides in increasing HAART access across the world, infrastructural barriers result in inconsistent access to treatment in many areas of the United States, such as the Deep South, and beyond, including parts of Asia and Africa. In Botswana, for example, where HAART access is universal, the annual mortality rate of PLWHA has decreased but has not fallen to expected levels (Bertozzi et al., 2006). And in the Deep South of the United States (Alabama, Mississippi, Louisiana, Georgia, North Carolina, South Carolina, Florida, Tennessee), issues related to socioeconomic disparities, religious culture, poverty, and stigma present barriers to treatment, thereby systematically limiting access to HIV treatment (Reif et al., 2015). Other factors, including low health and mental health literacy, co-occurring substance abuse, psychiatric illness, multimorbidity, and resistant disease represent additional barriers to HIV treatment and present appropriate targets for palliative care intervention. Palliative care, inherently holistic, addresses health promotion and HIV education (e.g., prevention, increased comfort, harm reduction, and treatment) to improve overall health and decrease transmission to others, fostering community linkages and referral relationships (WHO, 2010). It also uses interprofessional teams of physicians, nurses, clergy, social workers, pharmacists, psychologists, nutritionists, and substance use specialists to facilitate comprehensive, quality care.

Figure 2.1 illustrates and summarizes the challenges and opportunities facing HIV palliative care in the post-HAART era. Particular interventions addressing each of these appear later in this chapter.

As HIV comes to resemble other treatable but incurable chronic diseases, the definition and practice of palliative care contributing to quality of life of PLWHA will continue to evolve. "Old" paradigms of palliative care have broadened to consider focusing on symptom control in patients who may continue to live for an extended period, require active treatment for an HIV-related condition, and/or maintenance care for another comorbid condition simultaneously (Harding et al., 2005). This encompasses treatment provided from the time of diagnosis throughout the disease trajectory, including end-of-life care planning,

Biological	Psychological/Behavioral	Social
• Aging with HIV • Multimorbidity • Pain and physical symptoms • Medication toxicity and management of side effects	• Psychological symptoms and distress • Substance abuse • Medication adherence • Treatment adherence • Retention in primary care	• Stigma and discrimination • Global disparities in resource allocation and treatment access • Disease literacy

Figure 2.1 Summary of challenges and opportunities facing HIV palliative care in the post-HAART era

bereavement, and other family needs. In the post-HAART era, more integrated models providing comprehensive care for patients and families across the disease course must supplant false dichotomies of curative vs. palliative care (Selwyn & Forstein, 2003).

From a palliative care perspective, addressing HIV stigma is important because of its consistent and robust associations with negative health outcomes, including depression, poorer quality of life, and loneliness (Emlet & Hughes, 2016). The next section will address HIV stigma and its relation to palliative care more specifically.

HIV stigma

HIV stigma – that is, negative feelings toward persons, groups (Goffman, 1963), and communities with high rates of HIV infection (Herek, Capitanio, & Widaman, 2002) – continues to represent a major and well-documented social problem among those living with HIV (Emlet, 2007; Foster & Gaskins, 2009; Haile, Padilla, & Parker, 2011), particularly for older adults who face the potential of dual stigma based on HIV status and age (Emlet, 2007). This phenomenon, known as "layering," occurs when one experiences stigma not only from HIV, but also from the route of transmission (injection drug use, sex work) or personal characteristics (age, race, or gender). HIV stigma includes a complex array of intrapersonal and interpersonal experiences including enacted stigma (prejudice/discrimination), internalized stigma (the internal acceptance of negative attributes and beliefs about people living with HIV), and anticipated stigma (the anticipation of enacted stigma) (Earnshaw & Chaudoir, 2009).

HIV-related stigma especially pervades parts of the rural Deep South of the United States and can decrease an individual's willingness to undergo HIV testing, to disclose HIV status, or to access treatment (Gielen, O'Campo, Faden, & Eke, 1997; Stall et al. 1996). Although little is known about differences in stigma globally, particularly between sub-Saharan Africa (with its high rates of HIV infection and prevalence) and the United States, it has been theorized that the stigma is more pronounced in rural areas of the Deep South (Foster, 2007) because of lack of medical access, social conservatism, and infrastructural barriers. The effects of stigma magnify for PLWHA in rural areas particularly when there is a deficit of trained medical professionals. If available, points of care in rural areas often are geographically dispersed (Heckman, 2006). Effectively addressing HIV in rural African American communities requires decreasing stigma through increased awareness and providing accurate information about HIV. For example, one of the authors conducted a faith-based stigma intervention which successfully decreased stigma in rural AA congregational members in rural Alabama (Payne Foster, 2017).

Little literature addresses effective strategies to increase access to care in rural communities, illustrating an area requiring further study. We explore the role of stigma in accessing hospice and palliative care through case examples later in this chapter.

Behavioral interventions in palliative care for persons living with HIV/AIDS

Professionals providing palliative care to those considered vulnerable – such as people diagnosed with HIV and older adults – need to understand the particular issues relevant to these populations. Professionals working with vulnerable populations should familiarize themselves with the goals of palliative care and understand how this type of care may assist chronically and seriously ill people achieve maximum quality of life. Additionally, the importance of collaboration between medical and mental health professionals cannot be overstated. Further, the organizational structures in which palliative care services are provided should be continuously evaluated for responsiveness and effectiveness, particularly relative to quality of life of people receiving care. Healthcare policies must be flexible to accommodate all those who may be in need of palliative care services (Goeren, 2011).

Assessment of potential psychosocial interventions in the pre- and post-HAART eras (and beyond) is key to accessing the most effective means to achieve patients' treatment goals. HIV palliative social workers, for instance, provide education needed by patients and family caregivers (as well as to professionals) who may not understand the complex psychological and social issues inherent throughout the disease process. Education may focus on:

- overall wellness
- self-care
- caregiving
- stress management
- basics and myths about HIV
- functions of the immune system
- knowledge of HIV course of illness with and without HAART
- knowledge of comorbid conditions
- importance of adherence especially in light of changing therapies, health disparities, and challenges to continuity of care
- knowledge of palliative care, hospice, and the scope of these services
- AIDS phobia or stigma
- resources and supports pre- and post-disclosure to help with coping with the disease

Ongoing assessment is essential in the areas of patient and caregiver "total" pain, as influenced by psychosocial aspects and needs for counseling, legal assistance, mental health, and substance abuse referrals. In addition, regarding the issue of grief and bereavement, assessment related to multiple HIV-related illness and the deaths of others is essential. Education and counseling should be provided that relates to the attitudes and beliefs of the patient and their wider social network throughout the course of the disease progression. In the HAART era, additional considerations can be noted regarding assessment for potential interventions. Potential interventions after assessment of HIV patients for palliative care include: recovery into wellness, recovery into chronic illness, lifelong treatment adherence, fear of failure of HARRT (and without options for further treatment), emerging long-term survivor medical conditions previously not seen in the disease course, and recent sero-conversion and related reactions.

Psychosocial interventions are also very important in the course of treatment of HIV/AIDS, particularly during palliative care. These interventions are integral to maximizing quality of life of patients and families throughout the disease trajectory. To achieve that, advocacy is needed for the importance of mental health interventions for both patients and caregivers, and social workers must be seen as essential providers on the interprofessional team.

As a part of the tool kit of behavioral interventions, spiritual or faith-based approaches can maintain a sense of hope and provide additional support to the individual living with HIV and the family as well. Also, mental health professionals and pastoral counselors can provide support to medical clinicians who may worry that acknowledging the inevitability of death will cause patients to lose hope. Most patients, however, understand that they are getting sicker, and they expect clinicians to initiate discussions about death and dying (Johnston, Pfeifer, & McNutt, 1995; Lo, McLeod, & Saika, 1986; Selwyn & Arnold, 1998). It is important to recognize that patients can hope for many things other than the cure of their illness. For example, they can hope for good control of their symptoms so they can spend meaningful time with family and friends, heal troubled relationships, create a legacy, and say good-bye. As in other developmental stages throughout life, the process of dying can be a time of emotional and spiritual growth and provide an opportunity to deepen relationships and find greater meaning (Block, 2001). Many physicians do, however, feel comfortable in helping patients to refocus on more realistic medical goals, thereby reinstating hope into what may be perceived as a hopeless situation (Clayton, Butow, Arnold, & Tattersall, 2005; Pantilat,1999).

In HIV/AIDS palliative care, using interprofessional teams can address larger social, spiritual, and mental health needs of patients. That is, including a member of the faith, social services and mental health professions as a part of palliative care teams can address the wide variety of patient needs and concerns though the course of illness. Addressing spiritual, emotional, social, and existential concerns is best implemented through a team approach with professionals of different but complementary backgrounds. Further, members of the team can support one another in their own emotional reactions to caring for patients with serious illness. They can help serve as a buffer for each other in facing potential compassion fatigue as they repeatedly grieve the deaths and worsening of patients for whom they have provided care at a critical time in life (Block, 2001).

Although the role of the interprofessional team is particularly important in HIV care when medical interventions are available and working successfully to get a patient to an undetectable viral load, the role of the interprofessional team is equally important when the HIV patient is at the end of life. At this vulnerable time, HIV patients and family members/friends may perceive an abandonment by the medical team, especially as clinic visits become less frequent or stop altogether. It is important to reassure patients that choosing to terminate curative medical treatment and/or choosing palliative or hospice care does not signify "giving up" on providing quality care (Ludwig & Chittenden, 2008).

With palliative care, psychosocial support does not end with the death of the patient. The palliative care team can reach out to survivors and provide bereavement support or referrals for bereavement counseling. Writing letters or making phone calls to loved ones after a death can be incredibly meaningful at this time. In addition, family members or friends may have lingering questions that providers can address in these phone calls (Ludwig & Chittenden, 2008).

Comorbid conditions and therapeutic interventions in HIV palliative care

The literature has established that depression and its treatment are very important in palliative care (Ganzini, Goy, & Dobscha, 2008). In a nationally representative probability sample of 2,864 American adults participating in the HIV Care Services and Utilization Study, 12-month prevalence rates for major depression were estimated as 36% (Safren et al., 2012). Depression not only causes significant distress and functional impairment, but it can also interfere with HIV treatment and care. For example, depressed mood puts patients at a particular disadvantage through its associations with more rapid CD4 cell growth and faster HIV viral load increase (Safren et al., 2012), progression to AIDS, mortality, and most likely due to poor adherence to HAART treatment (Ganzini et al., 2008).

Given the association of depression to poor self-care and management with HIV, therapeutic interventions should focus on interrupting the cycle of depression with poor adherence. The most common and successful of these interventions is Cognitive Behavioral Therapy for Adherence and Depression (CBT-AD), based on traditional CBT approaches for the treatment of depression combined with intervention techniques applicable to persons with chronic illness in general. Designs that integrate adherence counseling with CBT for depression have demonstrated success in increasing adherence as well as reducing pain and depressive symptoms in HIV positive persons diagnosed with depression (Safren et al., 2012).

Notably, the integration of CBT-AD principles into the repertoire of interventions in palliative care settings continues to increase. Among patients with advanced cancer, for example, CBT interventions weaved into palliative care have been shown to reduce depressive symptoms and improve adaptive coping processes among symptomatic patients (Daniels, 2015). Again, this also highlights the importance of access to an interprofessional team (expected in the palliative care approach) that is composed of psychologists and social workers who are specifically trained to administer these interventions.

Second to depression, many PLWHA must manage issues related to substance abuse. For example, one in four people living with HIV/AIDS reports using alcohol or drugs to an extent requiring treatment (Substance Abuse and Mental Health Services Administration, 2017). A challenging aspect to effective palliative pain treatment seen in other chronic medical conditions is prescription and adherence to opioid medications to treat pain. Patients who have "recovered" from substance abuse often express concern about becoming "addicted" again, yet effective pain management may involve use of opioid analgesics within the context of palliative care. Thus, management of pain in palliative care may require specific skills in the clinician treating individuals with prior or current substance abuse and addiction.

Strengths and gaps in research

Research on the impact of chronic pain in patients with HIV and the approaches to its management in rural settings has been limited (Merlin et al., 2013). A secondary diagnoses, such as mental illness or substance abuse, can greatly affect key health behaviors such as medication adherence and retention in care and can be challenging not only for the patient, but for their families and providers. Research that tests and identifies best practices for palliative care management is limited and must be conducted to meet the needs of people living with HIV/ AIDS with various psychiatric disorders in the post-HAART period. Lastly, comorbidities with progressive, chronic diseases that are typified by gradual deterioration until death, such as Hepatitis C, end-stage renal disease, and liver failure, highlight the need to use hospice care at the end of the palliative care model when managing patients with these conditions. Best practices for these situations for PLWHA also need to be developed and tested.

Harding and colleagues (2005) reviewed 22 studies using meta-analysis and found that, although home palliative care and inpatient hospice care significantly improved HIV patient outcomes vis-a-vis pain and symptom control, anxiety, insight, and spiritual well-being, the current body of research appears to lack studies using quasi-experimental methods studying the effects of palliative care outcomes among PLWHAs. Studies that have attempted to standardize and evaluate measures of palliative care include a set of methodological limitations, including small sample sizes, attrition, selection bias in recruitment and gate-keeping (particularly among those with advanced disease), and lack of successful previous models of randomized clinical trials (RCTs) as a foundation for future work (Harding et al., 2005). Conclusions cannot be drawn regarding the comparative benefits of palliative care in studies without the necessary rigor in research design. Issues related to the most effective symptom management for HIV and its co-morbidities that may occur in the later stages of the disease (e.g., inadequate nutritional and dietary intake) are understudied. Since these symptoms may be most distressing to PLWA and their families, research must address this gap (Breitbart et al., 1998; Merlin et al., 2013; Wood, Whittet, & Bradbeer, 1997).

Although AIDS treatment is more accessible in developed countries, the lack of access to HAART in other places throughout the world may change the palliative and hospice needs of patients, especially in developing countries where disparities exist. For example, the need for palliative and hospice care may be even higher given the disparity in access to HAARTs. Best practices from developed countries could be beneficial globally, especially strategies that are efficient and low cost. Therefore, evidence-informed interventions that address the unique factors related to culture and other diverse characteristics of individuals and their families would be ideal. Complementary integrative medicine (such as the use of traditional healers) and strategies for acceptance of these among various cultures are anecdotally reported but confirming research is needed (Sepulveda, Marlin, Yoshida, & Ullrich, 2002; Harding et al., 2005). Additionally, some individuals may not choose palliative or hospice care, and how their needs for care may be met needs to be identified as well.

Another gap in research has to do with accurate descriptions of the exact need for HIV/AIDS hospice/palliative care within the larger hospice/palliative care arena. For example, provider data from a hospice highlighted staff concern that the low number of HIV/AIDS referrals prevented them from maintaining skills needed specifically in the clinical and behavioral care of HIV patients. The lack of consistent exposure to HIV/AIDS patients might limit quality care and result in substandard care given to these patients (Harding et al., 2005).

Cultural and diversity issues in treatment delivery

The Palliative Care Strategy for HIV and other diseases (Family Health International, 2009) identifies six interlinked concepts that are central to successful palliative care service delivery. According to the dictates of this strategy, palliative care should be:

1 Provided through a continuum of care;
2 Integrated into existing service hubs;
3 Developed to deliver coordinated services;
4 Offer a comprehensive package of care that includes HAART; opportunistic infection (OI) prevention, and treatment and prevention for positives;
5 Be family centered; and,
6 Tailored to the specific needs of different populations.

Implied in at least three of these – namely concepts three, five, and six – is consideration of diversity and culture in both the application and delivery of palliative care services – from the formation of interprofessional teams to sensitively targeting the unique needs of PLHWA and their families. The ensuing section

18 Christina P. Parker et al.

will briefly describe and explore cultural and diversity issues confronting palliative and hospice care for HIV disease.

Diversity issues

Cultivating diverse interprofessional teams in resource-limited settings

Palliative care for HIV is a necessarily holistic enterprise because of its physical, emotional, spiritual, and psychosocial features (WHO, 2015). One profession or individual cannot be expected to have the skills to make the necessary assessment, institute the necessary interventions, and provide ongoing monitoring. Accordingly, the tendency to manage HIV from a purely biomedical perspective represents an obsolete paradigm at odds with the principles and demands of modern palliative care for the disease.

To best address the catalogue of holistic and diverse care needs of PLHWA, *interprofessional teams* are critical. Teams may be composed of members from a single facility of both clinic and community members, but the interprofessional diversity of those teams is typically predicated on the resources and settings in which those teams are embedded. In resource-limited settings, such as in developing regions of Africa, India, or in the Deep South of the United States, teams may be small – simply including a doctor, nurse, or a pharmacist. In others, they are more comprehensive and can include the aforementioned care agents plus social workers, nutritionists, physiotherapists, community home-based caregivers, psychologists, and spiritual counselors (Family Health International, 2009). Disparities in the diversity of interprofessional teams are notable because, when palliative care is interdisciplinary, quality of life outcomes are typically improved for families and patients, and the burden on available health services is lessened.

The Integrated Community-based Home Care model (ICHC), which recruits and trains professionally supervised community caregivers and volunteers to administer home-based palliative care, represents a promising avenue to addressing disparities in resource-poor communities facing high patient demand, underdeveloped care systems, and limited access to pharmacological treatments (Defilippi, 2005). However, more training, funding, and support are required to strengthen these programs and extend their reach (Ludwig & Chittenden, 2008). Additional challenges include the validation of alternative models for implementing effective and efficient palliative care programs in different cultural and socioeconomic climates (Sepulveda et al., 2002).

Tailoring care to needs of diverse and emerging populations

Effective palliative care services must also consider the diversity of the populations they serve, especially because needs of HIV positive drug users, sex workers, men who have sex with men, older adults, and migrants, for example, are likely to be heterogeneous (Family Health International, 2009). In areas where

PLWHA are predominantly drug users, for example, addiction and addiction treatment may be considered to promote better understanding of issues related to hypersensitivity to pain, pain management for injecting drug users on opioid substitution therapy, and fears related to further addiction.

Among some immigrant communities and cultures, the severity of HIV stigma may prevent patients from disclosing their HIV status, possibly leading to a reduced uptake of HIV-related palliative and hospice care services (Wood et al.,1997). Reassurance about confidentiality and the option of discrete services, in combination with cultural competence, are particularly important in cases such as these. Where issues of language and cross-cultural communication arise, palliative care services should consider using interpreters to administer accurate and culturally informed advice (Wood et al., 1997).

Clinical advances notwithstanding, growing evidence suggests that aging with HIV disease presents unique challenges (High et al., 2012). Seropositive older adults must confront complex physiological and psychosocial issues (High et al., 2012) related to increased morality (Centers for Disease Control and Prevention [CDC], 2013; Lohse et al., 2007), delayed or late diagnosis (CDC, 2013), as well as accelerated or accentuated aging (Pathai, Bajilan, Landay, & High, 2014) that younger cohorts typically do not. Stigma and ageism – related not only to the disease itself, but to aging with it – have been implicated in the fragility of seropositive older adults' informal social support networks and their relative isolation from them (Emlet, 2006; Fredriksen-Goldsen et al., 2011; Shippy, Cantor, & Brennan, 2004). Care providers must also recognize cohort differences in attitudes toward homosexuality and, therefore, the possibility that many older adults – particularly men who have sex with men – may not have disclosed their sexual orientation to their friends or family. Accordingly, it behooves palliative care teams to consider psychological services for the unique distress that may accompany aging with HIV disease and to recognize the possibility of heteronormative biases imposed upon older adults.

Cultural issues

Racial/ethnic differences in attitudes toward palliative and hospice care

African Americans (AAs) and other minorities appear to underuse palliative and hospice care, even when they have access to this care (Crawley et al., 2000). Compared to their non-Hispanic White (NHW) counterparts, who represent 83% of patients participating in hospice and palliative care, AAs represent only 8%. Explanations for the underuse of care services among AA appear tied to a catalogue of historical, social, cultural, economic, and religious reasons (Crawley et al., 2000). These racial/ethnic differences highlight the importance of honoring differences in cultural and familial preferences in selecting and using palliative and hospice care.

Other challenges and considerations

Finally, delivery of effective HIV palliative care relies on recognizing challenges in its delivery at levels of the disease, population, community and country. Table 2.2 summarizes some of these barriers and challenges associated with delivery of HIV/AIDS palliative care.

Ethical issues

There are four primary bioethical principles: autonomy, beneficience, nonmaleficence and justice. For healthcare providers, care should act toward the best interests of the patient and not cause harm. Especially in the care of PLWHA in palliative and hospice care, the ethical issues of autonomy and justice play an important role. For them, autonomy means that the patient has the right to choose the type of care desired. The right to refuse medical treatment also exists. Further care should be equitable and accessible to all regardless of race, gender, religion, or socioeconomic status.

Palliative and hospice care often presents ethical issues, but these may be even more pronounced in HIV/AIDS care, particularly in resource-limited settings such as in the rural Deep South of the United States and in sub-Saharan Africa, areas of significant health disparity. For example, in areas with extreme poverty, basic healthcare services are often scarce or unavailable; thus, palliative or hospice care often goes unprioritized. Additionally, pain medications generally prescribed in palliative care, such as opioid medications, may not be available. Many countries are using alternative models such as integrated community-based home care models to adapt to lack of resources. Further, these areas lack training opportunities for health professionals in the basic tenets of HIV infection (and varying risk factors for older adults) and palliative care.

Table 2.2 Challenges in delivery of HIV/AIDS palliative care

Domain	Associated barriers and challenges
Disease-specific	• Stigma of disease • Fear of contagion • Erratic, episodic disease • Multiple medical comorbidities
Population-specific	• Stigmatized lifestyles • Lifestyle-related treatment issues • Access to, and attitudes toward, medical services • Maintaining continuity of care via multidisciplinary teams
Community and country-specific	• Impoverished communities • Developing countries • Limitations in resources • Limitations in integration of public and private care services

Adapted from: http://hab.hrsa.gov/abouthab/special/palliativecasestudy.html

Elder's (1998) principles of lifespan development assume connections between individual lives and the historical and socioeconomic context in which these lives unfold. He conceptualized the life course as a sequence of socially defined events and roles that the individual enacts over time, tethered to the following core principles: 1) human agency, 2) historical time and place, 3) timing, and 4) linked lives. It assumes that, to a large extent, people follow normative, standard, gendered patterns (social pathways) regarding the proper behavior at a particular age and the proper sequence of transitions (e.g., education, employment, marriage, parenthood). Cultural preferences, ethical prescriptions, and institutionalized policies shape these gender and age-specific pathways; thus, deviations therefrom can invite social and cultural sanctions.

Aging with HIV or acquiring it in later life conforms well to this idea. For example, health professionals frequently fail to identify and adequately serve HIV-infected older adults; thus, HIV-infected persons over 50 often remain hidden, under-diagnosed, and poorly treated. One of the challenges facing physicians is correctly identifying HIV infection in older adults, particularly because initial complaints present as non-constitutional symptoms, including fatigue, weight loss, and fever, that mimic the often subtle presentation of common diseases of aging. Ageist beliefs that older adults are not sexual, monogamous, or heterosexual compound these challenges. Thus, lack of clinical suspicion and the parallel lack of identifying at-risk behavior among older adults themselves add unnecessarily to the potential of late diagnosis of HIV among older people.

HIV and AIDS have affected millions of children and families. This may lead to other unique ethical issues that have to do with protection and advocacy for key vulnerable populations such as children, which must be addressed. During the 30 years of the global HIV epidemic, an estimated 17 million children lost one or both parents because of death due to AIDS. A staggering 90% of these children live in sub-Saharan Africa. In addition, 3.4 million children under age 15 are living with HIV. Despite some decline in HIV adult prevalence worldwide and increased access to treatment, the number of children affected by or at risk for HIV infection remains alarmingly high. In 2015, 23% of pregnant women living with HIV did not have access to HAARTs to prevent transmission to their infants. In the same year, around 150,000 children became infected with HIV; this equates to 400 children a day (UNAIDS, 2016).

Families and communities have led a massive response to protect, care for, and support children affected by HIV and AIDS. Since 2003, the U.S. President's Emergency Plan for AIDS Relief (PEPFAR) has provided more than $2 billion in funding and technical support and has greatly enhanced these efforts. These investments have enabled children to stay in school, strengthened households, and ensured that parents are able to continue their roles as primary caregivers. Please see the following for additional details: (www.usaid.gov/what-we-do/global-health/hiv-and-aids/technical-areas/orphans-and-vulnerable-children-affected-hiv).

International palliative care models and integrated community palliative care

Internationally, the impact of HIV/AIDS has produced many innovative responses to the need for care and support for adults and children – including the development of community-based models of palliative care (Family Health International, 2009). In countries such as South Africa and Ethiopia, as well as other low-resource settings, comprehensive community initiatives are providing training to help increase local capacity for implementing palliative care treatments.

South Africa: integrated community palliative care

In South Africa, an integrated community palliative care (ICPC) model links existing health systems with community care support mechanisms like home-based care, hospice, and support groups to provide different levels of palliative care activities and build sustainability. Guiding principles of this model include: family-centeredness, sustainability, comprehensiveness, and team integration. ICPC integrates support throughout the entire holistic health system, including primary healthcare facilities and their interprofessional teams, HAART sites and their interdisciplinary care teams, community and home-based care groups, support groups, and communities and families themselves. The integrated service delivery of ICPC makes it possible to provide a full continuum of palliative care from diagnosis to end-of-life care and bereavement.

Each component of the ICPC model is critical to its success, but of paramount importance is the integration of complementary, comprehensive palliative care and wellness services into the existing health structure and community-based providers. Provision of integrated services is the only way that all the continuum of care needs can be met. No one health provider can address all the physical, emotional, social, and spiritual needs of holistic palliative care and wellness support that a pediatric and/or adult or older adult client has. Thus, the ICPC model embraces a team approach for meeting these complex, chronic care needs.

Under this model, health professionals, caregivers, and other members of the interprofessional team are trained in palliative care. Additionally, palliative care training with traditional healers and pastors has also assisted in bringing a holistic approach to the ICPC program. Data suggest that patients and their families experienced an improvement in their quality of care, and beneficial links between facility- and community-based services have strengthened the continuum of care (Family Health International, 2009).

Ethiopia: community and home-based care (CHBC)

Like South Africa, Ethiopia has also has been exerting commendable efforts in implementing comprehensive community and home-based care through community mobilization in 14 communities since October 2004. The program has made a significant difference in quality of life at the individual, family, and community level.

Ethiopia's community and home-based care model is the result of unique partnerships between community organizations, non-governmental organizations, and governmental organizations. From the start, the implementing non-governmental organizations, concerned governmental organizations and control offices, and health bureaus have worked together to identify and mobilize *idirs* or traditional burial societies. Regional prevention and control offices and health bureaus provide funds to fulfill the needed supplies (medical and nonmedical items and food). Local administrations provide shelter, in most cases free of rent, and construction materials for renovation, rent-free offices for community and home-based care, and land for patients whose health status has improved to substitute for income.

Data suggest these programs have reduced levels of self-stigmatization and increased communication between PWLHA and their families, neighbors, and visitors (Family Health International, 2009). Participants report being satisfied with the service and are active in identifying new clients as well as organizing self-help groups. At the family level, there is less stigmatization of family members with signs and symptoms of HIV, and families are willing to accept community and home-based caregivers into their households. There is improved acceptance of the skills transferred from the caregivers to family members or neighbors in caring for the patients.

In order to fully describe treatment settings for PLWHA and issues surrounding palliative care, especially as they relate to changes in attitudes and practices over time as well as urban versus rural differences, the authors conducted and analyzed two interviews/case studies. These interviews were conducted with healthcare providers in facilities in two under-resourced areas of the southeastern United States: one urban and one rural. The case examples were chosen to display issues of diversity and culture in palliative and hospice care in HIV/AIDS patients.

Case examples

In the United States, HIV/AIDS has decreased or stabilized in many regions, but the Deep South of the United States – including its many rural areas – remains a hotbed of HIV incidence (Reif et al., 2015). In 2016, the authors conducted two interviews with HIV/AIDS health professionals to better understand the evolving use and application(s) of hospice and palliative care for PWLHA in Alabama over the last ten years. Case example 1 captures our interview with Ms. Mel Prince, LCSW, Executive Director of Selma AIDS Information and Resources

(AIR), an AIDS service organization (ASO) located in rural Alabama. Case example 2 includes an interview with James Raper, DSN, CRNP, JD, FANNP, FAAN, the Director of the 1917 HIV/AIDS Outpatient Clinic in Birmingham, Alabama. Analyses and discussion questions follow each case study.

Case example 1

"I am the Director of an AIDS Service Organization (ASO) in rural Alabama and I have been working there off and on for about 20 years. I remember back in the early days of the epidemic in the mid-90s up until about five years ago (2010), the stigma was horrible for our clients. One of the worst examples of stigma happened when I went to visit a patient who was being cared for by a hospice worker. I observed her not wanting to touch the patient's slippers with her hand, but instead sliding it over and picking it up with her feet. I was livid when I saw that behavior and I angrily told her so. I also reported her treatment of our client to her immediate supervisor and I never saw her again. Other barriers to care were apparent in the old days when we literally did not have anywhere to take patients when they needed end-of-life care. First of all, there were only about three hospices in the state [of Alabama] that would take AIDS patients and none of them were close to us. I remember taking patients across state lines and driving them in our vehicles many miles away in Mississippi or adjacent states to get them access to services. I'm talking a one and half hour drive – one way.

But times have changed and gotten better. For one thing, we don't have as many patients who need hospice/palliative care because of the medicines. In the last five years, I have only had two patients, both in their 30s who needed palliative/hospice care. And they had gotten to that point because they refused to take their medicines. The other thing that has gotten better is that there are many more hospice/palliative care services available. Unlike the old days, the companies offering services are knocking at our door to provide services. That is very different from the early days. I believe it is because health care workers are getting better educated about HIV, therefore decreasing their fear of transmission for themselves and for residents of nursing homes, or hospices. Additionally, I know that people fear using services if they don't live in their own private home. For example, if they live in an apartment or public housing, they are afraid of what people "might say." So although stigma still exists, it has gotten better."

Questions

1   What features of Elder's life course approach can be applied to this case study?
2   What ethical dilemmas present themselves in this case study? And, how much treatment does a healthcare provider actually provide to a patient that is non-adherent to a treatment regimen?
3   How might cultural competency issues complicate these ethical dilemmas?

Case example 2

"In the early years (1995 – before HAART), in the time of AZT etc. people were dying every week. We had several deaths a week every week. That's just how it was. In 1996, research on protease inhibitors started and gradually became commercially available; it was just a matter of just getting patients on medications through compassionate use programs from drug companies. There was only one company in the entire US that provided access to Indinavir (protease inhibitor) and there was such a national need for it. There was one company that coordinated all of the demand for the drug in one central location, I believe it was in Philadelphia. [. . .] So, in those days, we had a lot of people die. My first partner died in 93. We never talked about hospice care [when Steve was dying]. The doctor just always told us when the end comes, I'll be here for you. We did have home health though.

Today, we have hospice companies who regularly call on us at the 1917 clinic – making us aware of the services they provide which is tremendously different from 10–20 years ago. But yeah, they routinely want to call on us. They meet with our social workers. They even provide continuing education credit. So they are actively looking for eligible patients to enroll. When we have had patients who we enrolled in hospice, they'll oftentimes come that day while that patient is in clinic and make the first engagement in the presence of the social worker, the care provider, and the patient. Oftentimes, the intake will happen here in the clinic [. . .] it's clearly a business model now.

We've had trouble with getting patients in nursing homes. That's been a challenge. But even that now seems to be a lot better. We now have nursing homes that are very receptive to our clients so we will contact them (at least 3). We have some of our residents who are permanent residents of the nursing homes – not just for end of life. They are very receptive and the patients seem satisfied with their care there." "In the early years, there was clearly the stigma of HIV. But now like I said, they [hospice] are coming looking for people."

Questions

1 Why are hospice and palliative care services more receptive in the 2010s to caring for HIV/AIDS patients?
2 How is the stigma confronting HIV/AIDS patients different from 10–12 years ago? How is it the same? How can hospice and palliative care manage this barrier?
3 How can nursing homes and other institutional care models be modified to accommodate the needs of HIV/AIDS patients?

Case example discussion

One thing that became clear after conducting the interviews was that the perceptions and realities of both AIDS health workers were very different depending on their geographic location and access to resources. The first provider (rural) reported experiencing more perceived discrimination in referring patients for hospice/palliative care than the second provider (urban). It is conceivable that, given the 1917 clinic's affiliation with a large university medical center, the second provider may not have had these experiences because their clinic offers in house palliative care services and associations with external hospice providers.

The first provider shared her experiences of the lack of cultural competency among hospice care service providers in her rural area. This may be influenced by the fact that the provider in Case # 1 was an African American female and the provider in Case #2 was a NHW male. Perhaps racial and gender differences as well as geographic differences in perception and interactions may play a role. More recently, research regarding implicit bias or perceptions acknowledges that often people are not consciously aware of their stereotyping, discrimination, or prejudice, which makes it harder to correct (Banaji & Greenwald, 2013).

Another distinction between the two care service providers was that the second provider examined the agency's data on all deaths that had occurred in the clinic during the previous few years and found that none of the clients (mainly AA males) had accessed hospice care.

> Additionally, both revealed that palliative care, particularly for pain, probably was underused either because of lack of provider referral or aforementioned cultural barriers with patients and their families.
>
> Another area of concern for the provider in Case Example #1 was that the burden of care was often on the families who do not have enough support, (psychosocial, financial). She believed that consideration to involve hospice and palliative care may be low on the list of priorities within these family systems. Both providers gave insight into areas for research and clinical practice for the future.

Practice implications/summary

It is clear that caring for persons living with HIV is continually changing with the development of more effective HIV medications and regimens and as access becomes more of a reality for patients globally. As patients age, use of palliative/hospice care will be important in maximizing the quality of life for individuals who will most likely have comorbidities. These comorbidities, such as heart disease and diabetes, as well as those with a shorter trajectory of deterioration just prior to death – like cancer and Hepatitis C – can affect their lifespan and quality of life. Additionally, other intersectionalities such as low socioeconomic status, substance abuse and addiction, interpersonal violence, race, sexual orientation, etc. may add complexity for PLWHA, particularly as they receive palliative care.

The integration of primary care providers with specialists such as infectious disease physicians will be crucial for managing the long-term health maintenance of the HIV patient. The incorporation of mental health providers as members of the interprofessional healthcare team, including 1) mental health specialists to manage depression, 2) pharmacists who can manage drug toxicities with use of multiple drugs, 3) pastoral care counselors, 4) complementary and alternative medicine practitioners and others who facilitate a holistic care delivery approach according to the individual's needs. For example, spirituality/religion has been reported as a very vital component in health and healing and may help maintain hope during times of crisis, particularly among PWLHA (Emlet & Hughes, 2016). Social workers, pastoral counselors, or psychologists in palliative and hospice care can work together and be ideal team leaders to address the psychosocial, spiritual (and medical) challenges often accompanying chronic disease.

Health providers must be familiar with the interprofessional approach provided by palliative and hospice care in order to recommend it to patients with HIV who could benefit. Additionally, training should target an understanding of healthcare preferences that are often influenced by cultural beliefs. This could be important in combatting the barriers to utilization of palliative and hospice care among culturally and ethnically diverse as well as geographically diverse populations.

While hospice care covers the last six months of life, palliative care services can focus on keeping HIV patients comfortable and increasing the quality of their lives as early as the initial diagnosis. Palliative care is not solely provided to terminal patients, and there is clinical evidence that PWLHA need pain and symptom management throughout the disease trajectory that would be available within the context of palliative care.

Conclusion

In summary, the needs of HIV/AIDS patients have changed over the course of the epidemic, from acute support in a rapid trajectory toward death, to support for long-term and chronic issues because of longer life expectancies as well as acute needs. Ongoing research should be conducted in the areas of 1) pain control, 2) co-infections and other comorbid diseases and the need for palliative care, and 3) psychosocial interventions to identify best practices in working with PLWHA throughout the course of the disease. In addition, health professionals need ongoing education and training to keep current on effective treatments, psychosocial issues, and challenges facing PLWHA. This education should include cultural awareness of the particular needs of diverse vulnerable populations including ethnic and racial minorities and those who live in rural areas of the United States, particularly because HIV/AIDS disproportionately affects them and their communities. The case examples presented here can provide some insight into the wide range and disparity that may exist in treatment and services available to PLWHA, as well as the continuing presence of stigma and discrimination those receiving health, palliative, and hospice care – particularly urban and rural African Americans – face in the Deep South of the United States. This may also be seen as providing additional context for addressing these issues for similar populations globally.

Acronyms for chapter

AIDS   Acquired Immunodeficiency Syndrome
HAART   Highly active antiretroviral treatment
HIV   Human Immunodeficiency Virus
PLWHA   People living with HIV/AIDS

References

Banaji, M. R., & Greenwald, A. G. (2013). *Blind spot: Hidden biases of good people.* New York, NY: Delacorte Press.

Bertozzi, S., Padian, N. S., Wegbreit, J., DeMaria, L. M., Feldman, B., Gayle, H., . . . Musgrove, P. (2006). HIV/AIDS prevention and treatment. Chapter 18: HIB/AIDS Prevention and

Treatment. In D. T. Jamison, J. G. Breman, A. R. Measham, et al. (Eds.), *Disease control priorities in developing countries*. Washington, DC: The International Bank for Reconstruction and Development/The World Bank. Retrieved from www.ncbi.nlm.nih.gov/books/NBK11782/Co-published by New York: Oxford University Press.

Block, S. D. (2001). Psychological considerations, growth, and transcendence at the end of life: the art of the possible. *Journal of the American Medical Association, 285*(22), 2898–2905.

Breitbart, W., Passik, S., McDonald, M. V., Rosenfield, B., Smith, M., Kaim, M., & Funesti-Esch, J. (1998). Patient-related barriers to pain management in ambulatory AIDS patients. *Pain, 76*(1–2), 9–16.

Centers for Disease Control and Prevention. (2013). Diagnoses of HIV infection among adults aged 50 years and older in the United States and dependent areas, 2007–2010. *HIV Surveillance Supplemental Report, 18*(3), 1–70. Retrieved from www.cdc.gov/hiv/pdf/statistics_2010_HIV_Surveillance_Report_vol_18_no_3.pdf

Clayton, J. M., Butow, P. N., Arnold, R. M., & Tattersall, M. H. (2005). Fostering coping and nurturing hope when discussing the future with terminally ill cancer patients and their caregivers. *Cancer, 103*(9), 1965–1975.

Crawley, L., Payne, R. P., Bolden, J., Payne, T., Washington, P., & Williams, S. (2000). Palliative and end-of-life care in the African American community. *The Journal of the American Medical Association, 284*(19), 2518–2521.

Daniels, S. (2015). Cognitive behavior therapy for patients with cancer. *Journal of the Advanced Practitioner in Oncology, 6*(1), 54–56.

Defilippi, K. (2005). Integrated community-based home care: Striving towards balancing quality with coverage in South Africa. *Indian Journal of Palliative Care, 11*, 34–36.

Earnshaw, V. A., & Chaudoir, S. R. (2009). From conceptualizing to measuring HIV stigma: A review of HIV stigma mechanism measures. *AIDS Behavior, 13*(6), 1160–1177.

Elder, G. H. (1998). The life course as developmental theory. *Child Development, 6*(1), 1–12.

Emlet, C. A. (2006). "You're awfully old to have *this* disease": Experiences of stigma and ageism in adults 50 years and older living with HIV/AIDS. *The Gerontologist, 46*(6), 781–790.

Emlet, C. A. (2007). Experiences of stigma in older adults living with HIV/AIDS: A mixed-methods analysis. *AIDS Patient Care and STDs, 21*(10), 740–752. doi:10.1089/apc.2007.0010

Emlet, C. A., & Hughes, A. K. (2016). Older adults with HIV/AIDS. In D. Kaplan & B. Berkman (Eds.), *The Oxford handbook of social work in health and aging* (2nd ed., pp. 363–372). New York: Oxford University Press.

Family Health International. (2009). *Palliative care strategy for HIV and other disease*. Retrieved from www.inpracticeafrica.com/~/media/Guidelines/FHI_HIV_Palliative.pdf

Foster, P. H. (2007). Use of stigma, fear, and denial in development of a framework for prevention of HIV/AIDS in rural African American communities. *Family and Community Health, 30*(4), 318–327.

Foster, P. H., & Gaskins, S. (2009). Older African Americans' management of HIV/AIDS stigma. *AIDS Care, 21*(10), 1306–1312.

Fredriksen-Goldsen, K. I., Kim, H.-J., Emlet, C. A., Erosheva, E. A., Muraco, A., Petry, H., et al. (2011). *The health report: Resilience and disparities among lesbian, gay, bisexual and transgender older adults*. Seattle, WA: Institute for Multigenerational Health.

Ganzini, L., Goy, E., & Dobscha, S. K. (2008). Prevalence of depression and anxiety in patients requesting physicians' aid in dying: Cross sectional survey. *BMJ, 337*, a1682.

Gielen, A. C., O'Campo, P., Faden, R. R., & Eke, A. (1997). Women's disclosure of HIV status: Experiences of mistreatment and violence in an urban setting. *Women and Health, 25*(3), 19–31. doi:10.1300/J013v25n03_02

Goeren, W. (2011). Social work, HIV disease, and palliative care. In T. Altilio & S. Otis-Green (Eds.), *Oxford textbook of palliative social work*. New York, NY: Oxford University Press.

Goffman, E. (1963). *Stigma: Notes on the management of spoiled identity*. New York: Simon and Shuster.

Haile, R., Padilla, M. B., & Parker, E. A. (2011). "Stuck in the Quagmire of an HIV Ghetto": The meaning of stigma in the lives of older black gay and bisexual men living with HIV in New York City. *Culture, Health & Sexuality, 13*(4), 429–442. http://doi.org/10.1080/13691058.2010.537769

Harding, R., Karus, D., Easterbrook, P., Raveis, V., Higginson, I., & Marconi, K. (2005). Does palliative care improve outcomes for patients with HIV/AIDS? A systematic review of the evidence. *Sexually Transmitted Infections, 81*(1), 5–14. http://doi.org/10.1136/sti.2004.010132

Heckman, B. D. (2006). Psychosocial differences between whites and African Americans living with HIV/AIDS in rural areas of 13 US states. *The Journal of Rural Health, 22*(2), 131–139.

Herek, G. M., Capitanio, J. P., & Widaman, K. F. (2002). HIV-related stigma and knowledge in the United States: Prevalence and trends, 1991–1999. *American Journal of Public Health, 92*(3), 371–377.

High, K. P., Brennan-Ing, M., Clifford, D. B., Cohen, M. H., Currier, J., Deeks, S. G., . . . Volberding, P. (2012). HIV and aging: State of knowledge and areas of critical need for research: A report to the NIH Office of AIDS Research by the HIV and Aging Working Group. *Journal of Acquired Immune Deficiency Syndrome, 60*(Suppl. 1), S1–S18. doi:10.1097/QAI.0b013e31825a3668

Johnston, S. C., Pfeifer, M. P., & McNutt, R. (1995). The discussion about advance directives: Patient and physician opinions regarding when and how it should be conducted: End of life study group. *Archives of Internal Medicine, 155*(10), 1025–1030.

Justice, A., & Falutz, J. (2014). Aging and HIV: An evolving understanding. *Current Opinion in HIV and AIDS, 9*(4), 291–293.

Lo, B., McLeod, G. A., & Saika, G. (1986). Patient attitudes to discussing life-sustaining treatment. *Archives of Internal Medicine, 46*(8), 1613–1615.

Lohse, N., Hansen, A. B., Pedersen, G., Kronborg, G., Gerstoft, J., Sorensen, H. T., . . . Obel, N. (2007). Survival of persons with and without HIV infection in Denmark, 1995–2005. *Annals of Internal Medicine, 146*(2), 87–95.

Ludwig, A., & Chittenden, E. (2008). Palliative care of patients with HIV. *In HIV In Site Knowledge Base chapter*. Accessed from: http://hivinsite.ucsf.edu/InSite?page=kb-03-03-05

Merlin, J. S., Cen, L., Praestgaard, A., Turner, M., Obando, A., Alpert, C., . . . Frank, I. (2012). Pain and physical and psychological symptoms in ambulatory HIV patients in the current treatment era. *Journal of Pain and Symptom Management, 43*(3), 638–645. http://doi.org/10.1016/j.jpainsymman.2011.04.019

Merlin, J. S., Tucker, R. O., Saag, M. S., & Selwyn, P. A. (2013). The role of palliative care in the current HIV treatment era in developed countries. *Topics in Antiviral Medicine, 21*(1), 20–26.

Moore, R. D., & Chaisson, R. E. (1999). Natural history of HIV infection in the era of combination antiretroviral therapy. *AIDS, 1*(14), 1933–1942.

Nightengale, S., Winston, A., Letendre, S., Michael, B., McArthur, J.C., Khoo, S., & Solomon, T. (2014). Controversies in HIV-associated neurocognitive disorders. *The Lancet Neurology, 13*, 1139–1151.

Pantilat, S. Z. (1999). Care of dying patients: Beyond symptom management. *Western Journal of Medicine, 171*(4), 253–256.

Parker, R., Stein, D. J., & Jelsma, J. (2014). Pain in people living with HIV/AIDS: A systematic review. *Journal of the International AIDS Society, 17*(1), 18719. http://doi.org/10.7448/IAS.17.1.18719

Pathai, S., Bajillan, H., Landay, A. L., & High, K. P. (2014). Is HIV a model of accelerated or accentuated aging? *Journals of Gerontology: A Biological Sciences Medical Sciences, 69*(7), 833–842. doi:10.1093/gerona/glt168

Payne Foster, P. (2017). PI for Project FAITHH (Faith-based Anti-stigma Initiative to Heal HIV/AIDS), a CDC-funded intervention to decrease HIV stigma in African American rural Alabama congregational members.

Pierson, C. M., Curtis, J. R., & Patrick, D. L. (2002). A good death: A qualitative study of patients with advanced AIDS. *AIDS Care, 14*(5), 587–598.

Reif, S., Pence, B. W., Hall, I., Hu, X., Whetten, K., & Wilson, E. (2015). HIV diagnoses, prevalence and outcomes in Nine Southern States. *Journal of Community Health, 40*(4), 642–651.

Safren, S. A., O'Cleirigh, C. M., Bullis, J. R., Otto, M. W., Stein, M. D., & Pollack, M. H. (2012). Cognitive behavioral therapy for adherence and depression (CBT-AD) in HIV-infected injection drug users: A randomized controlled trial. *Journal of Consulting and Clinical Psychology, 80*(3), 404–415. doi:10.1037/a0028208

Selwyn, P. A., & Arnold, R. (1998). From fate to tragedy: The changing meanings of life, death, and AIDS. *Annals of Internal Medicine, 129*(11), 899–902.

Selwyn, P. A., & Forstein, M. (2003). Overcoming the false dichotomy of Curative vs Palliative care for late-stage HIV/AIDS: "Let me live the way I want to live, until I can't". *JAM, 290*(6), 806–814. doi:10.1001/jama.290.6.806

Sepulveda, C., Marlin, A., Yoshida, T., & Ullrich, A. (2002). Palliative care: The World Health Organization's global perspective. *Journal of Pain and Symptom Management, 24*(2), 91–96.

Shippy, R. A., Cantor, M. H., & Brennan, M. (2004). Social networks of aging gay men. *Journal of Men's Studies, 13*(1), 107–120.

Stall, R., Hoff, C., Coates, T. J., Paul, J., Phillips, K., Ekstrand, M., . . . Diaz, R. (1996). Decisions to get HIV tested and to accept antiretroviral therapies among gay/bisexual men: Implications for secondary prevention efforts. *Journal of Acquired Immune Deficiency Syndromes and Human Retrovirology, 11*(2), 151–160.

Substance Abuse and Mental Health Services Administration. (2017). *HIV, AIDS, and viral hepatitis.* Rockville, MD: National Institute of Health.

United States President's Emergency Plan for AIDS Relief [PEPFAR]. (2006). *HIV/AIDS palliative care guidance: Comprehensive HIV/AIDS care services in the President's Emergency Plan for AIDS Relief.* Retrieved from www.pepfar.gov/reports/guidance/75827.htm

Wood, C. G., Whittet, S., & Bradbeer, C. S. (1997). ABC of palliative care: HIV infection and AIDS. *BMJ: British Medical Journal, 315*(7120), 1433–1436.

World Health Organization. (2010). *Priority interventions: HIV/AIDS prevention, treatment and care in the health sector.* Retrieved from http://apps.who.int/iris/bitstream/10665/44418/1/9789241500234_eng.pdf

World Health Organization. (2015). *Palliative care.* Retrieved from www.who.int/mediacentre/factsheets/fs402/en/

World Health Organization HIV/AIDS Department. (2018). *HIV/AIDS: Data and statistics.* Retrieved from www.who.int/hiv/data/en/

Chapter 3

Serious mental illness and palliative care

Julia Kasl-Godley and Kimberly E. Hiroto

Serious mental illness (SMI) is defined as a mental, behavioral, or emotional disorder (excluding developmental and substance use disorders), diagnosable currently or within the past year, of sufficient duration to meet diagnostic criteria specified within the Diagnostic and Statistical Manual of Mental Disorders (DSM-5, APA, 2013) and resulting in serious functional impairment that substantially interferes with, or limits, one or more major life activities. A World Health Organization (WHO) World Mental Health Survey across 28 different countries found lifetime prevalence rates of SMI from 0.8%–6.8% among adults (Kessler et al., 2009). In the United States, approximately 2.7% of adults age 50 and over had SMI in the past year (Substance Abuse and Mental Health Services Administration, 2017). Approximately 8 million deaths, or an estimated 14.3% of all deaths worldwide each year, are attributable to mental illness (Walker, McGee, & Druss, 2015). Compared to the general population, people with SMI have a 13- to 30-year shorter life expectancy (Chang et al., 2011; Viron & Stern, 2010; Vreeland, 2007), though mortality risk differs with age, gender, and ethnicity (Chang et al., 2010).

Individuals with SMI are at greater risk for medical illness and have higher morbidity and more severe functional impairments than adults without SMI (Weissman, Pratt, Miller, & Parker, 2015). Increased morbidity and mortality are due to behavioral factors as well as disparities in healthcare access, utilization, and quality of care (De Hert et al., 2011). Among people with SMI, higher incidence of smoking, poor diet and exercise, substance abuse, unsafe sexual behaviors, and medication nonadherence increase risk for medical disorders (Goldberg et al., 2013; Lawrence & Kisely, 2010). Atypical antipsychotics, mood stabilizers, and antidepressants – all commonly prescribed for people with SMI – can have a deleterious impact on physical health through increasing risk of obesity, Type 2 diabetes, cerebrovascular disease, and metabolic disorders (De Hert et al., 2011).

Additionally, there often is a lack of clarity amongst providers about who should be responsible for preventive care and physical disease management in individuals with SMI (Lawrence & Kisely, 2010). For example, in comparison to the general population, individuals with SMI are less likely to receive routine cancer screening and are more likely to present with metastatic disease, lower rates of surgery, and fewer chemotherapy sessions (Kisely, Crowe, & Lawrence, 2013). They also have a lower likelihood of receiving specialized interventions for cardiovascular disease or circulatory medications despite having a high incidence of coronary artery disease (De Hert et al., 2011). Furthermore, healthcare providers often experience discomfort and difficulty caring for people with SMI (Zolnierek & Clingerman, 2012).

Individuals with SMI also experience difficulties accessing care due to incarceration, transportation difficulties, limited financial resources, limited-to-no medical insurance, and stigma from both individuals in the community and medical providers (Morgan, 2016). They may have limited support systems, which can have an impact on their ability to access and navigate the healthcare system. Even when they do access care, individuals with SMI may not be able to identify or describe their problems clearly, leading to misdiagnosis or delays in treatment. They also may be reluctant to seek medical treatment, in part out of fear of psychiatric hospitalization, and they may be unable to tolerate interventions or adhere to treatment as prescribed (Lawrence & Kisely, 2010).

SMI and palliative care

Very little is known about rates of SMI in palliative care populations or how often individuals with SMI seek out or receive palliative care (Chochinov, Martens, Prior, & Kredentser, 2012; Lloyd-Williams, Abba, & Crowther, 2014). Using the 2.7 percent, 12-month prevalence rate for adults age 50 or older, and the nearly 1.4 million Medicare beneficiaries who received hospice services in 2015 (NHPCO Facts and Figures: Hospice Care in America, 2017,), roughly 37,800 hospice recipients in the US are likely to have SMI. One New Zealand study suggests that individuals with SMI are less likely to receive palliative care (3.5 times less) than those without SMI (Butler & O'Brien, 2017). However, another study across six VA medical centers found that DNR status at the time of death did not vary as a function of mental health diagnosis (Bailey et al., 2012). Furthermore, Ganzini, Socherman, Duckart, and Shores (2010) found that veterans with schizophrenia dying from cancer, though less likely to receive home hospice due to lack of a caregiver, had otherwise comparable if not better end-of-life care than their non-mentally ill counterparts. The authors suggest that their findings might have been different if they examined individuals who were transient and/or nonadherent to their treatment and were not integrated into a healthcare system. In the US, the Veterans Administration (VA) has a highly integrated medical, palliative care, and mental health service.

Nonetheless, palliative and hospice care often require that individuals have a home and family members or friends involved in their care, yet estrangement from family and lack of family support, social isolation, homelessness, and addictions are prevalent amongst individuals with SMI (Ganzini et al., 2010). Stigma and limited knowledge about mental health among palliative care providers also can widen healthcare disparities (Stienstra & Chochinov, 2006; Tarzian, Neal, & O'Neil, 2005). For example, McCasland (2007) found that hospice nurses caring for psychiatric patients expressed lack of knowledge, anxiety, fears for their own safety, dislike of caring for those with SMI, and a belief that it is "not our role." In addition, individuals with SMI often are viewed as too medically ill to be in an inpatient psychiatric setting and too psychiatrically ill to be on a medicine unit. Qualitative research addressing the intersection of SMI and end-of-life care highlights this theme of "no right place to die" (Morgan, 2016, p. 38). Providers in medical or psychiatric settings feel ill equipped to tend to patients' psychiatric or medical needs, respectively (Bloomer & O'Brien, 2013; Zolnierek & Clingerman, 2012). Consulting palliative care teams or consult/liaison mental health providers can help fill this gap, although underresourced medical settings may not have access to these specialized services. Where such individuals seek treatment may depend on the local resources available to them and the team's ability to manage their needs.

Little guidance is available on interventions or policies to improve the care of persons with SMI who develop cancer or other conditions requiring palliative care, with the exception of dementia (e.g., van der Steen et al., 2014). This paucity argues for the need for integration of palliative care and mental health care, particularly amongst psychologists and psychiatrists, and for examples of good practices for how mental health teams can engage more fully with palliative care (e.g., Fairman & Irwin, 2013; Kasl-Godley, King, & Quill, 2014).

A few innovative models have been piloted, though outcome data are not yet available. For example, the Integrated Mental Health and Palliative Care Task project (IMhPaCT; Taylor et al., 2012) was a service improvement initiative funded by the Australian Department of Health and Aging to enhance the quality of care for individuals with SMI and life-limiting illnesses. It sought to (1) increase the mental health knowledge of palliative care clinicians and palliative care knowledge of mental health providers through workshops, observation of assessment processes, and access to educational programs, and (2) improve palliative care to individuals living with SMI through the development and evaluation of a triage tool, along with the use of validated case conferencing. IMhPaCT was informed by a demonstration project developed and implemented by the Massachusetts Department of Mental Health to improve access to advance care planning and end-of-life care among individuals with SMI that incorporated cross-training, modeling, self-directed learning modules, and liaison roles (Foti, 2003). As another example, the Mehac Foundation in India (http//www.mehacfoundation.org) has piloted partnerships between community mental health and palliative care programs in an attempt to strengthen the psychosocial component in the delivery of palliative care.

Though not specifically developed for individuals with SMI receiving palliative care, chronic care and integrated care models address some of the problems in treating this population. The premise of the chronic care model is that healthcare systems need to address both acute problems and chronic conditions; otherwise,

Serious mental illness and palliative care   35

healthcare systems will become increasingly inefficient and ineffective, with expenditures rising without concomitant improvements in population health. Palliative care for SMI is, in essence, a chronic care model. Chronic disease self-management programs have been adapted with promising outcomes for more targeted use in psychiatric clinics and rehabilitation settings that serve individuals with SMI (e.g., Goldberg et al., 2013). For example, individuals with chronic medical conditions and SMI showed significant improvements in patient activation and greater likelihood of using primary care medical services after participating in a program incorporating self-management tasks found to be common across chronic health conditions (i.e., action planning and feedback, modeling of behaviors and problem-solving by participants, reinterpretation of symptoms, and training in specific disease management techniques; Druss et al., 2010).

Finally, peer patient navigator programs help patients make sense of the complicated healthcare system and enhance treatment engagement. These programs might be adapted to assist people with SMI manage physical health concerns by more fully engaging in healthcare over the long term (e.g., Corrigan, Pickett, Batia, & Michaels, 2014). Adaptations would need to consider how cognitive, emotional, and interpersonal challenges of SMI affect navigation skills (e.g., McKibbin et al., 2006).

Substance use disorders and other specific psychiatric disorders

Given the high comorbidity among SMI and substance use disorders, we next review substance use disorders in addition to specific serious mental disorders. Throughout, we include a case example to demonstrate the complexity of providing palliative care to persons with SMI.

Case example

Substance use disorders and the case of Mr. S

Mr. S is a 68-year-old non-Hispanic White male Vietnam combat Veteran with non-small cell lung cancer, Type II diabetes, and chronic obstructive pulmonary disease (COPD). He initially opted for chemotherapy to treat his lung cancer but after finding the symptom burden during chemotherapy to be intolerable, he decided to pursue a self-ascribed holistic approach. His primary care provider (PCP) subsequently referred him to palliative care for symptom management and also to primary care mental health because he reported symptoms of PTSD, anxiety, and depression with passive suicidal ideation. The primary care psychologist consulted with Mr. S's providers to clarify his decision to discontinue chemotherapy and to clarify concerns they may have. The primary and palliative care physicians both deemed him to have decisional capacity. The psychologist agreed to assess further and offer recommendations.

Mr. S described a long history of polysubstance use since returning from Vietnam, including heroin, methamphetamine, cannabis, and alcohol. He reported remaining abstinent from alcohol and illicit substances since the 1990s after completing residential treatment. However, he reported daily cannabis use to manage the cancer pain and saw this use as a holistic and natural remedy. Over time, the psychologist grew concerned about his cognitive functioning and mood (e.g., forgetting appointments, passive suicidal ideations), the etiologies of which were unclear, confounded by his cannabis use. Mr. S remained reluctant to try prescription pain medications due to concern about synthetic additives. However, with progressive cancer pain and through discussion and motivational enhancement, he eventually agreed to start prescription pain medications. He reported concerns for potential physiological dependency and worked with his PCP and pharmacist to evaluate his medications continually to ensure appropriate use and efficacy. The palliative care team served as consultants for pain management, with input from the psychologist given Mr. S's history of addiction. Mr. S refused to titrate back his cannabis.

Questions

1 How does Mr. S's history of polysubstance use influence your approach to discussing pain medications?
2 Each party (Mr. S., the psychologist, the primary care team, the palliative care consultants) has their respective concerns about pain medications. What might they be and why?

Of the 4.5 million adults age 50 and older living with substance use disorders, 11% have a comorbid SMI (Substance Abuse and Mental Health Services Administration, 2017). Among individuals living with cancer in the US and Canada, including those admitted to palliative care units or seen through outpatient palliative care services, the incidence of substance use disorders (alcohol and drug use) ranges from approximately 20%–38% (Barclay, Owens, & Blackhall, 2014; Braiteh, Osta, Palmer, Reddy & Bruera, 2007; Carmichael, Morgan, & Del Fabbro, 2016; Dev et al., 2011; Parsons et al., 2008). These rates are higher than a

Serious mental illness and palliative care 37

4% rate of high alcohol use in an Italian study of patients with advanced cancer, in which high-use individuals were more likely to be male and younger, independent of diagnosis and performance status (Mercadante et al., 2015). Substance use disorders may exacerbate suffering in palliative care patients, decrease quality of life, complicate management of other cancer-related symptoms, and distress family care partners (Dev et al., 2011; Krashin, Murinova, & Ballantyne, 2012; Passik & Theobald, 2000). Individuals with active substance use can be difficult to engage in treatment and less compliant with treatments (Morasco, Dukart, & Dobscha, 2011). Individuals with a past history of addiction may be at increased risk of relapse when prescribed controlled substances. Providers should acknowledge this risk (or fear thereof) and discuss nonpharmacological pain management interventions (Krashin et al., 2012).

The context of substance use disorders or fear of misuse can complicate pain management in individuals with cancer and other types of advanced serious illness. Cancer pain is undertreated in the US and Europe, with a third of patients not receiving pain medication proportional to their pain intensity (e.g., Greco et al., 2014), especially among US minorities (Fisch et al., 2012). Concern for substance use disorders, particularly opioid addiction and opioid misuse (that is, the taking of pain medication in any way not prescribed, whether intentionally or inadvertently and whether or not harm results) contributes to inadequate management. However, even individuals with clear risk factors for misuse or abuse may legitimately have moderate to severe pain. Providers must consider reasons for misuse, including poor pain control and pseudo-addiction (when patients have inadequate pain control and seek greater pain relief). High-risk individuals should be monitored for aberrant behavior, provided education on safe opioid use, and have emotional needs addressed (Kwon, Hui, & Bruera, 2015). Pain specialists, addiction specialists, oncologists, palliative care providers, and mental health providers can work collaboratively so that individuals can be forthcoming about fears of unmanaged pain, issues of misuse or addiction, and opioid risk management strategies (Pergolizzi et al., 2016).

Although there has been an increase in research and practice guidelines about opioid risk management for chronic, nonmalignant pain, less information is available about both the frequency of the problem and current practices regarding screening for substance use disorders, misuse, and diversion in patients and family members seen in palliative care clinics (Carmichael et al., 2016). One survey of palliative care programs in the US found less than half had policies for screening patients or their family members (Tan, Barclay, & Blackhall, 2015). Recommended screening tools include the CAGE (Ewing, 1984), CAGE-AID (Brown & Rounds, 1995), Addiction Behaviors Checklist (ABC) (Wu et al., 2006), and Opioid Risk Tool (ORT) (Webster & Webster, 2005), the latter of which assists with opioid risk management. Opioid risk management seeks to balance concerns about opioid misuse with the need for appropriate pain control. The goal is to minimize harm associated with opioid therapy while maintaining access to opioid therapy for control of pain (Pergolizzi et al., 2016). Risk management strategies include using pain monitoring tools (urine drug testing, pill counts, pain intensity assessments), treatment agreements, periodic pain assessments, and abuse-deterrent formulations and packaging (Pergolizzi et al., 2016).

Case example

Schizophrenia spectrum and other psychotic disorders and case example continued

Over the course of treatment, the treating psychologist developed growing concerns for Mr. S's general psychological functioning, especially in light of his passive suicidal ideations. For example, he reported grandiose plans to move to Peru (given his kinship with Peruvian culture) and open a medical clinic providing holistic, equitable services to the chronically and terminally ill. However, his plans for accomplishing this task were unrealistic and not well developed . He also was determined to maintain his holistic treatment for cancer despite the medical team's skepticism about its efficacy, especially as the window of time to pursue life-prolonging treatment was closing. The psychologist worried that Mr. S's decisions were influenced by his mental health. He agreed to a psychodiagnostic and neuropsychological assessment. Results showed no evidence of cognitive impairment or questionable capacity to make these medical decisions, although the neuropsychologist spoke with him about the effects of cannabis on attention, concentration, and memory. Nonetheless, both psychologists remained concerned that Mr. S may have possible underlying psychotic symptoms, given his odd and eccentric thought patterns and interpersonal style.

Questions

1 Given the information about Mr. S and the psychologists' concerns, what would you do next?
2 What might be some of the ethical concerns that arise in this case?
3 What more would you want to know about Mr. S and his psychology?

Individuals with schizophrenia experience higher morbidity and mortality compared to the general population (Chwastiak & Tek, 2009; Hendrie et al., 2014). They have higher rates of smoking, obesity, substance abuse, cardiovascular disease, COPD, and diabetes and suffer more postoperative complications

(Copeland et al., 2008; Hendrie et al., 2014). Delays between diagnosis of cancer and initiation of treatment result in persons with schizophrenia presenting with more advanced disease and higher likelihood of mortality (Irwin, Henderson, Knight, & Pirl, 2014), and they have a 15- to 25-year shorter life expectancy than the general population (Kisely et al., 2013; Saha, Chant, McGrath, 2007; Tran et al., 2009). Compared to the general population, people with schizophrenia are more likely to die in nursing homes and have lower utilization of hospital-based or community-based palliative care; individuals dying in nursing homes in general are less likely to have comprehensive palliative care compared to those dying in a hospital (Chochinov et al., 2012).

Several issues complicate the care of people living with schizophrenia and other psychotic disorders. Individuals may have withdrawn or bizarre affect that makes it difficult to build a therapeutic alliance. Disordered thought processes and communication and perceptual disturbances may make it difficult to obtain information. In addition, individuals with these disorders may be reluctant to seek medical treatment, be unable to tolerate or adhere to treatment, and may have limited support available to help them navigate care or advocate on their behalf. They also may be more likely to refuse treatment and demonstrate behaviors that disrupt care (Lawrence & Kisely, 2010).

Pain management may be particularly challenging in individuals with schizophrenia. They are less likely to receive pain medication, particularly amongst individuals dying of cancer, for unclear reasons. They may be less sensitive to pain and less able to communicate symptoms or verbalize pain, but, rather, become quieter, displaying affective flattening, or more inward symptoms (negative symptoms). Pain may be incorporated into delusions, thereby distorting the experience and reporting of pain (Webber, 2012). Collectively, these findings suggest providers should adopt a high index of suspicion when evaluating physical symptoms in individuals with schizophrenia (Irwin et al., 2014). In addition, it is important to establish communication between mental health providers and primary care providers when possible, given that patients may not provide full medical or psychiatric history. Family members, when available, can provide important collateral history, serve as advocates, or act as surrogate decision-makers (Irwin et al., 2014).

Case example

Mood disorders and case example continued

Mr. S scored positive on the PHQ-9 screen for depression. He acknowledged a long history of depression since returning from Vietnam, and his mental health notes also mentioned possible bipolar disorder, although he showed no current signs of this disorder. Ongoing drug use at the time confounded these diagnoses. He denied prior psychiatric hospitalizations but acknowledged isolated periods of manic-like episodes likely induced by illicit substances. He reported often using other drugs to counteract these effects, contributing to even more drug-related problems. As therapeutic rapport deepened, Mr. S disclosed a long history of suicidal ideation without prior attempts or known family history. He reflected back on experiences of losing battle buddies in Vietnam, grappling to understand why he survived and they did not. He also reflected on his cancer diagnosis, his hope for his family, and his wish that his children not see him die as a "frail and weak man."

Questions

1 Mr. S's prior mental health notes mentioned the possibility of bipolar disorder. What questions and possible concerns arise upon learning this information?
2 How would you clarify whether Mr. S's depression was driving his decision to pursue holistic treatment that he believed to be curative rather than well-established, evidence-based curative treatment?

Major depression amongst people living with advanced serious illness ranges from 5% to 50%, with an average prevalence of approximately 15% (Akizuki et al., 2016; Mitchell et al., 2011), though prevalence varies by setting (Walker et al., 2013) and disease type (Walker et al., 2014). Depression is the most common mental disorder in geriatric cancer patients, particularly at advanced disease stages (Parpa, Tsilika, Gennimata, & Mystakidou, 2015). A meta-analysis of mood disorders in oncological, haematological, and palliative care settings found a prevalence of approximately 15% for major depression, 19% for minor depression, 3% for dysthymia, and 19% for adjustment disorders (Mitchell et al., 2011).

Depressive symptoms may be associated with the disease process, treatment, and impact of illness. Symptoms may by triggered by functional dependence, loss of control/autonomy, loss of purpose and meaning in life, pain, previous history of depression, perception of oneself as a burden, poor support, concurrent stressors such as financial strain, and younger age (Goy & Ganzini, 2003; King, Heisel, & Lyness, 2005; Wilson, Lander, & Chochinov, 2009). Among palliative care patients, close to half have shown elevated depressive symptoms (Buzgova, Jarosova, & Hajnova, 2015), with depression associated with performance status, pain, desire for an early death, and distress related to symptom burden (Brenne et al., 2013; Lie et al., 2015; Rayner et al., 2011; Wilson et al., 2007). In addition, depression is an independent predictor of poor survival in patients with advanced cancer (Lloyd-Williams, Shiels, Taylor, & Dennis, 2009) and of rehospitalization and death in individuals with heart failure (Freedland et al., 2016).

A number of screening measures have been used to assess for depression in palliative care populations but with little consensus on the best tool (Mitchell et al., 2012). These measures include the Patient Health Questionnaire 9 (PHQ-9) (Andersen et al., 2014), the Beck Depression Inventory – Fast Score (BDI-FS; Neitzer, Sun, Doss, Moran, & Schiller, 2012), and the Palliative Care Outcome Scale (POS) items 7 (feeling depressed) and 8 (feeling good about yourself) (Antunes, Murtagh, Bausewein, Harding, & Higginson, 2015). In terms of assessing specific symptoms, sadness and tearfulness can represent a normative response to serious illness. However, prolonged sadness nearly every day, with little or no lifting of mood despite positive events, accompanied by other symptoms, suggests that major depressive disorder may be present. Careful assessment is key to differentiate between normative illness-related experiences and actual depressive disorders.

In terms of treatment, a series of collaborative care interventions for depression in individuals with advanced cancer which combined antidepressants, Problem Solving Therapy and Behavioral Activation, and care coordination between the primary care physician, psychiatrist, and oncologist (SMART-Oncology 2, SMART-Oncology 3) found reductions in depressive symptoms (Sharpe et al., 2014; Walker et al., 2014). Another treatment protocol, Managing Cancer and Living Meaningfully (CALM), developed for patients with advanced cancer and drawing upon relational and attachment theories in addition to existential psychotherapy, found reduced depression and anxiety and increased psychological growth (Lo et al., 2014; Nissim et al., 2012). Dignity Therapy, discussed in Chapter 5 in this volume, has been used with terminally ill patients with depression (e.g., Julião, Oliveira, Nunes, Carneiro, & Barbosa, 2014) with improvements in depression and anxiety. Importantly, more research is needed on the efficacy of other psychotherapeutic interventions for major depression (e.g., acceptance and commitment therapy, cognitive behavioral therapy) in those with advanced serious or terminal illnesses in order to compare and critique treatment approaches.

The empirical literature on bipolar disorder and palliative care is practically nonexistent. Individuals with bipolar disorder have substantial rates of medical burden (Sylvia et al., 2015) with increased incidence of asthma, cardiovascular disease, obesity, thyroid dysfunction, kidney disease, and Parkinson's disease (Forty et al., 2014). Given the high comorbidity of bipolar disorder with substance use disorders (SUD) and resultant complications in management (e.g., Kemp et al., 2009), caring for individuals with bipolar disorder in palliative care settings may be particularly challenging. Individuals with bipolar disorder and comorbid SUD evidence more mixed manic episodes, delayed recovery, more treatment resistant symptoms, and shorter periods of remission between episodes. Individuals are also at increased risk for suicidality. Substance use often is a means to manage other symptoms (sleep, racing thoughts, mood). In addition, impulsivity and impaired judgment may lead to excessive substance use, and a sense of invulnerability may lead to increased risk for relapse. It also is likely that, in some individuals, substance use may exacerbate bipolar disorder symptoms. The significant symptom overlap between substance use and bipolar disorder complicates differential diagnosis. Rigorous treatment of both the underlying affective and substance use disorder is important. Components can include education on the relationship between SUD and bipolar disorder, self-care, coping with risky situations, consequences of problem use, reasons to quit, and relapse prevention.

Case example

Suicidal ideation and desire for death and case example continued

Mr. S understood that chemotherapy might cure his cancer and prolong his life and that the window of time to pursue this option was quickly closing. As the cancer progressed to an advanced stage, he disclosed feeling "relieved" to receive a terminal diagnosis. He believed that declining chemotherapy for cancer created a loophole, allowing him to hasten his death and avoid suicide, which violated his spiritual beliefs. He reasoned that the holistic treatments would help him live long enough to address his family's needs and then retreat to Peru to live his remaining days alone. The psychologist remained concerned that Mr. S's mental health conditions were influencing his decisions, given his longstanding suicidal ideation. Even though the neuropsychologist deemed that he maintained decisional capacity, the primary care psychologist continued questioning whether Mr. S's belief systems and history of suicidality were influencing his decisions. She consulted with colleagues from different disciplines and sought guidance from the hospital bioethics committee. All supported her work with Mr. S and agreed that he has the capacity to make decisions others might not. The psychologist received emotional support from her colleagues and remained vigilant that her own beliefs and values did not adversely affect therapy.

Questions

1   As you reflect on Mr. S, what aspects of this case would you struggle with the most on a personal level? Why?
2   What ethical concerns come to mind with Mr. S's case, and how do you navigate them on both a personal and professional level?

Serious mental illness and palliative care   43

There is an elevated risk of suicide in individuals with cancer (Misono, Weiss, Fann, Redman, & Yueh, 2008), with vulnerability most heightened after learning of poor prognosis and when experiencing distress (Urban et al., 2013), though some suicides occur among individuals whose cancer can be cured. Additional risk factors for suicide include lack of social/family support, hopelessness, helplessness, diminished control, poor communication with healthcare providers, difficulties with making treatment decisions and with everyday living, substance use, and family history of suicide (Leung et al., 2013). Individuals with advanced serious illness often express a wish to die, a desire for hastened death, and/or a desire to receive aid in dying, regardless of its legality. The desire for hastened death or the wish to hasten death have been defined by an international consensus group as a reaction to suffering, in the context of a life-threatening condition, from which the individual can see no way out other than to accelerate death. This wish may be expressed spontaneously or after being asked about it, but it is distinguished from the acceptance of impending death or from a wish to die naturally, although preferably soon (Balaguer et al., 2016).

There are a variety of reasons, meanings, and functions to the desire for hastened death (Ohnsorge, Gudat, & Rehmann-Sutter, 2014). The wish to hasten death may arise in response to one or more factors, including physical symptoms (either present or anticipated), psychological distress (e.g., depression, hopelessness, fears, etc.), existential suffering (e.g., loss of meaning in life), or interpersonal issues (e.g., feeling that one is a burden) (Balaguer et al., 2016). Research suggests that 11%–55% of individuals in palliative care settings experience at least a transient desire to die, and 3%–20% experience a more pervasive desire. Desire for death is associated with depression, pain, fatigue and other physical symptoms, weak social support, diminished functional status, low quality of life, anxiety, and hopelessness. Prevalence of a diagnosed mental disorder among patients expressing a desire to die ranges from 47%–80% suggesting desire for death often is embedded in a broader context of psychological distress, but not always. For some, desire for death may reflect despair; for others, it may reflect letting go (Wilson et al., 2016).

Many healthcare providers feel unprepared or uncertain about how to respond to the wish for hastened death or requests for aid in dying (Hudson et al., 2006), yet there are few guidelines to help providers respond (Hudson et al., 2006). Healthcare professionals working with individuals with advanced illness need to ascertain the reasons and underlying intentions behind a desire for hastened death.

Individuals who express desire for hastened death may request aid in dying. Medical aid in dying is currently legal either through statute or court decision in several states in the US and countries in Europe and South America. Aid in dying is not considered suicide; consideration of aid in dying or request for aid in dying does not in and of itself indicate psychopathology. Psychologists and psychiatrists are given an evaluative role in determining an individual's capacity to end his/her life under aid in dying legislation, should a physician be concerned that a mental health condition is impairing judgment or decisional capacity. These professionals have the legal right to decline to participate in aid in dying activities, but they do not have the right to abandon their patients considering this option. Appropriate referrals are needed. However, because it is the discretion of the physician and not a requirement of the law that a mental health referral be made, concerns have arisen about whether nonpsychiatrically trained physicians are adequately sensitive to the role of depression and other mental health disorders in aid for dying requests (Werth, Benjamin, & Farrenkopf, 2000). Guidelines have been developed but are not detailed about how to make this determination (Orentlicher, Pope, & Rich, 2016; Young et al., 1997). Furthermore, whereas tests and assessments exist to evaluate decisional capacity and diagnosable disorders, they may not be validated or reliable in their use with individuals at the end of life who are considering aid in dying (Jull-Patterson, 2016). In addition, although psychologists have skills and knowledge in evaluating decision-making capacity, they may benefit from additional training in this area, as one's own values and experiences can affect capacity evaluations for aid in dying (e.g., Johnson, Cramer, Gardner, & Nobles, 2015; Johnson, Cramer, Conroy, & Gardener, 2014.)

Case example

Anxiety disorders and case example continued

As Mr. S's cancer spread, his anxiety increased, often triggered by pain, functional decline, and respiratory distress. He often expressed worry that he might choke while eating/drinking or suffocate due to shortness of breath. He also conveyed increased feelings of vulnerability as his mobility and independence decreased, which stood in stark contrast with his fiercely independent lifestyle. While still able to attend psychotherapy appointments, he found benefit in breathing, relaxation, and mindfulness exercises to help calm his distress.

Although anxiety disorders are not necessarily considered a serious mental illness, anxiety disorders in advanced serious and terminal illness warrant attention. Rates of generalized anxiety disorder and panic disorder are higher amongst individuals with COPD than the general population (Brenes, 2003). Prevalence of anxiety disorders amongst individuals living with advanced cancer ranges from 8%–18% (Spencer, Nilsson, Wright, Pirl, & Prigerson,

2010; Stark et al., 2002; Wilson et al., 2007), with a diagnosis of anxiety disorder associated with younger age, worse physical performance status, greater physical symptom burden and existential concerns, reduced social networks, and greater problems in the physician-patient relationship (Spencer et al., 2010; Wilson et al., 2007). For those living with advanced serious illness, the prevalence of anxiety ranges from 2%–33% (Buzgova et al., 2015; Kadan-Lottick, Vanderwerker, Block, Zhang, & Prigerson, 2005; Miovic & Block, 2007; Roth & Massie, 2007; Spencer et al., 2010), with an average prevalence of 10% (Mitchell et al., 2011).

In general, risk factors for anxiety include the underlying disease (pneumonia, pulmonary embolism, lung cancer, pleural effusion, COPD) and associated symptoms (pain, dyspnea), medications (e.g., adverse/paradoxical reactions to corticosteroids and stimulants), substance use, conditioned response to treatment (e.g., radiation, chemotherapy), history of diagnosable disorder (generalized anxiety disorder, obsessive compulsive disorder, panic), uncertainties/ fears of living with life-limiting illness, and time constraints for attending to unresolved issues. Individuals may experience fears focused on several different areas: medical intervention or treatment, symptoms and their capacity to cope with them, living in the face of incapacity, cognitive impairment, the dying process, concerns based on past experiences with death of significant others, the afterlife, leaving loved ones behind, being judged for past transgressions, and being rejected/abandoned (Gibson et al., 2006; Goy & Ganzini, 2003; Hendriksen et al., 2015).

A paucity of research exists on psychotherapeutic interventions for anxiety amongst individuals receiving palliative care or at end of life. Existing literature focuses primarily on cognitive behavioral therapy and mindfulness in addition to alternative therapies, including exercise, art, and aromatherapy (Smith, Cope, Sherner, & Walker, 2014). However, outcome data are limited. Greer and colleagues (2011) piloted a modified CBT intervention for anxiety among persons with terminal cancer. The modified treatment included psychoeducation and goal setting, relaxation training, coping strategies for cancer-related fears using cognitive therapy, and activity planning and pacing. In comparison to a waitlist control group, individuals receiving the modified CBT treatment demonstrated significant reductions in anxiety. Similarly, men with advanced prostate cancer in a mindfulness-based cognitive therapy (MBCT) showed reduced anxiety, improved mindfulness skills, and reductions in avoidance and fear of cancer recurrence (Chambers, Foley, Galt, Ferguson, & Clutton, 2012). The authors suggest that peer learning in a group format contributed to the effectiveness of this intervention. A systematic review of the efficacy of mindfulness-based cognitive therapy (MBCT) or stress reduction (MBSR) for individuals with cancer found gross improvements in anxiety and stress (Shennan, Payne, & Fenlon, 2011), though the studies were not specific to palliative care or end of life.

Case example

Posttraumatic stress disorder and case example continued

Mr. S reported experiencing combat trauma while in Vietnam but never disclosed the details, and the psychologist never asked. His report of trauma remained credible and was previously documented in prior mental health records. The psychologist understood that Mr. S had little time or emotional, psychological, or physical energy to process his trauma history, and the benefit of focusing on comfort outweighed the clinical utility of exploring this history further. She did, however, administer a self-report measure for PTSD in part to determine severity of symptoms and clarify the relative salience of symptom clusters. He denied significant intrusive symptoms, although his daily cannabis use likely served to mitigate PTSD symptoms. Cognitive and behavioral avoidance, emotional numbing, and interpersonal distancing manifested through limited trust, skepticism, and a tendency to isolate when feeling closed in or emotionally vulnerable. He attempted to keep the psychologist from getting too close, often keeping the discussion at an intellectual level and only occasionally disclosing emotional content. He would occasionally retreat to the woods after expressing increased vulnerability and on one occasion drove across state lines to work as a day laborer for extra money. However, as rapport and trust increased in therapy, and as his health declined, these occasions grew less frequent.

Questions

1 As the treating psychologist, how would you have navigated this balance of keeping Mr. S engaged and helping him process his end of life experience while also respecting his boundaries?
2 How might you integrate Mr. S's active PTSD symptoms into your clinical conceptualization? How would you then communicate this information to the primary treatment team, and how much would you disclose?

Posttraumatic stress disorder (PTSD) is associated with increased morbidity and mortality (Buckley, Mozley, Bedard, Dewulf, & Greif, 2004), particularly coronary artery disease (Ahmadi et al., 2011; Vaccarino et al., 2013) and a number of poor health behaviors, including smoking (Zen, Zhao, Whooley, & Cohen, 2012). Since the revision of the DSM-5 Criterion A for PTSD, it remains difficult to determine whether a cancer diagnosis in and of itself would suffice as an index trauma. However, prior to this revision, prevalence rates of PTSD from cancer ranged from 3% to 45% (Gold et al., 2012; Kangas, Henry, & Bryant, 2005) with the majority of studies reporting a range of 4% to 6% (French-Rosas, Moye, & Naik, 2011).

Those individuals with premorbid PTSD may experience a resurgence in symptoms when learning of and coping with any life-threatening illness and/ or facing their own mortality at the end of life, but there is limited research on PTSD in people with advanced, serious illness, or at the end of life (Feldman, 2011). Acknowledging one's mortality and reflecting on life is a normative process for those at end of life. Themes that surface in individuals with PTSD often involve existential distress, guilt, self-blame, moral injury, spiritual distress, and struggles with forgiveness. Moral injury, a topic gaining more attention, refers to the spiritual, emotional, psychological distress that often results from perceived violations of one's moral code (e.g., killing of civilians). These themes often are magnified at the end of life as individuals evaluate their lives and, for some, work to reconcile their relationship with their God or higher spirit. Chaplains can be powerful resources when themes of moral injury surface, allowing individuals to find self-forgiveness within a spiritual context. As individuals become increasingly more dependent on others for care, they may feel more physically and emotional vulnerable, exacerbating issues around trust. This outcome may be especially true for veterans and other service members (e.g., police officers, fire fighters) who may have primarily relied on their physical and cognitive dexterity and strength to defend against perceived threats.

Preoccupation with and worry over pain may trigger PTSD symptoms. Pain interference (disruption of activity or functioning because of pain or fear of pain) has been found to predict PTSD symptoms in palliative care patients, suggesting that daily awareness of pain interference may act as a reminder of cancer-related trauma and maintain the relationship between pain and PTSD-related symptoms (Roth, St. Cyr, Harle, & Katz, 2013). Pain anxiety (cognitive anxiety, escape/avoidance behaviors, fear of pain, physiological symptoms of anxiety) and pain catastrophizing (exaggerated negative mental set brought to bear during actual or anticipated pain experience characterized by rumination, magnification, helplessness) mediated the relationship between pain interference and PTSD-related symptoms (Roth et al., 2013).

A number of self-report measures exist to assess for signs and symptoms of PTSD but with no psychometric data for use in palliative care or hospice populations. The PTSD Checklist for the DSM-5 (PCL-5) (Blevins, Weathers, Davis, Witte, & Domino, 2015) is among the most commonly used measures. A lengthy structured interview, like the Clinician Administered PTSD Scale (CAPS-5) (Weathers et al., 2017), which takes between 40–60 minutes, may fatigue the patient. These measures can help clarify the salience of symptom clusters (e.g., intrusion symptoms, avoidance, negative mood/cognitions, hyper-arousal), which may help target treatment interventions.

Exposure-based therapies are generally viewed as the most efficacious for trauma-related disorders and include evidence-based treatments such as Pro-longed Exposure (PE) and Cognitive Processing Therapy (CPT). However, restructuring thoughts or processing trauma may be inappropriate or counter-therapeutic for those living with advanced and/or life-limiting illness (Greer, Park, Prigerson, & Safren, 2010). Considerations include individuals' cognitive abilities to consent to treatment, engage in and benefit from therapy, and carry-over information between sessions. As with all therapeutic interventions, the benefit must outweigh the risk of treatment. Critical to PTSD treatment is the ability to engage in additional coping strategies should intrusive symptoms surface (e.g., initiate grounding techniques or engage in mindfulness exercises). Often, processing the trauma experience can be counter-therapeutic for adults at the end of life due to the level of emotional distress that may surface. Instead, distraction or grounding techniques and general coping skills can be promoted to help manage emotional distress if/when intrusive symptoms emerge.

Therapeutic approaches, including acceptance and commitment and existential therapies, also can facilitate individuals' efforts to find meaning and process existential distress. Some individuals have never disclosed their traumas to anyone, including family, but feel the need to "confess" and tell their story before dying. Others may never have shared their histories with their families, often worried that their family may judge or think differently of them upon learning about their trauma, especially if the experiences involve perpetrating against another (e.g., combat killings, war crimes, etc.). If individuals volunteer this information, oftentimes listening nonjudgmentally to the person's story, bearing witness to their pain and resilience, and expressing compassion and empathy can go a long way.

Feldman, Sorocco, and Bratkovich (2014) proposed a stepwise psychosocial palliative care model for those with PTSD. Treatment occurs in three stages but progresses to the next stage only if the previous one did not effectively diminish symptoms. Stage I focuses on rapport-building through active listening, problem-solving strategies for practical issues, social/environmental modifications to prevent trauma triggers, and facilitation of communication between family, individual with PTSD, and providers. Stage II focuses on psychoeducation about PTSD and introduction of basic coping skills (relaxation and breathing retraining, thought-stopping, mindfulness-based interventions, and communication skills). In this stage, the provider also trains family members to help the individual with PTSD practice these skills. Stage III involves exposure-based interventions with emphasis on cognitive processing and meaning making. This stage is tailored to the individual's ability and is used only when prior stages do not sufficiently reduce symptoms. Providers are encouraged to use their clinical judgment when using this final stage, given the emotional, psychological, and existential distress this may evoke in the patient. Limited research exists on this proposed model of intervention, with hopes for more outcome data on its efficacy.

Conclusion

Individuals with serious mental illness experience increased morbidity and mortality as compared to the general population. Issues of substance use, psychosis, mood, anxiety, and trauma often complicate management and can create systemic, cultural, logistical, and individual barriers to medical and psychological help seeking. The palliative care and end-of-life needs of persons with SMI demand special attention due to the complexities of providing whole-person care.

Palliative and end-of-life care for individuals with SMI should include cross-training in palliative care and mental health, and individuals should have access to care that integrates families, mental health care, palliative care, other medical services, and social services. Professionals in mental health should be attentive to patients' general health and collaborate with patients' medical providers. In addition, mental health providers can share knowledge of SMI and related comorbidities with palliative care and hospice teams, and through cross-pollination, they can empower each other to provide high quality end-of-life care to this marginalized group. Indeed, doing so highlights the humanity of persons living with dying and recognizes the importance of psychological care at end of life. Mental health professionals also can work with the palliative care and hospice teams to provide psychoeducation on SMI, destigmatizing this label and demystifying the process of caring for psychiatrically complex patients. Mental health providers can share expectations for symptom improvement while recognizing the limits of treating longstanding psychiatric disorders. They can explore how individuals are managing their symptoms/illness and discuss behavioral management strategies and adaptive coping strategies.

For those working in hospital settings where mental health is integrated into medicine (e.g., consult-liaison psychiatry, behavioral health), opportunities for integration may be easier to find. Community hospice agencies and rural health clinics are less likely to employ mental health providers, despite the clear need for psychiatric and psychological services. Systemic barriers, including Medicare reimbursement, disincentivize hospice and palliative care services from hiring mental health professionals equipped to address SMI and other complicated mental health problems. Advocacy efforts are needed to provide equitable healthcare for the living and dying, for when would a person need more mental health support than when imminently facing their own death? Medical care at end of life is clearly valued, although not available to all. Mental health care, however, seems less valued as reflected by the systemic barriers to receiving this service. Advocacy efforts to this end are needed, lest we remain complicit with a system that institutionally disenfranchises the most vulnerable.

Research focused on the mental health needs of individuals with SMI at end-of-life is sorely missing. Similarly, studies demonstrating the efficacy of psychological treatment approaches for this population are equally absent. Increased attention to the needs of this vulnerable population at end of life is critical in order to provide appropriate, evidence-based care. Such research also may facilitate more in-depth discussions about SMI and death/dying, two topics that often evoke discomfort and uncertainty. Mental health providers can empower others to discuss these topics and give permission to explore the intersection of SMI and life-limiting illness in safe, supportive, and educational ways. Pursuing and advocating for research and clinical practice with the SMI population at end of life remains a critically and sorely undervalued avenue toward health equity and whole-person care.

References

Ahmadi, N., Hajsadeghi, F., Mirshkarlo, H. B., Budoff, M., Yehuda, R., & Ebrahimi, R. (2011). Post-traumatic stress disorder, coronary artherosclerosis, and mortality. *American Journal of Cardiology, 108*, 29–33.

Akizuki, N., Shimizu, K., Asai, M., Nakano, T., Okusaka, T., Shimada, K., . . . Uchitomi, Y. (2016). Prevalence and predictive factors of depression and anxiety in patients with pancreatic cancer: A longitudinal study. *Japanese Journal of Clinical Oncology, 46*(1), 71–77.

American Psychiatric Association. (2013). *Diagnostic and statistical manual of mental disorders* (5th ed.). Arlington, VA: Author.

Andersen, B. L., DeRubeis, R. J., Berman, B. S., Gruman, J., Champion, V. L., Massie, M. J., . . . for the American Society of Clinical Oncology. (2014). Screening, assessment, and care of anxiety and depressive symptoms in adults with cancer: An American Society of Clinical Oncology guideline adaptation. *Journal of Clinical Oncology, 32*(15), 1605–1619.

Antunes, B., Murtagh, F., Bausewein, C., Harding, R., & Higginson, I. J. on behalf of EURO IMPACT. (2015). Screening for depression in advanced disease: Psychometric properties, sensitivity, and specificity of two items of the Palliative Care Outcome Scale (POS). *Journal of Pain and Symptom Management, 49*(2), 277–288.

Bailey, F. A., Allen, R. S., Williams, B. R., Goode, P. S., Granstaff, S., Redden, D. T., & Burgio, K. L. (2012). Do-not-resuscitate orders in the last days of life. *Journal of Palliative Medicine, 15*(7), 751–759.

Balaguer, A., Monforte-Royo, C., Porta-Sales, J., Alonso-Babarro, A., Altisent, R., Aradilla-Herrero, A., et al. (2016). An international consensus definition of the wish to hasten death and its related factors. *PloS ONE, 11*(1), e0146184. http://doi.org/10.1371/journal. pone.0146184

Barclay, J. S., Owens, J. E., & Blackhall, L. J. (2014). Screening for substance abuse risk in cancer patients using the Opioid Risk Tool and urine drug screen. *Supportive Care in Cancer, 22*, 1883–1888.

Bloomer, M. J., & O'Brien, A. P. (2013). Palliative care for the person with serious mental illness: The need for a partnership approach to care in Australia. *Progress in Palliative Care, 21*(1), 27–31.

Braiteh, F., Osta, E., Palmer, J. L., Reddy, S. K., & Bruera, E. (2007). Characteristics, findings, and outcomes of palliative care inpatient consultations at a comprehensive cancer center. *Journal of Palliative Medicine, 10*(4), 948–955.

Brenes, G. A. (2003). Anxiety and chronic obstructive pulmonary disease: Prevalence, impact, and treatment. *Psychosomatic Medicine, 65*, 963–970.

Brenne, E., Loge, J. H., Kaasa, S., Heitzer, E., Knudsen, A. K., Wasteson, E., & the European Palliative Care Research Collaborative (EPCRC) (2013). Depressed patients with incurable cancer: Which depressive symptoms do they experience? *Palliative and Supportive Care, 11*(6), 491–501.

Brown, R. L., & Rounds, L. A. (1995). Conjoint screening questionnaires for alcohol and other drug abuse: Criterion validity in a primary care practice. *Wisconsin Medical Journal, 94*(3), 135–140

Buckley, T. C., Mozley, S. L., Bedard, B. S., Dewulf, A.-C., & Greif, J. (2004). Preventive health behaviors, health-risk behaviors, physical morbidity, and health-related role functioning impairment in veterans with post-traumatic stress disorder. *Military Medicine, 169*(7), 536–540.

Butler, H., & O'Brien, A. J. (2017). Access to specialist palliative care services by people with severe and persistent mental illness: A retrospective cohort study. *International Journal of Mental Health Nursing.* doi:10.1111/inm.12360. [Epub ahead of print].

Buzgova, R., Jarosova, D., & Hajnova, E. (2015). Assessing anxiety and depression with respect to the quality of life in cancer patients receiving palliative care. *European Journal of Oncology Nursing, 19*, 667–672.

Carmichael, A., Morgan, L., & Del Fabbro, E. (2016). Identifying and assessing the risk of opioid abuse in patients with cancer: An integrated review. *Substance Abuse and Rehabilitation, 7*, 71–79.

Chambers, S. K., Foley, E., Galt, E., Ferguson, M., & Clutton, S. (2012). Mindfulness groups for men with advanced prostate cancer: A pilot study to assess feasibility and effectiveness and the role of peer support. *Supportive Care in Cancer, 20*(6), 1183–1192.

Chang, C.-K., Hayes, R. D., Broadbent, M., Fernandes, A. C., Lee, W. E., Hotopf, M., & Stewart, R. (2010). All-cause mortality among people with serious mental illness (SMI), substance use disorders, and depressive disorders in southeast London: A cohort study. *BMC Psychiatry, 10*, 77.

Chang, C.-K., Hayes, R. D., Perera, G., Broadbent, M., Fernandes, A. C., Lee, W. E., . . . Stewart, R. (2011). Life expectancy at birth for people with serious mental illness and other major disorders from a Secondary Mental Health Care Case Register in London. *PLoS ONE, 6*(5), e19590. doi:10.1371/journal.pone.0019590

Chochinov, H. M., Martens, P. J., Prior, H. J., & Kredentser, M. S. (2012). Comparative health care use patterns of people with schizophrenia near the end of life: A population-based study in Manitoba, Canada. *Schizophrenia Research, 141*, 241–246.

Chwastiak, L. A., & Tek, C. (2009). The unchanging mortality gap for people with schizophrenia. *Lancet, 374*(9690), 590–592.

Copeland, L. A., Zeber, J. E., Pugh, M. J., Mortensen, E. M., Restrepo, M. I., & Lawrence, V. A. (2008). Postoperative complications in the seriously mentally ill: A systematic review of the literature. *Annals of Surgery, 248*(1), 31–38.

Corrigan, P. W., Pickett, S., Batia, K., & Michaels, P. J. (2014). Peer navigators and integrated care to address ethnic health disparities of people with serious mental illness. *Social Work in Public Health, 29*, 581–593.

De Hert, M., Correll, C. U., Bobes, J., Cetkovich-Bakmas, M., Cohen, D., Asai, I., . . . Leucht, S. (2011). Physical illness in patients with severe mental disorders, I: Prevalence, impact of medications and disparities in health care. *World Psychiatry, 10*, 52–77.

Dev, R., Parsons, H. A., Palla, S., Palmer, J. L., Del Fabbro, E., & Bruera, E. (2011). Undocumented alcoholism and its correlation with tobacco and illegal drug use in advanced cancer patients. *Cancer, 117*, 4551–4556.

Druss, B. G., Zhao, L., von Esenwein, S. A., Bona, J. R., Fricks, L., Jenkins-Tuckerd, S., . . . Lorig, K. (2010). The Health and Recovery Peer (HARP) program: A peer-led intervention to improve medical self-management for persons with serious mental illness. *Schizophrenia Research, 118*(1–3), 264–270.

Ewing, J. A. (1984). Detecting alcoholism. The CAGE Questionnaire. *JAMA, 252*(14), 1905–1907.

Fairman, N., & Irwin, S. A. (2013). Palliative care psychiatry: Update on an emerging dimension of psychiatric practice. *Current Psychiatry Reports, 15*(7), 374.

Feldman, D. B. (2011). Posttraumatic stress disorder at the end of life: Extant research and proposed psychosocial treatment approach. *Palliative & Supportive Care, 9*, 407–418.

Feldman, D. B., Sorocco, K. H., & Bratkovich, K. L. (2014). Treatment of posttraumatic stress disorder at the end-of-life: Application of the stepwise psychosocial palliative care model. *Palliative and Supportive Care, 12*, 233–243.

Fisch, M. J., Lee, J. W., Weiss, M., Wagner, L. I., Chang, V. T., Cella, D., . . . Cleeland, C. S. (2012). Prospective, observational study of pain and analgesic prescribing in medical oncology outpatients with breast, colorectal, lung, or prostate cancer. *Journal of Clinical Oncology, 30*(16), 1980–1988.

Forty, L., Ulanova, A., Jones, L., Jones, I., Gordon-Smith, K., Fraser, C., . . . Craddock, N. (2014). Comorbid medical illness in bipolar disorder. *The British Journal of Psychiatry, 205*, 465–472.

Foti, M. (2003). "Do it your way": A demonstration project on end-of-life care for persons with serious mental illness. *Journal of Palliative Medicine, 6*(4), 661–668.

Freedland, K. E., Carney, R. M., Rich, M. W., Steinmeyer, B. C., Skala, J. A., & Davila-Roman, V. G. (2016). Depression and multiple rehospitalizations in patients with heart failure. *Clinics of Cardiology, 39*(5), 257–262.

French-Rosas, L. N., Moye, J., & Naik, A. D. (2011). Improving the recognition and treatment of cancer-related posttraumatic stress disorder. *Journal of Psychiatry Practice, 17*, 270–276.

Ganzini, L., Socherman, R., Duckart, J., & Shores, M. (2010). End-of-life care for veterans with schizophrenia and cancer. *Psychiatric Services, 61*(7), 725–728.

Gibson, C. A., Lichtenthal, W., Berg, A., & Breitbart, W. (2006). Psychologic issues in palliative care. *Anesthesiology Clinics, 24*(1), 61–80.

Gold, J. I., Douglas, M. K., Thomas, M. L., Elliott, J. E., Rao, S. M., & Miaskowski, C. (2012). The relationship between posttraumatic stress disorder, mood states, functional status, and quality of life in oncology outpatients. *Journal of Pain and Symptom Management, 44*(4), 520–531.

Goldberg, R. W., Dickerson, F., Lucksted, A., Brown, C. H., Weber, E., Tenhula, W. N., . . . Dixon, L. B. (2013). Living well: An intervention to improve self-management of medical illness for individuals with serious mental illness. *Psychiatric Services, 64*(1), 51–57.

Goy, E., & Ganzini, L. (2003). End-of-life care in geriatric psychiatry. *Clinics of Geriatric Medicine, 19*(4), 841–856.

Greco, M. T., Roberto, A., Corli, O., Deandrea, S., Bandieri, E., Cavuto, S., & Apolone, G. (2014). Quality of cancer pain management: An update of a systematic review of undertreatment of patients with cancer. *Journal of Clinical Oncology, 32*(36), 4149–4154.

Greer, J. A., Park, E. R., Prigerson, H. G., & Safren, S. A. (2010). Tailoring cognitive-behavioral therapy to treat anxiety comorbid with advanced cancer. *Journal of Cognitive Psychotherapy, 24*, 294–313.

Greer, J. A., Traeger, L., Bemis, H., Solis, J., Hendriksen, E. S., Park, E. R., . . . Safren, S. A. (2011). A pilot randomized controlled trial of brief cognitive-behavioral therapy for anxiety in patients with terminal cancer. *Oncologist, 17*, 1337–1345.

Hendrie, H. C., Tu, W., Tabbey, R., Purnell, C. E., Ambuehl, A., & Callahan, C. M. (2014). Health outcomes and cost of care among older adults with schizophrenia: A 10-year study using medical records across the continuum of care. *American Journal of Geriatric Psychiatry, 22*(5), 427–436.

Hendriksen, E., Williams, E., Sporn, N., Greer, J., DeGrange, A., & Koopman, C. (2015). Worried together: A qualitative study of shared anxiety in patients with metastatic non-small cell lung cancer and their family caregivers. *Support Care Cancer, 23*, 1035–1041.

Hudson, P. L., Kristjanson, L. J., Ashby, M., Kelly, B., Schofield, P., Hudson, R., . . . Street, A. (2006). Desire for hastened death in patients with advanced disease and the evidence base of clinical guidelines: A systematic review. *Palliative Medicine, 20*(7), 693–701.

Hudson, P. L., Schofield, P., Kelly, B., Hudson, R., Street, A., O'Connor, M., . . . Aranda, S. (2006). Responding to desire to die statements from patients with advanced disease: Recommendations for health professionals. *Palliative Medicine, 20*, 703–710.

Irwin, K. E., Henderson, D. C., Knight, H. P., & Pirl, W. F. (2014). Cancer care for individuals with schizophrenia. *Cancer, 120*, 323–334.

Johnson, S. M., Cramer, R. J., Conroy, M. A., & Gardener, B. O. (2014). The role and challenges for psychologists in physician assisted suicide. *Death Studies, 38*(6–10), 582–588.

Johnson, S. M., Cramer, R. J., Gardner, B. O., & Nobles, M. R. (2015). What patient and psychologist characteristics are important in competency for physician-assisted suicide evaluations? *Psychology, Public Policy, and Law, 21*(4), 420–431.

Julião, M., Oliveira, F., Nunes, B., Carneiro, A. V., & Barbosa, A. (2014). Efficacy of dignity therapy on depression and anxiety in Portuguese terminally ill patients: A phase II randomized controlled trial. *Journal of Palliative Medicine, 17*, 1–8.

Jull-Patterson, D. (2016, Fall). Psychology's ethics and the End of Life Option Act. *California Psychological Association Newsletter, 35*.

Kadan-Lottick, N. S., Vanderwerker, L. C., Block, S. D., Zhang, B., & Prigerson, H. G. (2005). Psychiatric disorders and mental health service use in patients with advanced cancer: A report from the coping with cancer study. *Cancer, 104*(12), 2872–2881.

Kangas, M., Henry, J. L., & Bryant, R. A. (2005). Predictors of posttraumatic stress disorder following cancer. *Health Psychology, 24*(6), 579–585.

Kasl-Godley, J. E., King, D. A., & Quill, T. E. (2014). Opportunities for psychologists in palliative care: Working with patients and families across the disease continuum. *American Psychologist, 69*(4), 364–376.

Kemp, D. E., Gao, K., Ganocy, S. J., Caldes, E., Feldman, K., Chan, P. K., . . . Calabrese, J. R. (2009). Medical and substance use comorbidity in bipolar disorder. *Journal of Affective Disorders, 116*(1–2), 64–69.

Kessler, R. C., Aguilar-Gaxiola, S., Alonso, J., Chatterji, S., Lee, S., Ormel, J., Üstün, T. B., & Wang, P. S. (2009). The global burden of mental disorders: An update from the WHO World Mental Health (WMH) surveys. *Epidemiologia e Psichiatria Sociale, 18*(1), 23–33.

King, D. A., Heisel, M. J., & Lyness, J. M. (2005). Assessment and psychological treatment of depression in older adults with terminal or life-threatening illness. *Clinical Psychology: Science and Practice, 12*(3), 339–353.

Kisely, S., Crowe, E., & Lawrence, D. (2013). Cancer-related mortality in people with mental illness. *JAMA Psychiatry, 70*(2), 209–217.

Krashin, D., Murinova, N., & Ballantyne, J. (2012). Management of pain with comorbid substance abuse. *Current Psychiatry Reports, 14*, 462–468.

Kwon, J. H., Hui, D., & Bruera, E. (2015). A pilot study to define chemical coping in cancer patients using the Delphi Method. *Journal of Palliative Medicine, 18*(8), 703–706.

Lawrence, D., & Kisely, S. (2010). Inequities in healthcare provision for people with severe mental illness. *Journal of Psychopharmacology, 24*(Suppl. 4, 11), 61–68.

Leung, Y. W., Li, M., Devins, G., Zimmermann, C., Rydall, A., Lo, C., & Rodin, G. (2013). Routine screening for suicidal intention in patients with cancer. *Psycho-Oncology, 22*(11), 2537–2545.

Lie, H. C., Hjermstad, M. J., Fayers, P., Finset, A., Kaasa, S., & Loge, J. H., on behalf of the European Palliative Care Research Collaborative (EPCRC). (2015). Depression in advanced cancer: Assessment challenges and associations with disease load. *Journal of Affective Disorders, 173*, 176–184.

Lloyd-Williams, M., Abba, K., & Crowther, J. (2014). Supportive and palliative care for patients with chronic mental illness including dementia. *Current Opinions in Supportive and Palliative Care, 8*(3), 303–307.

Lloyd-Williams, M., Shiels, C., Taylor, F., & Dennis, M. (2009). Depression: An independent predictor of early death in patients with advanced cancer. *Journal of Affective Disorders, 113*, 127–132.

Lo, C., Hales, S., Jung, J., Chiu, A., Panday, T., Rydall, A., . . . Rodin, G. (2014). Managing Cancer and Living Meaningfully (CALM): Phase 2 trial of a brief individual psychotherapy for patients with advanced cancer. *Palliative Medicine, 28*(3), 234–242.

McCasland, L. A. (2007). Providing hospice and palliative care to the seriously and persistently mentally ill. *Journal of Hospice and Palliative Nursing, 9*(6), 305–313.

McKibbin, C. L., Patterson, T. L., Norman, G., Patrick, K., Jin, H., Roesch, S., . . . Jeste, D. V. (2006). A lifestyle intervention for older schizophrenia patients with diabetes mellitus: A randomized controlled trial. *Schizophrenia Research, 86*(1–3), 36–44.

Mercadante, S., Porzio, G., Caruselli, A., Aielli, F., Adile, C., Girelli, N., & Casuccio, A. on behalf of the Home Care-Italy Group (HOCAI). (2015). The frequency of alcoholism in patients with advanced cancer admitted to an acute palliative care unit and a home care program. *Journal of Pain and Symptom Management, 49*(2), 254–257.

Misono, S., Weiss, N. S., Fann, J. R., Redman, M., & Yueh, B. (2008). Incidence of suicide in persons with cancer. *Journal of Clinical Oncology, 26*(29), 4731–4738.

Mitchell, A. J., Chan, M., Bhatti, H., Halton, M., Grassi, L., Johansen, C., & Meader, N. (2011). Prevalence of depression, anxiety, and adjustment disorder in oncological, haematological, and palliative-care settings: A meta-analysis of 94 interview-based studies. *The Lancet Oncology, 12*(2), 160–174.

Mitchell, A. J., Meader, N., Davies, E., Clover, K., Carter, G. L., Loscalzo, M. J., . . . Zabora, J. (2012). Meta-analysis of screening and case finding tools for depression in cancer: Evidence based recommendations for clinical practice on behalf of the Depression in Cancer Care consensus group. *Journal of Affective Disorders, 140*, 149–160.

Miovic, M., & Block, S. (2007). Psychiatric disorders in advanced cancer. *Cancer, 110*(8), 1665–1676.

Morasco, B. J., Duckart, J. P., & Dobscha, S. K. (2011). Adherence to clinical guidelines for opioid therapy for chronic pain in patients with substance use disorder. *Journal of General Internal Medicine, 26*(9), 965–971.

Morgan, B. D. (2016). "No right place to die": Nursing attitudes and needs in caring for people with serious mental illness at end-of-life. *Journal of the American Psychiatric Nurses Association, 22*(1), 31–42.

Neitzer, A., Sun, S., Doss, S., Moran, J., & Schiller, B. (2012). Beck Depression Inventory-Fast Screen (BDI-FS): An efficient tool for depression screen in patient with end-stage renal disease. *Hemodialysis International, 16*, 207–213.

NHPCO Facts and Figures: Hospice Care in America. (2017, September). Alexandria, VA: National Hospice and Palliative Care Organization.

Nissim, R., Freeman, E., Lo, C., Zimmermann, C., Gagliese, L., Rydall, A., . . . Rodin, G. (2012). Managing Cancer and Living Meaningfully (CALM): A qualitative study of a brief individual psychotherapy for individuals with advanced cancer. *Palliative Medicine, 26*(5), 713–721.

Ohnsorge, K., Gudat, H., & Rehmann-Sutter, C. (2014). What a wish to die can mean: Reasons, meanings and functions of wishes to die, reported from 30 qualitative case studies of terminally ill cancer patients in palliative care. *BMC Palliative Care, 13*, 38.

Orentlicher, D., Pope, T. M., & Rich, B. A. (2016). Clinical criteria for physician aid in dying. *Journal of Palliative Medicine, 19*(3), 259–262.

Parpa, E., Tsilika, E., Gennimata, V., & Mystakidou, K. (2015). Elderly cancer patients' psychopathology: A systematic review aging and mental health. *Archives of Gerontology and Geriatrics, 60*, 9–15.

Parsons, H. A., Delgado-Guay, M. O., Osta, B. E., Chacko, R., Poulter, V., Palme, L., & Bruera, E. (2008). Alcoholism screening in patients with advanced cancer: Impact on symptom burden and opioid use. *Journal of Palliative Medicine, 11*(7), 964–968.

Passik, S. D., & Theobald, D. E. (2000). Managing addiction in advanced cancer patients: Why bother? *Journal of Pain and Symptom Management, 19*, 229–234.

Pergolizzi, J. V., Zampogna, G., Taylor, R., Gonima, E., Posada, J., & Raffa, R. B. (2016). A guide for pain management in low and middle income communities: Managing the risk of opioid abuse in patients with cancer pain. *Frontiers in Pharmacology, 7*(42), 1–9.

Rayner, L., Lee, W., Price, A., Monroe, B., Sykes, N., Hansford, P., . . . Hotopf, M. (2011). The clinical epidemiology of depression in palliative care and the predictive value of somatic symptoms: Cross-sectional survey with four-week follow up. *Palliative Medicine, 25*(3), 229–241.

Roth, A. J., & Massie, M. J. (2007). Anxiety and its management in advanced cancer. *Current Opinions in Supportive and Palliative Care, 1*, 50–56.

Roth, M. L., St. Cyr, K., Harle, I., & Katz, J. D. (2013). Relationship between pain and post-traumatic stress symptoms in palliative care. *Journal of Pain and Symptom Management, 46*(2), 182–191.

Saha, S., Chant, D., & McGrath, J. (2007). A systematic review of mortality in schizophrenia: Is the differential mortality gap worsening over time? *Archives of General Psychiatry, 64*(10), 1123–1131.

Sharpe, M., Walker, J., Hansen, C. H., Martin, P., Symeonides, S., Gourley, C., . . . for the SMaRT Oncology-2 Team. (2014). Integrated collaborative care for comorbid major depression in patients with cancer (SMaRT Oncology-2): A multicenter randomised controlled effectiveness trial. *The Lancet, 384*, 1099–1108.

Smith, P. R., Cope, D., Sherner, T. L., & Walker, D. K. (2014). Update on research-based interventions for anxiety in patients with cancer. *Clinical Journal of Oncology Nursing, 18*, 5–16.

Shennan, C., Payne, S., & Fenlon, D. (2011). What is the evidence for the use of mindfulness-based interventions in cancer care? A review. *Psychooncology*, *20*(7), 681–697.

Spencer, R., Nilsson, M., Wright, A., Pirl, W., & Prigerson, H. (2010). Anxiety disorders in advanced cancer patients: Correlates and predictors of end-of-life outcomes. *Cancer*, *116*, 1810–1819.

Stark, D., Kiely, M., Smith, A., Velikova, G., House, A., & Selby, P. (2002). Anxiety disorders in cancer patients: Their nature, associations, and relation to quality of life. *Journal of Clinical Oncology*, *20*(14), 3137–3148.

Stienstra, D., & Chochinov, H. M. (2006). Vulnerability, disability and palliative end-of-life care. *Journal of Palliative Care*, *22*, 166–174.

Substance Abuse and Mental Health Services Administration. (2017). *Key substance use and mental health indicators in the United States: Results from the 2016 National Survey on Drug Use and Health* (HHS Publication No. SMA 17–5044, NSDUH Series H-52). Rockville, MD: Center for Behavioral Health Statistics and Quality, Substance Abuse and Mental Health Services Administration. Retrieved from www.samhsa.gov/data/

Sylvia, L. G., Shelton, R. C., Kemp, D. E., Bernstein, E. E., Friedman, E. S., Brody, B. D., . . . Calabrese, J. R. (2015). Medical burden in bipolar disorder: Findings from the Clinical and Health Outcomes Initiative in Comparative Effectiveness for Bipolar Disorder study (Bipolar CHOICE). *Bipolar Disorders*, *17*(2), 212–223.

Tan, P. D., Barclay, J. S., & Blackhall, L. J. (2015). Do palliative care clinics screen for substance abuse and diversion? Results of a national survey. *Journal of Palliative Medicine*, *18*(9), 752–757.

Tarzian, A. J., Neal, M. T., & O'Neil, J. A. (2005). Attitudes, experiences, and beliefs affecting end-of-life decision-making among homeless individuals. *Journal of Palliative Medicine*, *8*(1), 36–48.

Taylor, J., Swetenham, K., Myhill, K., Picot, S., Glaetzer, K., & van Loon, A. (2012). IMh-PaCT: An education strategy for cross-training palliative care and mental health clinicians. *International Journal of Palliative Nursing*, *18*(2), 290–294.

Tran, E., Rouillon, F., Loze, J. Y., Casadebaig, F., Philippe, A., Vitry, F., & Limosin, F. (2009). Cancer mortality in patients with schizophrenia: An 11-year prospective cohort study. *Cancer*, *115*(15), 3555–3562.

Urban, D., Rao, A., Bressel, M., Neiger, D., Solomon, B., & Mileshkin, L. (2013). Suicide in lung cancer: Who is at risk? *Chest*, *144*(4), 1245–1252.

Vaccarino, V., Goldberg, J., Rooks, C., Shah, A. J., Veledar, E., Faber, T. L., . . . Bremner, J. D. (2013). Post-traumatic stress disorder and incidence of coronary heart disease: A twin study. *Journal of the American College of Cardiology*, *62*, 970–978.

van der Steen, J. T., Radbruch, L., Hertogh, C. M., de Boer, M. E., Hughes, J. C., Larkin, P., . . . European Association for Palliative Care (EAPC). (2014). White paper defining optimal palliative care in older people with dementia: A Delphi study and recommendations from the European Association for Palliative Care. *Palliative Medicine*, *28*(3), 197–209.

Viron, M. J., & Stern, T. A. (2010). The impact of serious mental illness on health and healthcare. *Psychosomatics*, *51*(6), 458–465.

Vreeland, B. (2007). Bridging the gap between mental and physical health: A multidisciplinary approach. *Journal of Clinical Psychiatry*, *68*(Suppl. 4), 26–33.

Walker, E. R., McGee, R. E., & Druss, B. G. (2015). Mortality in mental disorders and global disease burden implications: A systematic review and meta-analysis. *JAMA Psychiatry*, *72*(4), 334–341.

Walker, J., Hansen, C. H., Martin, P., Sawhney, A., Thekkumpurath, P., Beale, C., . . . Sharpe, M. (2013). Prevalence of depression in adults with cancer: A systematic review. *Annals of Oncology*, *24*, 895–900.

Walker, J., Hansen, C. H., Martin, P., Symeonides, S., Gourley, C., Wall, L., . . . for the SMaRT Oncology-3 Team. (2014). Integrated collaborative care for major depression comorbid with poor prognosis cancer (SMaRT Oncology-3): A multicenter randomised controlled trial in patients with lung cancer. *The Lancet, 15*, 1168–1176.

Walker, J., Hansen, C. H., Martin, P., Symeonides, S., Ramessur, R., Murray, G., & Sharpe, M. (2014). Prevalence, associations, and adequacy of treatment of major depression in patients with cancer: A cross-sectional analysis of routinely collected clinical data. *Lancet Psychiatry, 1*, 343–350.

Weathers, F. W., Bovin, M. J., Lee, D. J., Sloan, D. M., Schnurr, P. P., Kaloupek, D. G., Keane, T. M., & Marx, B. P. (2017). The Clinician-Administered PTSD Scale for DSM-5 (CAPS-5): Development and initial psychometric evaluation in military veterans. *Psychological Assessment*. May 11 doi: 10.1037/pas0000486. [Epub ahead of print].

Webber, T. (2012). End of life care for people with mental illness. *Journal of Ethics in Mental Health, 7*, 1–4.

Webster, L. R. & Webster, R. (2005). Predicting aberrant behaviors in opioid-treated patients: Preliminary validation of the opioid risk tool. *Pain Medicine, 6*(6), 432–442.

Weissman, J., Pratt, L. A, Miller, E. A,, & Parker, J. D. (2015). *Serious psychological distress among adults: United States, 2009–2013. NCHS data brief, no 203*. Hyattsville, MD: National Center for Health Statistics.

Werth, J. L., Benjamin, G. A., & Farrenkopf, T. (2000). Requests for physician-assisted death: Guidelines for assessing mental capacity and impaired judgement. *Psychology, Public Policy and the Law, 6*(2), 348–372.

Wilson, K. G., Chochinov, H. M., Skirko, M. G., Allard, P., Chary, S., Gagnon, P. R., . . . Clinch, J. J. (2007). Depression and anxiety disorders in palliative cancer care. *Journal of Symptom Management, 33*(2), 118–129.

Wilson, K. G., Dalgleish, T. L., Chochinov, H. M., Chary, S., Gagnon, P. R., Macmillan, K., . . . Fainsinger, R. L. (2016). Mental disorders and the desire for death in patients receiving palliative care for cancer. *British Medical Journal Supportive & Palliative Care, 6*, 170–177.

Wilson, K. G., Lander, M., & Chochinov, H. M. (2009). Diagnosis and management of depression in palliative care. In H. M. Chochinov & W. Breitbart (Eds.), *Handbook of psychiatry in palliative medicine* (2nd ed., pp. 39–68). New York: Oxford University Press.

Wu, S. M., Compton, P., Bolus, R., Schieffer, B., Pham, Q., Baria, A., Van Vort, W., Davis, F., Shekelle, P., & Naliboff, B. D. (2006). The Addiction Behaviors Checklist: validation of a new clinician-based measure of inappropriate opioid use in chronic pain. *Journal of Pain and Symptom Management, 32*, 342–351.

Young, E. W., Marcus, F. S., Drought, T., Mendiola, M., Ciesielski-Carlucci, C., Alpers, A., . . . Ross, C. (1997). Report of the Northern California Conference for Guidelines on Aid-in-Dying: Definitions, differences, convergences, conclusions. *Western Journal of Medicine, 166*(6), 381–388.

Zen, A. L., Zhao, S., Whooley, M. A., & Cohen, B. E. (2012). Post-traumatic stress disorder is associated with poor health behaviors: Findings from the heart and soul study. *Health Psychology, 31*, 194–201.

Zolnierek, C. D., & Clingerman, E. M. (2012). A medical-surgical nurse's perceptions of caring for a person with severe mental illness. *Journal of the American Psychiatric Nurses Association, 18*(4), 226–235.

Chapter 4

Person-centred end-of-life care for individuals living with dementia in the United Kingdom

Jane Chatterjee and Murna Downs

Introduction

Dementia is now recognised as a terminal disease, yet palliative approaches have only recently been applied to dementia, and access to hospice services are the exception rather than the rule. The European Association for Palliative Care (EAPC) has provided the first definition of palliative care in dementia. In its framework, it advocates a partnership between palliative care and dementia care specialists to ensure that optimum end-of-life care is received by people living with dementia.

Palliative approaches applied to dementia have much in common with person-centred dementia care. These approaches recognise the multiplicity of influences on quality of life and the range of domains affected at end of life – physical, medical, psychological, emotional, spiritual, and social. In this chapter, we will consider the role of hospices in supporting people living and dying with dementia and provide an overview of evidence-based, clinically informed, palliative and person-centred approaches for this diverse range of people and their families. We illustrate these approaches with examples of best practice and case studies.

Dementia

Dementia refers to a collection of cognitive and functional impairments that are caused by a number of neurodegenerative diseases. The most commonly occurring of these are Alzheimer's disease and vascular dementia (Stephan & Brayne, 2008). They are terminal conditions in that, if someone living with dementia does not die from some other life-limiting illness, then they will die from complications caused by the advanced stages of dementia. The course of dementia is often protracted and unpredictable, with a comparable symptom burden at the end of life as other terminal conditions, including cancer and heart failure (Sampson, Burns, & Richards, 2011). Prognosis varies from a few years to more than 10, with the median survival from diagnosis reported as 4.5 years (Xie, Brayne, Matthews, & Medical Research Council Cognitive Function and Ageing Study Collaborators, 2008).

The prevalence of dementia increases with age; in the United Kingdom (UK), one in 14 people over the age of 65 has dementia, which increases to one in six people over the age of 80. There are currently around 850,000 people living with dementia in the UK, and this number is expected to rise to over a million by 2025 (Alzheimer's Society, 2014). With the demographics of ageing populations, the World Health Organisation (2012) has identified dementia as a global health challenge.

We know that approximately one in three people over the age of 65 will either die with, or from, dementia (Alzheimer's Association, 2017). It has become the leading cause of death in England and Wales (Office for National Statistics, 2015). Many older people who have dementia also live with comorbidities. Seven out of 10 people living with dementia in the UK live with an additional 4.6 chronic illnesses (Guthrie, Payne, Alderson, McMurdo, & Mercer, 2012). As such, people living with dementia may die from another terminal illness such as cancer or heart failure. In some cases, although dementia is not the main cause of death, its interaction with other conditions can complicate and exacerbate their effects. People living with end-stage dementia will be severely cognitively and functionally impaired, likely confined to bed, have very limited or no language skills, incontinent of urine and faeces, and have difficulty coordinating chewing and swallowing leading to dysphagia. As this extreme frailty impedes recovery from illness, infection, in particular aspiration pneumonia, is the most likely cause of death (Alzheimer's Society, 2012b; Cox & Cook, 2002). Despite the significant numbers who will die with or from dementia, there are continued reports of people dying with dementia receiving suboptimal end-of-life care, with inappropriate hospital admissions, futile treatments, and poor management of end-of-life symptoms (Sampson et al., 2011).

Palliative care

The central role of palliative care in ensuring quality of care for people living with dementia is increasingly recognised in the UK and internationally. Over the last decade UK national strategies for end-of-life care (Department of Health, 2008a; Department of Health Northern Ireland, 2010; National Palliative and End of Life Care Partnership, 2015; Scottish Government, 2015; Welsh Government, 2017) and for dementia care (Department of Health, 2009a; Department of Health Northern Ireland, 2011; Welsh Assembley, 2011; Scottish Government, 2016) address end-of-life care for people with dementia by advocating a partnership approach where dementia and palliative care specialists can complement each other. The EAPC (2013) emphasises the value of national strategies in raising the profile of end-of-life care and influencing policy makers.

Given the complexities created by declining cognitive function and behavioural changes, it is increasingly recognised that the traditional model of palliative care, with its roots in cancer care, may lack suitability for people with dementia (National Council for Palliative Care, 2009). Van der Steen and colleagues (2014) report on a proposed new model of palliative care developed by the EAPC which aims to address the unique features of dying with dementia, a focus lacking in traditional models. These include (Porsteinsson & Antonsdottir, 2015):

- memory problems,
- communication difficulties,
- visual and perceptual difficulties,
- coordination difficulties,
- hallucinations and delusions,
- disorientation,
- changes in a person's mood and behaviour.

In an effort to address the paucity of research in this field, the EAPC conducted a Delphi study to gain consensus on defining optimal palliative care for older people with dementia (van der Steen, et al., 2014). Through evidence from literature, guidelines and, where available, empirical studies, the EAPC (2013) provided recommendations for practice, policy, and research, categorised under the following domains:

- Applicability of palliative care
- Person-centred care, communication and shared decision-making
- Setting care goals and advance care planning
- Continuity of care
- Prognostication and timely recognition of dying
- Avoiding overly aggressive, burdensome or futile treatment
- Optimal treatment of symptoms and providing comfort
- Psychosocial and spiritual support
- Family care and involvement
- Education of the healthcare team
- Societal and ethical issues

People with dementia are a diverse group with respect to age, ethnicity, sexual orientation, income, and education. A poorer quality of end-of-life care and a lower diagnosis rate for dementia is reported for people from black and minority ethnic communities, compared to their white British counterparts. It is generally recognised that for these communities there are various potential barriers to accessing palliative and dementia care services including: lack of cultural and religious sensitivity; discrimination, or fear of it; communication barriers; different cultural views regarding discussing death and the understanding of dementia; and assumptions that families are more prepared to care for their relatives at home (All-Party Parliamentary Group on Dementia, 2013; Dixon, King, Matosevic, Clark, & Knapp, 2015; National Palliative and End of Life Care Partnership, 2015). If diversity is not fully recognised it could lead to oversimplified solutions to meeting the palliative care needs for people living with dementia. These issues will be explored throughout the chapter by referring to EAPC (2013) recommendations and following the case examples of three diverse individuals:

Case example

June is an 82-year-old lady with vascular dementia, heart failure, and diabetes. She has been admitted to a hospice for assessment of her pain.

Michal is a 65-year-old man with Lewy body dementia and lung cancer. His condition has deteriorated, and he has been admitted to a hospice for a period of assessment.

Aamira is an 87-year-old lady with advanced Alzheimer's disease living in a care home. She is nursed in bed, is incontinent, and eats small amounts of soft diet.

Hospice care

Dame Cicely Saunders (1967), founder of the modern hospice movement, developed the model of 'total pain' to recognise the multifaceted, interdependent nature of suffering, with physical, emotional, spiritual, and social domains. In the UK, hospices offer specialist palliative care as inpatient, outpatient, community, and day services to people with cancer and nonmalignant terminal conditions. A multidisciplinary hospice team supports patients with complex needs. Hospices also offer consultation and training to generalists providing end-of-life care. Hospice UK (2015), a national charity, acknowledge that, while the proportion of people with a nonmalignant diagnosis accessing specialist palliative care services is increasing, hospices' response to dementia remains generally small. It argues that under the Equality Act (2010) hospices have a legal and moral commitment to ensure equal access to the service, which should be adapted to meet the specific needs of people with dementia. It reports on organisational concerns around the suitability of hospice environments and the level of resources and staff skills in dementia care; some fearing a 'tsunami' effect with growing numbers of people with dementia needing support. Hospice UK (2015) does not, however, suggest that all people with dementia who are dying require admission to hospice inpatient units; arguably they may be better supported in their usual place of care where they can avoid the stress of unfamiliar care staff and environments. Coining the term 'hospice-enabled dementia care', Hospice UK (2015) advocates that hospices not only adapt their current services but also adopt a facilitative role, reaching out to the local community and care providers to work in partnership, envisaging that this will create more person-centred and individualised ways of working, depending on the needs of the community and existing services. This chapter will look at initiatives taken by some UK hospices towards providing equitable care for people living and dying with dementia.

Person-centred dementia care

Saunders' hospice movement has a lot in common with Tom Kitwood's (1990) seminal work on person-centred dementia care. For Kitwood, the experience of living with dementia was a function of the dynamic relationship between the person's neurological condition and the extent to which the person's psychological, social, and emotional needs were being met. Kitwood's (1997) enriched model of dementia care proposes that personhood is upheld when an individual is supported in meeting their psychological needs for comfort, attachment, inclusion, occupation, identity, and love. He paid particular attention to the potential of interactions, relationships, and the social environment to meet these needs. He advocated psychological and social approaches to promote well-being and quality of life. For Kitwood, communication is central to our relationships with others and to all aspects of care (Downs & Collins, 2015). While dementia may limit a person's scope for communicating, we can enable and enhance a person's residual abilities to communicate through a supportive social environment (Kitwood, 1990).

Dementia care specialists identify ways of supporting communication through using skills such as a calm approach, gestures, asking short questions, allowing response time, addressing sensory impairments, and minimising distractions (Social Care Institute for Excellence, 2009). Augmentative communication is also advocated: using written words and pictures to enhance understanding of what is spoken and reduce demands on a person's language skills and memory. Studies show that this approach can improve social and conversational skills for people with mild to moderate dementia as well as help them to stay focused and organise their thoughts (Bourgeois, Dijkstra, Burgio, & Allen-Burge, 2001; Murphy, Gray, & Cox, 2007).

It is increasingly recognised that, as language becomes compromised, people living with dementia express their needs through nonverbal behaviour (Allan & Killick, 2008). This expression of unmet need can be erroneously considered inevitable symptoms of living with dementia and labelled as 'challenging behaviour' (Downs, Small, & Froggatt, 2006). A more person-centred, unmet-needs understanding of behaviour suggests that the challenge rests with the carers to identify the cause, meaning, or agenda of the behaviour. Kitwood (1990) advises that knowing about a person, including their life story, can help care staff anticipate their needs and understand their emotions; short-term memory problems lead them to draw on past experiences to understand their current situation. Furthermore, studies suggest that understanding a person's routines, habits, and

Dementia and end-of-life care in the UK   63

needs allows changes in their behaviour to be identified and understood in context, making it easier to differentiate between different causes of distress such as physical pain, hunger, fatigue, and anxiety (Cohen-Mansfield & Creedon, 2002; Falls & Stevens, 2004). The 'This is me' leaflet (Alzheimer's Society, 2017) is an initiative that encourages familiar carers to record such information about the person with dementia, to be made available for those caring for them who may lack familiarity.

Case example

June had a leg ulcer that required daily dressings. Despite trying different dressings to promote comfort, June would remove them. When she took off her cardigan she would fold it neatly with the arms tucked in. Her family told staff that June had worked in a department store. It was found that if she was given items to fold she was less likely to remove her dressings.

Key elements of quality end-of-life care for people with dementia

Symptom assessment

The holistic nature of symptom assessment is fundamental to palliative care. Holistic assessment takes into account the physical, psychosocial, and emotional dimensions of a person's experience of living with a life-limiting condition. Common physical symptoms at end of life, regardless of disease process, include pain, breathlessness, nausea, and vomiting, often compounded towards the end of life by general debility, infection, and anxiety. The gold standard for holistic assessment is a person's self-report. This is because many symptoms are subjective, and even those with overt signs have an affective component (McCaffery, 1968; Pace, Treloar, & Scott, 2011). As already discussed, individuals living with dementia may have difficulty understanding, expressing, and reporting how they feel. These limitations to assessment are the likely cause of there being a gross disparity in the treatment of pain and other symptoms. Numerous studies have demonstrated that pain is underassessed, underreported, and undertreated in people with dementia (Lichtner et al., 2014). We know that people with hip fracture and advanced dementia received a third of the analgesics administered to their counterparts without dementia (Morrison & Siu, 2000).

While self-report should always be sought, this may become difficult given minimal verbal expression or increasing reliance on behavioural expression

(Hadjistavropoulos, Fitzgerald, & Marchildon, 2010). The majority of research in symptom assessment for people living with dementia considers pain assessment. Most studies use convenience samples and quasi-experimental designs with low levels of evidence. Based on the available evidence, guidelines have been developed by experts. There are two main ways pain is assessed: through self-report and observation.

It is important to ask the person about their pain, as some people with dementia will likely find it difficult to initiate such conversations with others. There is no specific level of cognition that determines whether a person can report the presence of pain; a minimum response could be a nod or a hand squeeze. Asking questions using alternative words for pain such as hurting, aching, sore, or uncomfortable can be helpful as well as using supportive and augmentative communication skills. Assessment should take place when the person is moving about as well as when they are resting as they may forget pain encountered on movement when they are no longer active (American Geriatrics Society, 2002; Hadjistavropoulos et al., 2010; Royal College of Physicians, British Geriatrics Society, & British Pain Society, 2007). Unidimensional assessment tools to measure pain intensity come in various formats using images, numbers, words, and colour gradation. Studies suggest that these show adequate reliability and validity for use with people with mild to moderate dementia (Hadjistavropoulos et al., 2010). A person's preference for a particular assessment tool may be influenced by their education, personality, and culture, as well as level of cognitive impairment (Curtiss, 2010; DeWaters, Popovitch, & Faut-Callahan, 2003). For example, someone who worked as an accountant may prefer to use a numerical rating scale, whereas others may prefer the more visual representation of the Iowa Pain Thermometer (Herr, Spratt, Garand, & Li, 2007).

There is little evidence on the use of self-report multidimensional assessment tools considering other aspects of pain. Some studies show that a significant number of nursing home residents with dementia could locate their pain by pointing to themselves or to a body diagram and use pain descriptors shown as words on flash cards (Ferrell, Ferrell, & Rivera, 1995; Wynne, Ling, & Remsberg, 2000). Pain descriptors are words collated by Melzack and Torgerson (1971) to help a person describe the nature and quality of their pain. Bennett (2001) added sensory related descriptors to identify patients whose pain has a neuropathic element. These pain descriptors include words like burning, heavy, sharp, stabbing, squeezing, shock-like, pins, and needles. Displaying these as words and pictures supports assessment in some people with dementia who can understand the representation (Chatterjee, 2012). It is recommended that assessment tools be explained to the person at a time when their pain is least severe (DeWaters, Popovitch, & Faut-Callahan, 2003). There may be times when pain is so overwhelming it hinders a person's ability to use typical assessment tools.

Dementia and end-of-life care in the UK 65

> **Case example**
>
> Michal rang the nurse call alarm from the bathroom. He told the nurse that he had almost fallen. When he was asked if he had pain he said 'no' but lay on his bed with his eyes closed. He was asked if he had any discomfort or if it hurt or ached anywhere and it became apparent he had a headache. On further questioning it became clear that he would become dizzy when he got his headaches. He was started on regular analgesics and over the next couple of days Michel spent less time lying down. His family reported that some of his 'old self' had returned.

This example highlights the importance of combining self-report assessment with observation of a person's behaviour. Recognising Michal's continued distress led the nurse to pursue the assessment using short, direct questions and different adjectives to describe pain and discomfort.

When a person is unable to communicate verbally, observation of their non-verbal behaviour becomes central to the assessment of their symptoms. Numerous behavioural observation tools have been developed to assess pain in people with advanced dementia. Herr, Bursch, Ersek, Miller, and Swafford (2010), in a systematic review, evaluated 14 tools, rating their validity, reliability, feasibility, and ability to identify six categories of behavioural indicators of pain defined by the American Geriatrics Society (2002):

- facial expressions
- vocalisations
- body movements
- changes in interpersonal interactions
- changes in activity patterns
- changes in mental status.

The Pain Assessment Checklist for Seniors with Limited Ability to Communicate (PACSLAC) (Fuchs-Lacelle & Hadjistavropoulos, 2004) and the Pain Assessment in Advanced Dementia (PAINAD) (Warden, Hurley, & Volicer, 2003) are psychometrically the most robust. The PAINAD is brief, taking no more than a couple of minutes to complete; the PACSLAC is more comprehensive, with more items to consider (Herr et al., 2010). One study found that 75% of nurses rated the PACSLAC as more clinically useful for people with dementia than the PAINAD (Zwakhalen, Hamers, & Berger, 2006). Herr and colleagues recommend PACSLAC and PAINAD to be used in conjunction, with PACSLAC implemented monthly for ongoing screening and PAINAD on a more regular basis to monitor response to interventions. Lichtner and colleagues (2014) in their meta-analysis involving 28 observational tools could not recommend the use of any one over another based on the available evidence. They identified methodological limitations to the studies and a lack of theory underpinning tool development, recommending further research into the psychometric properties. Some authors question the value of such standardisation when measuring subjective phenomena, suggesting that gathering information from different carers, who may pick up on different behavioural cues, will provide a broader picture (Golafshani, 2003; Regnard et al., 2007; Snow et al., 2004). All the tools recognise that people with dementia may express pain in atypical ways, such as through anger or withdrawal (Herr et al., 2010).

Some authors argue that observational tools do not differentiate between pain and distress. Regnard et al. (2007) questions the content validity of the observational tools designed for pain assessment, given the lack of evidence of specific behaviours that distinguish pain from other causes of distress in people with severe communication difficulties. Distress may be physical pain or discomfort (such as nausea or constipation), psychosocial or spiritual pain, or a combination of these (Pace et al., 2011). Jordan, Regnard, O'Brien, and Hughes (2012) suggest the potential for false identification of pain if the wider concept of distress is not considered. Regnard et al. (2007) established that each person has their own language of distress and identified it as a change from the person's normal behaviour. They suggest that distress might go undetected if observational tools look only for common cues such as those categorised by the American Geriatric Society (2002).

The Disability Distress Assessment Tool (DisDAT) (Regnard et al., 2007) is recommended as an end-of-life care resource by National Council for Palliative Care (2009). It was developed to support carers who intuitively understand an individual's distress cues but lack confidence in their observations. It helps carers to document the range and subtleties of the behaviours they see, making explicit their implicit understanding. It records a person's content and distressed behaviour, so that distress is recognised when there is a change. This aids the detection of distress cues unique to the individual, as what may be content behaviour for one person, such as sitting quietly, could be distressed behaviour for another. Ideally, those who know the person well should be supported to complete the DisDAT. This understanding can then be used by others caring for the person who may be a visiting clinician or the care team if they are transferred to a different care environment. Regnard and colleagues (2007) suggest that, if there is no one familiar with the person's behaviour, the DisDAT can be used to make a baseline record. This may be the case if a person's decline in cognition has been rapid or the person has been living on their own and there is no one familiar with their behaviour. Their study showed that professional and family carers found the DisDAT useful. It could be argued that involving the family increases its feasibility and its individualised approach makes it applicable across cultures.

It is important to note that behavioural observation tools, including observational pain assessment tools, are only the first step. Once distress is identified, it is necessary to determine the cause (Pace et al., 2011). The EAPC (2013) recommends that behavioural distress be managed systematically where psychosocial approaches are considered first. These can be tailored to an individual through information given by the familiar carers. Such measures can help to reduce unnecessary use or dose escalation of medication, limiting the burden of unwarranted side effects. Opioids can cause constipation and, if used inappropriately, exacerbate confusion (National Council for Palliative Care, 2009). Antipsychotic medications may be effective against some distressing neuropsychiatric symptoms, such as hallucinations, but they have potentially severe adverse side effects and there is universal concern that they are often prescribed inappropriately (Banerjee, 2009).

A stepwise approach is offered by the Serial Trial Intervention (Kovach et al., 2006). Cohen-Mansfield's (2008) Treatment Routes for Exploring Agitation model provides a similar systematic approach to identifying the underlying need being expressed by the person's behaviour. A randomised controlled study showed that when the Serial Trial Intervention was used by nursing home nurses they were more persistent in their assessment approaches, leading to improved management and lower levels of discomfort experienced by the residents. In a further study, it was identified that, despite training, nurses underidentified changes in behaviour of residents with dementia, particularly more subtle changes, thus at times failing to trigger the use of the protocol (Kovach, Logan, Joosse, & Noonan, 2012). This finding emphasises the importance of identifying distress in the first instance. While the EAPC (2013) endorse such a stepwise approach, they caution against a delay in the use of appropriate medication to treat identifiable physical symptoms, giving the example of opioids for the early treatment of severe physical pain and/or breathlessness. This shows the need for clinical judgement.

Case example

When Aamira was first admitted to the care home she could walk independently and say a few words in Hindi, her mother tongue. Although she had learnt English she had reverted to speaking Hindi as her dementia progressed. It was also recognised that Aamira would like to sit in a particular chair in the conservatory next to plants and a water feature. Although normally quiet, she would shout if someone else was sitting in this chair. Some staff felt that she should not get her own way all the time and would challenge her. Aadit, her husband, completed the 'This is me' leaflet for her and it was identified that Aamira was a devout Hindu. He explained that the water feature and flowers would be a focus for her prayers. Understanding this made staff more receptive to her needs.

As Aamira's dementia progressed she stopped speaking and became unable to weight bear. It became necessary to use a hoist to lift her out of bed. Aamira's limbs would become rigid and she would shout 'arrh' when she was being moved in bed or with the hoist. She had a low dose transdermal analgesic (opioid) patch for arthritis. The care staff thought this must not be strong enough and she was experiencing pain when they were moving her. The GP increased the patch strength. Over the next couple of days Aamira called out less but became drowsy and stopped eating and drinking. The community palliative care team felt that she may be suffering the side effects of the increased opioid dose. Her analgesic patch was reduced back to the original strength and within a couple of days she became alert again. An assessment (DisDAT) was completed and Aamira's behaviour recorded over time. When she was content her body relaxed, she would make eye contact, smile and move her limbs freely. It was noticed that she would tense her body and call out at other times, for example, with any sudden loud noise. It was concluded that the vocalisation 'arrh' was one component of her language of distress and her distressed behaviour in these instances was likely a result of fear rather than pain. The care staff found that if they approached Aamira calmly, spoke reassuringly to her and held her close while she was being moved, she would be less distressed. The care staff also learnt a few words of Hindi with which to comfort Aamira.

One afternoon, although Aamira was sat in her usual chair, her body was tense and she was murmuring 'arrh' rhythmically. One member of staff wondered if she was chanting her prayers but others were concerned that this was not her usual behaviour. They looked for potential causes of distress; she was not constipated and she did not appear thirsty or hungry. This behaviour continued even when Aadit was visiting. The GP was called and the completed DisDAT was shown as evidence that this was her way of expressing distress. On physical examination the GP diagnosed a chest infection and suggested Aamira was likely experiencing pain with breathing. Oral antibiotics were prescribed as well as an additional oral analgesic to be given 'as required' for her comfort until the infection resolved.

Dementia and end-of-life care in the UK   69

> **Questions**
>
> 1 Drawing on this scenario, what are the key issues for a holistic assessment for people with dementia who cannot communicate their needs?
> 2 How useful are behavioural observation assessment tools? What would ensure that such tools are culturally sensitive?
> 3 What are the risks of always interpreting a person's distressed behaviour as pain?

Making decisions about care and treatment

The EAPC's (2013) framework for people living with dementia starts from the point of diagnosis. It stresses that a person's goals and priorities for care may change throughout the course of dementia. Prolongation of life may become less appropriate as dementia progresses while maintenance of function and maximisation of comfort more so, with maximisation of comfort the main priority of care when living with severe dementia. As such, decisions may differ, depending on where on the trajectory of living with dementia the person is. It is noteworthy that engaging people with dementia in these decisions will become compromised as the disease progresses.

For people with dementia and their families, knowing when end of life is approaching may assist with decision-making. However, this prognostication is notoriously difficult and, perhaps not surprisingly, considerable research attention is now being paid to this area of end-of-life care. In the UK, a prognostic indicator tool has been developed to help to determine the onset of end-stage dementia (Gold Standard Framework, 2011). It includes:

- low functional levels
- weight loss for no apparent cause or with reduced oral intake
- recurrent infections such as urinary and aspiration pneumonia
- high-grade pressure sores.

It is not meant to be prescriptive, and prognostication for people with dementia remains problematic. The end stage is protracted and uncertain. For some people living with dementia, it can last a year or more while, for others, concurrent conditions can accelerate their decline. Melis and colleagues (2013) found that multimorbidity was related to a faster rate of decline in people with dementia compared to those without dementia. Prognostication challenges are likely to contribute to the poor uptake of palliative care and hospice services.

In England and Wales, the Mental Capacity Act (2005) and Deprivation of Liberty Safeguards (Department of Health, 2009b) are legal frameworks for safeguarding people who lack capacity to make decisions for themselves. Similar legislation is in place in Scotland (Scottish Government, 2000), while for Northern Ireland many of the same principles are applied under common law. In these circumstances decisions about treatment and care should not be based on the chances of survival alone but should take account of:

- the burden and benefits of various treatments
- the person's quality of life
- the person's degree of suffering
- the person's known or perceived wishes and values.

This forms a basis of best-interest decision-making, which should be made through consensus among healthcare professionals and the family carers. Furthermore, anything done for or on behalf of a person who lacks capacity should be done in their best interests and in a way that is least restrictive (Department of Health, 2009b; Mental Capacity Act, 2005). In bioethics, principlism sees autonomy as the dominant ethical principle based on the individual and their right to make choices. When, through lack of capacity, a person is unable to maintain autonomy, the principles of beneficence (to do good) and nonmaleficence (to avoid doing harm) predominate (Beauchamp & Childress, 2001). Pace and colleagues (2011) suggest that it is not always possible to foresee the outcome of decisions to know whether these principles are achievable. Gillick (2012) points to the ongoing debate that asks if, given the extent of cognitive decline, a person with advanced dementia is the same person they were in the earlier stages of the disease. This leads to questions about whether, in advanced dementia, a person's previously expressed wishes should be upheld to support their autonomy, even if this conflicts with the principle of beneficence. Gillick (2012) recommends a measured approach, taking both perspectives into account. Baldwin (2008) suggests that for people who lack the capacity to make decisions, promoting personhood should be at the centre of ethical reasoning. Kitwood (1997, p. 8) sees personhood as "a standing or status that is bestowed upon one human being by others, in the context of relationship and social being"; thus, decisions need to be made in the context of the person's relationship with others.

Case example

Plans were made for June to be discharged from the hospice inpatient unit. Her family reported that since her admission to the hospice she had become more confused and more dependent on others. In a best

> interest decision meeting it was decided for June to be admitted to a care home. June was present during the discussion but continued to affirm that she wanted to go home. The family revealed that prior to June's admission to the hospice they had rearranged her house in order to keep her bed downstairs. This had caused her distress and she would ask to go home not recognising that she was at home. They also reported times in the hospice, during their visits, when she was relaxed and happy and thought that she was at home. June's wish to go home was likely an expression of insecurity and loss of independence. If June was discharged home the stress on the family could have a negative impact on her relationship with them. Through admission to a care home the family could continue to visit regularly, help the staff to know her better and put personal items in her room. Attending to June's needs in this way could help maintain her personhood and minimise the impact of this decision.

The EAPC (2013) recommends avoiding overly aggressive, burdensome, and futile treatments. The ethical principle of ordinary and extraordinary treatments states that there is no moral obligation to commit to extraordinary treatments. These are interventions that cause severe pain or suffering and have a high risk of morbidity or mortality or have a low chance of success (Hughes & Dove, 2006). There is evidence suggesting that aggressive medical treatments for acute infection, malnutrition, and dehydration show limited life-prolonging effects in people living with advanced dementia, as they do not halt the dementia progression (Meier, Ahronheim, Morris, Beskin-Lyons, & Morrison, 2001; Mitchell, Kiely, & Hamel, 2004). EAPC (2013) identifies studies that show a high risk of delirium and decompensation for people with dementia who are hospitalised, as well as shorter survival rates compared to hospitalised patients without dementia. With the distress caused by a lack of understanding of invasive procedures and new environments, the threshold at which treatments become classified as extraordinary is likely lower for people with dementia than for those without. When decisions concern medical treatments and there is no legally appointed advocate for the person who lacks capacity, the physician is ultimately responsible, following consultation with the wider healthcare team and family carers (General Medical Council, 2010). Within a family, members may have different values and interpretations of their culture and the perceived wishes of the person with dementia (Connolly, Sampson, & Purandare, 2012). Winter and Parks (2008) show that uncertainty or family discord is associated with stronger preferences for life-prolonging treatments and a weaker emphasis on a palliative care approach. Zarit and Zarit (2008) advocate case review meetings where anyone involved in the care of the person with dementia meet together to receive the same information, air their views and discuss the benefits and burdens of different scenarios. If the situation remains unresolved a second medical opinion is advocated (General Medical Council, 2010). In England and Wales, if legal advice is required the Court of Protection has the power to determine the lawfulness of any act relating to a patient's care or treatment (Mental Capacity Act, 2005).

Case example

Aamira had little appetite but seemed to enjoy a semolina milk pudding Aadit brought in for her. It was a family recipe. Recently he would spend several hours trying to get her to eat just a small amount. The care home staff saw that this was causing distress to them both. In a meeting with the GP it was explained that the most likely cause of Aamira's poor appetite and swallowing difficulties was the irreversible progression of her dementia. The option of feeding via a tube into her stomach and the potential burden and benefits were considered against the alternative of maximising comfort alone. Aadit was against enteral feeding. Their daughter questioned her father about his beliefs and felt it would be wrong to just give up. He explained that when diagnosed with dementia, Aamira had said she did not want treatment that would prolong her life. The GP identified that Aamira had an oral fungal infection and prescribed anti-fungal medication to relieve symptoms of a sore mouth. Aamira seemed to enjoy her semolina pudding again although she continued to lose weight. A couple of months later she developed a chest infection. The GP prescribed oral antibiotics but Aadit questioned whether this treatment would be against her wishes. It was discussed that prior to the infection, Aamira seemed content and smiled when her family visited. As she did not object to taking the oral medication, treating the chest infection would seem appropriate as it could alleviate symptoms and restore her quality of life. The likelihood of reoccurring infection was discussed and it was decided that when the treatment and/or side-effects became overly burdensome or require a hospital admission, alternative measures to manage symptoms of pain, breathlessness and fever within the care home would be the best option.

Dementia and end-of-life care in the UK 73

> **Questions**
>
> 1 What are the underpinning ethical principles in this scenario?
> 2 Why might Aadit not have spoken earlier to his daughter about Aamira's wishes? What effect might a conflict of opinion have had on decision-making at this stage? If unresolved how might it have affected the family in their bereavement?
> 3 What might have been the consequences if something had happened to Aadit and he was unable to be an advocate for Aamira? How could these potential consequences be avoided?

Family carers tend to feel unprepared for the role of proxy decision-maker, particularly during times of crises and emotional strain (Forbes, Bern-Klug, & Gessert, 2000). Advance care planning is identified as a way of relieving family carer stress by helping them understand their family member's wishes (Sampson & Burns, 2013). It is a process of structured discussions between an individual with dementia, their family and healthcare providers to identify and document: understanding of their illness and its progression, personal goals of care and preferences for future treatment and care. This takes place while they have decision-making capacity in anticipation of deterioration in their condition and potential loss of capacity (National Council for Palliative Care, 2008). An advance care planning discussion may result in one or more outcomes. In England and Wales, these would be classified as: a statement of preferences and wishes; Advance Decision to Refuse Treatment; appointment of a legal advocate-Lasting Power of Attorney for 'health and welfare' and/or 'property and affairs.' Under the Mental Capacity Act (2005) the latter two are legally binding, if valid and applicable, and although the former is not legally binding, it is obligatory that it is taken into account when a best interest decision is being made.

Advance care planning is embedded in UK policies such as the *End of Life Care Strategy* (Department of Health, 2008a) and the National Institute for Health and Care Excellence (2010) quality statement for dementia. Although the proposed benefits of advance care planning may include reducing inappropriate hospital admissions and allowing greater choice about where a person wishes to die, there is limited evidence on the implications for people with dementia. They would need to engage with advance care planning early in their disease trajectory while they can still hold meaningful conversations and have capacity to make informed decisions. For some, this would mean they are being asked to consider the end of their life at a time when they are coming to terms with a diagnosis of dementia. For others this 'window of opportunity' may be missed due to a delay in diagnosis (Harrison Dening, Jones, & Sampson,

2012; Sampson & Burns, 2013). In the UK, there are attempts to address this: the Alzheimer's Society UK runs a national dementia awareness campaign highlighting the benefits of seeking a diagnosis; GPs are given training and incentives to diagnose dementia and begin the process of advance care planning (National Health Service England, 2015). EAPC (2013) emphasises the need to respect a person's choice if they do not wish to engage in conversations about their future. Harrison Dening and colleagues (2012) found that, even with mild dementia, individuals can find it difficult to think about how the future will be for them and are likely to establish their views based on their current situation. Equally this could be the case for anyone with a long-term condition; it is found that preferences for care often change as people adapt to their illness and gain an understanding of its progression (Sampson & Burns, 2013). The need for an ongoing process of review is highlighted in policy (Department of Health, 2008a), but for people with dementia this can become difficult to implement as they lose decision-making capacity (EAPC, 2013). In this respect, if a person with dementia wishes to make an Advance Decision to Refuse Treatment while they have the capacity, care should be taken to ensure that it will not inadvertently compromise their quality of life and comfort at a later stage.

The EAPC (2013) suggest that, in many situations, a nuanced approach to advance care planning for people with dementia is appropriate. This could involve, with consent, family carers from early on who can continue to participate in the review process when the person loses decision-making capacity. The Mental Capacity Act (2005) states that an individual must be given all practicable support to make their own decisions and should be involved in conversations concerning their care for as long as possible; even when they lack decision-making capacity, they can continue to express their feelings and emotions. It may be necessary to identify an appropriate time of day when the person is more alert and uses supportive and augmentative communication techniques. EAPC (2013) further identifies the need for awareness of different perspectives among culturally diverse populations regarding discussions about the end of life. In some cultures, there may be stigmatisation concerning terminal illness, paternalism around decision-making, and religious beliefs regarding the sanctity of life (Johnstone & Kanitsaki, 2009). The EAPC (2013) proposes that the process could begin by considering in general terms an individual's values, preferences and wishes, not all of which may be related to the end of life; having conversations around prioritising goals of care can help healthcare staff translate these into treatment options at a later stage; and the naming of an advocate at diagnosis. Healthcare professionals, particularly those working in generalist settings, voice concern about the skills required to have advance care planning conversations. They report a lack of time given the need for sensitivity and regular review. Specific skills in assessing capacity, managing difficult conversations and end-of-life decision-making are needed, particularly when decisions are treatment related (Robinson, Dickinson, Clark, Hughes, &, Exley, 2012). These are well developed in palliative care specialists, who could work in

Dementia and end-of-life care in the UK 75

collaboration with other care providers to support people with dementia in the earlier stages. Hospice UK (2015) reports on a partnership between a hospice group and a GP federation to deliver a holistic memory service.

Maximising comfort care

As we have already discussed, people living with more advanced dementia are likely to be dependent, frail, and susceptible to pressure ulcers and infection for an extended period as well as having difficulty reporting their feelings of discomfort. The EAPC (2013) acknowledges the value of nursing care in providing comfort towards the end of life, with meticulous attention to position changes and hygiene needs. Eating and drinking can continue to be a form of pleasure and socialisation. Guidance suggests that people with dementia should be encouraged to eat and drink by mouth for as long as possible and when dysphagia occurs due to the progression of dementia, small amounts of soft diet and thickened fluids be offered at frequent intervals with the person sitting upright. When the severity of the swallowing difficulty causes choking and distress, or appetite is lacking, keeping a person's mouth moist and lips soft is the priority (EAPC, 2013; Summersall & Wight, 2004). Enteral feeding, via a feeding tube, is not recommended, except in circumstances where dysphagia is considered to be transient rather than caused by the severity of the dementia (National Institute for Health and Care Excellence, 2016). This is based on evidence that it has a significant burden and does not prevent weight loss due to cachexia (wasting of the body) resulting from advance disease or aspiration pneumonia caused by saliva or reflux of gastric contents (Finucane, Christmas, & Travis, 1999).

Optimising comfort is linked to personhood through the focus on promoting dignity and quality of life (EAPC, 2013). In this regard, studies have found that psychosocial interventions such as music, art, reminiscence, and group activities foster social interaction and reduce levels of distress in nursing home residents with dementia (Lawrence, Fossey, Ballard, Moniz-Cook, & Murray, 2012). Stacpoole, Hockley, Thompsell, Simard, and Volicer (2014) suggest that people with advanced dementia risk being marginalised and isolated when their ability to engage in meaningful activity becomes limited; one survey shows that, at the end of their lives, people with dementia were frequently found to have unmet emotional needs (Alzheimer's Society, 2012a). The End of Life Namaste Care program for People with Dementia – Namaste meaning 'to honour the spirit within' – was developed in care homes in the United States of America (USA) by Professor Joyce Simard. It looks to engage people with advanced dementia primarily through their senses. It takes place in a calm dedicated environment where a group of residents are supported by care staff who are always present and know the individuals' specific likes and life stories. This way, care is individualised with appropriate music, therapeutic touch, colour, scents, snacks, and drinks. Families are encouraged to take part in the activities and are supported to understand dementia and its progression. A study showed that there is generally a reduction in the severity of neuropsychiatric symptoms and distress behaviours in care home residents with advanced dementia who participate in the programme. Family and care staff also expressed positive experiences of greater awareness of end-of-life issues, closer relationships, and developing new skills (Simard & Volicer, 2010). Stacpoole and colleagues (2014) demonstrated similar results in four of the five care homes in their study. In the fifth care home, the Namaste Care program lacked effectiveness; ineffective medical and nursing practices were identified with residents experiencing consistently high scores for distress. They concluded that stable leadership, adequate staffing, and good medical and nursing support were conditions required for the programme to be effectively integrated into the culture of a care home with minimal extra resources. In the UK, some hospices, working collaboratively with care homes, have implemented the programme (Hospice UK, 2015).

Support for family carers

A family carer is someone who gives unpaid care and support to a relative, partner or friend (Department of Health, 2008b). Brodaty and Donkin (2009) report that carers for people living with dementia are found to have higher levels of psychological stress and lower levels of well-being and physical health, compared to carers of older people who do not have dementia. They suggest that this is likely because the period of dependency is often protracted and carers need to adapt to a changing relationship with their loved one, learning to understand their behavioural expressions while becoming less able to draw on their partnership. Supporting family carers, who provide 80% of care for older people in the UK (Nolan & Ryan, 2011), is recognised as a UK government priority through national policies including the Carers Strategy (Department of Health, 2008b). This proposes that carers be respected as expert care partners and supported to maintain their physical and mental health, social contacts and to avoid financial hardship. National Institute for Health and Care Excellence (2011) states that family carers should be offered an assessment to identify their own needs. Despite this link to policy, Hospice UK (2015) suggests that there is limited availability of carer support services. Alzheimer's Society UK (2012a) reports that around 50% of carers for people with dementia do not get sufficient support, which impacts on their health, leading to earlier admission of their relative to long-term care. Healthcare professionals need to support carers to develop resilience through social and practical support, along with education that underpins their role as carer and prepares them for potential eventualities (EAPC, 2013; Nolan & Ryan, 2011).

Coping with Caregiving is a complex psychological intervention first developed in the USA and adapted within the UK National Health Service to be delivered to dementia carers. The intervention was evaluated through the START (STrAtegies for RelaTives), randomised control study (Sommerlad, Manela, Cooper, Rapaport, & Livingston, 2014). It comprised eight sessions that took place

Dementia and end-of-life care in the UK   77

on a one-to-one basis in the carer's home. These included: education about dementia, carer stress, communication skills; how to access emotional support; strategies to manage difficult situations; relaxation techniques; and planning for the future. It was found that carers who had not been enrolled in the programme were seven times more likely to be anxious or depressed, compared to those who participated in it. Participants commented that they felt more prepared for the future and better able to cope as challenges emerged; they reported the benefit of sharing their concerns and validating their feelings with professionals (Sommerlad et al., 2014). A similar programme has been adopted by a UK hospice where participants benefit from attending the day service facilities. Recognising that many carers experience difficulty in leaving the person they care for, a parallel programme of support and occupation for the person with dementia is run in the same building (Crowther, Knight, Jones, & Hawkins, 2016). This way, carers gain peer as well as professional support at a time when social isolation can be a problem. While the Namaste Care program predominantly supports people with advanced dementia and their carers, this intervention can allow hospices to make contact at an earlier stage in the dementia trajectory.

Carers can experience grief reactions due to the various losses during the dementia trajectory. A spouse may feel the loss of companionship, affection, shared responsibilities, and a future planned together. Adult children may experience loss of support, advice, affection, and assistance or loss of the family kinkeeper (Zarit & Zarit, 2008). If formal support is required, carers can feel guilty at relinquishing their caring role (Shanley, Russell, Middleton, & Simpson-Young, 2011). The commonly described emotions considered to be normal to the grieving process and described in seminal research include: shock, numbness, disbelief; distress and anger; and depression and despair (Bowlby, 1980; Parkes, 1976). It is generally accepted that people will likely experience some or all of these reactions (Kübler-Ross, 2009). Owen, Goode, and Haley (2001) suggest that anticipatory grief, in anticipation of a loved one's death, can lessen the impact of grief after bereavement. Oyebode (2008) proposes that it can be difficult for carers of people with dementia to engage with anticipatory grief when they are not able to say important things to their loved one because of their communication difficulties or they are providing an exhaustive routine of personal care. Hospices offer holistic support to carers through psychosocial and complementary therapies, as well as pre- and post-bereavement services. In a survey, 92% of hospices reported that they provided this service to family carers of people with dementia who access their service (Hospice UK, 2015). It could be argued that an understanding of the specific stresses and emotional risk factors for carers of people with dementia could help tailor this support. The 'Goals of Care' model shows bereavement support to be prioritised after death, but EAPC (2013) identifies that families may need early and ongoing support to allow for anticipatory grief.

Older adults will commonly experience bereavement through the death of peers as well as losses associated with declining physical and mental health. Despite this likelihood, there appears to be little evidence, based on a few phenomenological studies, concerning the impact of grief on people with dementia. Grief and Myran (2006) suggest cognitive impairment can impede the normal mechanisms of grief and bereavement. They report on studies of people with moderate to severe dementia experiencing depression and anxiety, grief-related themes manifesting in delusions, and the continual reexperiencing of grief. Alzheimer's Scotland (2011) note that the person with dementia may confuse a present loss with an earlier one or they may not be able to retain the information that the person has died. Factors influencing a person's grief include the extent of the cognitive impairment, the relationship to the deceased person, and the person's ability to express their loss. Carers and care staff find it difficult to know what to say when a person with dementia asks for a loved one who is deceased. Current advice is based mainly on expert opinion, which suggests a trial of different approaches: a gentle reminder that the person has died may be enough for some but distressing for others if it seems they are hearing the news for the first time; responding to the person's emotion may allow them to feel supported without the need to answer their questions directly; using reminiscence and rituals may support their grieving process. Distraction is advocated as a last resort if the grief reaction appears too painful in that moment. It is further advised that, once the most suitable approach is identified, it should be communicated between all family and professional carers to ensure it is used consistently (Alzheimer's Scotland, 2011; Grief & Myran, 2006; Oyebode, 2008). Hospices need to consider their approach to supporting both patients with dementia and their family members, who are faced with loss, grief, and bereavement. If the deceased person was their main carer, they will not only experience the significant loss of relationship, it will impact on all aspects of their life.

Case example

June's family found it hard to understand why she called out for John, her deceased brother, rather than her husband who died two years ago. It transpired that June had looked after John when their parents died and blamed herself for his early death. June would sometimes mistake her son for John and sometimes became distressed thinking that it was her son who had died. The best way of supporting June was identified and staff and family followed this approach. If June called out for John she was encouraged to talk about him and was reassured that she had done all she could to look after him. Before her son visited staff or family would talk to her about him so her thoughts were of her son when he arrived. Photographs helped June to focus her thoughts and memories.

Approaches to embedding quality end-of-life care for people with dementia

This chapter has highlighted some of the skills, knowledge, and commitment required by professionals and carers to provide optimal care for people with dementia at the end of life. Here we discuss the role of training, leadership, and organisational development in embedding a palliative and person-centred approach to care for people with dementia at the end of life. Education in person-centred dementia care, advocated by the National Dementia Strategy (Department of Health, 2009a) and the EAPC (2013), can help hospice staff adapt their practice to provide palliative care that is tailored to the needs of people with dementia who access their service. It can also influence the end-of-life care support and education they give to community teams, particularly nursing homes where up to 80% of residents are living with dementia (Alzheimer's Society, 2014). It is widely recognised that education alone rarely leads to lasting practice change (Bowers, 2008). This is highlighted in the study by Kovach et al. (2012) where, despite training, nurses continued to underidentify distress behaviours in residents with dementia. Key requisites for a sustained and effective development of practice include not only a critical mass of staff trained with the necessary skills and knowledge, but also leaders to drive the change (Cameron & Green, 2009). Roberts, Nolet, and Gatecliffe (2008) propose that for leaders to be effective in delivering person-centred care within an organisation, they will need to create a shared vision amongst all stakeholders and provide opportunities for staff to develop new knowledge, skills, and ways of working. This in turn can reduce staff resistance to change, increase their job satisfaction and lower their levels of stress.

A 'train the trainer' model creates a resourceful way of disseminating training and developing champions to act as leaders. In this model experts train a core group of staff within an organisation to facilitate a programme of learning for their colleagues (Connell, Holmes, Voelkl, & Bakalar, 2002). Using this 'train the trainer' model in collaboration between a UK hospice and the University of Bradford we developed and piloted a dementia care training programme for staff in six hospices. Addressing Health Education England's framework for Core Skills Education and Training Framework (Skills for Health, Health Education England and Skills for Care, 2015) we offered foundation level training for all hospice staff and volunteers who have contact with patients and families. Clinical staff were provided a further intermediate level training in enhanced communication and end-of-life care. Evaluation of the programme found that in five of the six hospices the trained facilitators were delivering a rolling programme of training and an increase in confidence in caring for people with dementia was generally reported by hospice staff. The facilitators were also engaged in initiatives such as: introducing specific tools, promoting environmental changes, engaging in networking, developing dementia strategies for their hospice, and taking further studies in dementia care. They reported evidence of significant changes to practice, recognising that with the training being given to diverse groups of staff (for example, a consultant, physiotherapist, and volunteer attending the same foundation training session), supporting people with dementia was becoming everyone's concern. It is noteworthy that time commitments for delivering and attending training were identified as potential barriers to effectively maintaining the programme of training.

Case example

When Michal was first admitted to the Hospice he would be quite restless, continuously walking about, which would make him breathless. His family brought in his favourite music to encourage him to sit quietly in his room but this was not effective. One day Michal sat in a spare chair next to the ward clerk at the reception desk. Michal had been a headmaster and it was recognised that he was most content sitting behind a desk. The majority of the Hospice staff had completed foundation dementia care training and realised the value of working with Michal's reality in which he was still a headmaster. The ward clerk supplied him with pen and paper and everyone, from consultant to hospitality assistant, understood that they could engage with him best when he was sat there. Now Michal would sit for long periods arranging his papers. A suitable chair with a pressure relieving cushion was provided.

Organisational change is a further requirement for developing practice. Organisational commitment is necessary to ensure time, support, and resources are available (Moran & Avergun, 1997). As already discussed, Stacpoole and colleagues (2014) found the Namaste Care program failed to be implemented effectively in one care home where there was a lack of resources and leadership. Organisations respond to external change drivers such as evidence of need and national policy (Moran & Avergun, 1997). With dementia identified as a healthcare priority, Hospice UK (2015) urges that as a minimum hospices commit to a plan to offer appropriate support and care for people dying with dementia accessing their services. They also appeal for hospices to go further and develop new ways of working through collaboration with other organisations. Palliative care is appropriate from the time of diagnosis of a life-limiting condition and can be offered alongside supportive and life prolonging treatments (National Council for Palliative Care, 2015). Hospice UK (2015) proposes that while hospices may play a small part in the overall care provision

Dementia and end-of-life care in the UK   81

for people with dementia, timely contribution of their expertise can be of significant benefit at different points on the disease trajectory. This fits with UK and international policy advocating integrated systems where palliative care is embedded into health and social care to offer appropriate support for people living with chronic life limiting conditions (Hasselaar & Payne, 2016). This chapter has identified some examples of UK hospices being involved in collaborative programmes such as working with memory clinics, delivering the Namaste Care program in care homes, and providing post diagnosis support to people with dementia and their families. Other examples include dementia care specialists being based within hospices, recruitment of hospice staff with a background in mental health care, and exchange programmes between dementia care and hospice care staff (Hospice UK, 2015). In this way, hospices are beginning to be seen as key players in supporting people living and dying with dementia in the communities they serve; realising the ambitions of the end-of-life care strategy (Department of Health, 2008a) in providing quality end-of-life care for all regardless of disease or place of care.

Conclusion

In this chapter, we have drawn on the rich traditions of palliative and person-centred care to describe the evidence base available to guide care of people with dementia at the end of life. Our focus on symptom assessment, making decisions, maximising comfort care, and support for family carers has allowed us to comment on the diversity of experience of living with dementia at the end of life. We need to continue to develop the evidence base and to ensure human rights for people with dementia across the trajectory of living with dementia. Quality end-of-life care should not be confined to innovative research programmes or evident only in pockets of best practice. It should be a fundamental aspect of health and social care for some of the most vulnerable members of our society.

Hospices have a responsibility to provide equitable access to their services for people living with dementia. This could be achieved through individual hospices developing a dementia strategy. Support at a strategic level is necessary to ensure that time, resources, and structures are available. Strategic aims and goals derived from scoping exercises can promote change that is appropriately targeted. A practice development approach would encourage the implementation of best practice through a cyclical process of action planning and evaluation. A paucity of research is highlighted across all the areas explored in this chapter, highlighting a critical unmet need. Hospices are traditionally dedicated to research as well as clinical practice, education, and training. Engagement in specific research projects concerning symptom management, end-of-life decision-making, quality of life at the end of life, and bereavement support would maintain a pivotal role for hospices in supporting the palliative care needs of people with living with dementia.

References

Allan, K., & Killick, J. (2008). Communication and relationships: An inclusive social world. In M. Downs & B. Bowers (Eds.), *Excellence in dementia care: Research into practice* (pp. 212–229). Maidenhead: Open University Press.

All-Party Parliamentary Group on Dementia. (2013). *Dementia does not discriminate: The experiences of black, Asian and minority ethnic communities* (Report). Retrieved from www.alzheimers. org.uk/download/downloads/id/1857/appg_2013_bame_report.pdf

Alzheimer's Association. (2017). *2017 Alzheimer's disease facts and figures* (Report). Retrieved from www.alz.org/documents_custom/2017-facts-and-figures.pdf

Alzheimer's Scotland. (2011). *Loss & bereavement in people with dementia* (Information Sheet 42). Retrieved from www.alzscot.org/assets/0000/0176/loss_bereavement.pdf

Alzheimer's Society. (2012a). *Dementia 2012: A national challenge* (Report). Retrieved from www.alzheimers.org.uk/download/downloads/id/1389/alzheimers_society_dementia_2012-_full_report.pdf

Alzheimer's Society. (2012b). *My life until the end: Dying well with dementia* (Report). Retrieved from www.alzheimers.org.uk/downloads/download/945/my_life_until_the_end_dying_well_with_dementia

Alzheimer's Society. (2014). *Dementia UK update* (Report). Retrieved from www.alzheimers. org.uk/download/downloads/id/2323/dementia_uk_update.pdf

Alzheimer's Society. (2017). *This is me* (Leaflet). Retrieved from www.alzheimers.org.uk/download/downloads/id/3423/this_is_me.pdf

American Geriatrics Society. (2002). The management of persistent pain in older persons: Clinical practice guideline. *Journal of the American Geriatrics Society, 50*(Suppl. 6), S205–S224.

Baldwin, C. (2008). Toward a person-centred ethic in dementia care: Doing right or being good? In M. Downs & B. Bowers (Eds.), *Excellence in dementia care: Research into practice* (pp. 103–118). Maidenhead: Open University Press.

Banerjee, S. (2009). *The use of antipsychotic medication for people with dementia: Time for action* (Report). Retrieved from www.rcpsych.ac.uk/pdf/Antipsychotic%20Bannerjee%20Report.pdf

Beauchamp, T., & Childress, J. (2001). *Principles of biomedical ethics.* Oxford: Oxford University Press.

Bennett, M. (2001). The LANSS pain scale: The Leeds assessment of neuropathic symptoms and signs. *Pain, 92*(1), 147–157.

Bourgeois, M. S., Dijkstra, K., Burgio, L., & Allen-Burge, R. (2001). Memory aids as an augmentative and alternative communication strategy for nursing home residents with dementia. *Augmentative Alternative Communication, 17*(3), 196–210.

Bowers, B. (2008). A trained and supported workforce. In M. Downs & B. Bowers (Eds.), *Excellence in dementia care: Research into practice* (pp. 414–437). Maidenhead: Open University Press.

Bowlby, J. (1980). *Attachment and loss: Loss, sadness and depression* (Vol. 3). New York: Basic Books.

Brodaty, H., & Donkin, M. (2009). Family caregivers of people with dementia. *Dialogues in Clinical Neuroscience, 11*(2), 217–228.

Cameron, E., & Green, M. (2009). *Making sense of change management: A complete guide to the models, tools and techniques of organizational change.* London: Kogan Page Publishers.

Chatterjee, J. (2012). Improving pain assessment for patients with cognitive impairment: Development of a pain assessment toolkit. *International Journal of Palliative Nursing, 18*(12), 581–590.

Cohen-Mansfield, J. (2008). The language of behaviour. In M. Downs & B. Bowers (Eds.), *Excellence in dementia care: Research into practice* (pp. 187–211). Maidenhead: Open University Press.

Cohen-Mansfield, J., & Creedon, M. (2002). Nursing staff members' perceptions of pain indicators in persons with severe dementia. *Clinical Journal of Pain, 18*(1), 64–73.

Connell, C. M., Holmes, S. B., Voelkl, J. E., & Bakalar, H. R. (2002). Providing dementia outreach education to rural communities: Lessons learned from a train-the-trainer program. *Journal of Applied Gerontology, 21*(3), 294–313.

Connolly, A., Sampson, E. L., & Purandare, N. (2012). End-of-life care for people with dementia from ethnic minority groups: A systematic review. *Journal of the American Geriatrics Society, 60*(2), 351–360.

Cox, S., & Cook, A. (2002). Caring for people with dementia at the end of life. In J. Hockley & D. Clark (Eds.), *Palliative care for older people in care homes* (pp. 86–103). Buckingham: Open University Press.

Crowther, J., Knight, H., Jones, S., & Hawkins, J. (2016). Dementia carer wellbeing programme: Innovative and creative support for carers of people with dementia. *Ehospice*. Retrieved from www.ehospice.com/uk/Default/tabid/10697/ArticleId/18572/

Curtiss, C. P. (2010). Challenges in pain assessment in cognitively intact and cognitively impaired older adults with cancer. *Oncology Nursing Forum, 37*(Suppl.), 7–16.

Department of Health. (2008a). *End of life care strategy: Promoting high quality care for all adults at the end of life*. London: Department of Health. Retrieved from www.gov.uk/government/uploads/system/uploads/attachment_data/file/136431/End_of_life_strategy.pdf

Department of Health. (2008b). *Carers at the heart of 21st-century families and communities*. London: Department of Health. Retrieved from http://webarchive.nationalarchives.gov.uk/20130107105354/www.dh.gov.uk/prod_consum_dh/groups/dh_digitalassets/@dh/@en/documents/digitalasset/dh_085338.pdf

Department of Health. (2009a). *Living well with dementia: A national dementia strategy*. London: Department of Health. Retrieved from www.gov.uk/government/uploads/system/uploads/attachment_data/file/168220/dh_094051.pdf

Department of Health. (2009b). *The Mental Capacity Act Deprivation of Liberty Safeguards*. London: Department of Health. Retrieved from www.legislation.gov.uk/ukpga/2005/9/pdfs/ukpga_20050009_en.pdf

Department of Health Northern Ireland. (2010). *Living matters dying matters: A palliative and end of life care strategy for adults in Northern Ireland*. Retrieved from www.health-ni.gov.uk/sites/default/files/publications/dhssps/living-matters-dying-matters-strategy-2010.pdf

Department of Health Northern Ireland. (2011). *Improving dementia services in northern: A regional strategy*. Retrieved from www.health-ni.gov.uk/sites/default/files/publications/dhssps/improving-dementia-services-2011.pdf

DeWaters, T., Popovitch, J., & Faut-Callahan, M. (2003). An evaluation of clinical tools to measure pain in older people with cognitive impairment. *British Journal of Community Nursing, 8*(5), 226–234.

Dixon, J., King, D., Matosevic, T., Clark, M., & Knapp, M. (2015). *Equity in the provision of palliative Care in the UK: Review of evidence*. London: The Personal Social Services Research Unit. Retrieved from www.mariecurie.org.uk/globalassets/media/documents/policy/campaigns/equity-palliative-care-uk-report-full-lse.pdf

Downs, M., & Collins, L. (2015). Person-centred communication in dementia care. *Nursing Standard, 30*(11), 37–41.

Downs, M., Small, N., & Froggatt, N. (2006). Explanatory models of dementia: Links to end-of-life care. *International Journal of Palliative Nursing, 12*(5), 209–213.

Equality Act. (2010). Retrieved from www.legislation.gov.uk/ukpga/2010/15/contents

European Association for Palliative Care. (2013). Recommendations on palliative care and treatment of older people with Alzheimer's disease and other progressive dementias.

Supplement to the White Paper Published on Palliative Medicine 2013, *0*(0), 1–13. Retrieved from www.eapcnet.eu/LinkClick.aspx?fileticket=xhe-DLmfNb4%3D

Falls, D., & Stevens, J. (2004). Carers' perceptions of pain in people with dementia: A grounded theory approach. *Australian Journal of Holistic Nursing*, *11*(2), 3–11.

Ferrell, B. A., Ferrell, B. R., & Rivera, L. (1995). Pain in cognitively impaired nursing home patients. *Journal of Pain and Symptom Management*, *10*(8), 591–598.

Finucane, T. E., Christmas, C., & Travis, K. (1999). Tube feeding in patients with advanced dementia: A review of the evidence. *Journal of American Geriatric Society*, *282*(14), 1365–1370.

Forbes, S., Bern-Klug, M., & Gessert, C. (2000). End-of-life decision making for nursing home residents with dementia. *Journal of Nursing Scholarship*, *32*(3), 251–258.

Fuchs-Lacelle, S., & Hadjistavropoulos, T. (2004). Development and preliminary validation of the pain assessment checklist for seniors with limited ability to communicate (PACSLAC). *Pain Management Nursing*, *5*(1), 37–49.

General Medical Council. (2010). *Treatment and care towards the end of life: Good practice in decision making*. London: General Medical Council. Retrieved from www.gmc-uk.org/End_of_life.pdf_32486688.pdf

Gillick, M. R. (2012). Doing the right thing: A geriatrician's perspective on medical care for the person with advanced dementia. *Journal of Law, Medicine & Ethics*, *40*(1), 51–56.

Golafshani, N. (2003). Understanding reliability and validity in qualitative research. *The Qualitative Report*, *8*(4), 597–607.

Gold Standard Framework. (2011). *The GSF Prognostic Indicator Guidance*, *4*. Retrieved from www.goldstandardsframework.org.uk/cdcontent/uploads/files/General%20Files/Prognostic%20Indicator%20Guidance%20October%202011.pdf

Grief, C. J., & Myran, D. D. (2006). Bereavement in cognitively impaired older adults: Case series and clinical considerations. *Journal of Geriatric Psychiatry and Neurology*, *19*(4), 209–215.

Guthrie, B., Payne, K., Alderson, P., McMurdo, M. E., & Mercer, S. W. (2012). Adapting clinical guidelines to take account of multimorbidity. *British Medical Journal*, *345*, e6341.

Hadjistavropoulos, T., Fitzgerald, T. D., & Marchildon, G. P. (2010). Practice guidelines for assessing pain in older persons with dementia residing in long-term care facilities. *Physiotherapy Canada*, *62*(2), 104–113.

Harrison Dening, K., Jones, L., & Sampson, E. L. (2012). Preferences for end of life care: A nominal group study of people with dementia and their family carers. *Palliative Medicine*, *27*(5), 409–417.

Hasselaar, J., & Payne, S. (Eds.). (2016). *Integrated palliative care InSup-C*. The Netherlands: Nijmegen, Radboud University Medical Center. Retrieved from www.insup-c.eu/IntegratedPalliativeCare2016.pdf

Herr, K., Bursch, H., Ersek, M., Miller, L. L., & Swafford, K. (2010). Use of pain-behavioral assessment tools in the nursing home: Expert consensus recommendations for practice. *Journal of Gerontological Nursing*, *36*(3), 18–29.

Herr, K., Spratt, K. F., Garand, L., & Li, L. (2007). Evaluation of the Iowa pain thermometer and other selected pain intensity scales in younger and older cohorts using controlled clinical pain: A preliminary study. *Palliative Medicine*, *8*(7), 585–600.

Hospice UK. (2015). *Hospice enabled dementia care: The first steps*. London: Hospice UK. Retrieved from www.hospiceuk.org/docs/default-source/What-We-Offer/Care-Support-Programmes/dementia-network/hospice-enabled-dementia-care-the-first-steps.pdf?sfvrsn=0

Hughes, J. C., & Dove, P. (2006). The ethics of end-of-life decisions in severe dementia. In J. C Hughes (Ed.), *Palliative care in severe dementia* (pp. 45–54). London: MA Healthcare Limited.

Johnstone, M. J., & Kanitsaki, O. (2009). Ethics and advance care planning in a culturally diverse society. *Journal of Transcultural Nursing, 20*(4), 405–416.

Jordan, A., Regnard, C., O'Brien, J. T., & Hughes, J. C. (2012). Pain and distress in advanced dementia: Choosing the right tools for the job. *Palliative Medicine, 26*(7), 873–878.

Kitwood, T. (1990). The dialectics of dementia: With particular reference to Alzheimer's disease. *Aging and Society, 10*(2), 177–196.

Kitwood, T. (1997). *Dementia reconsidered: The person comes first.* Buckingham: Open University Press.

Kovach, C. R., Logan, B. R., Joosse, L. L., & Noonan, P. E. (2012). Failure to identify behavioural symptoms of people with dementia and the need for follow-up physical assessment. *Research in Gerontological Nursing, 5*(2), 89–93.

Kovach, C. R., Logan, B. R., Noonan, P. E., Schildt, A. M., Smerz, J., Simpson, M., & Wells, T. (2006). Effects of the Serial Trial Intervention on discomfort and behavior of nursing home residents with dementia. *American Journal of Alzheimer's Disease and Other Dementias', 21*(3), 147–155.

Kübler-Ross, E. (2009). *On Death and Dying: What the dying have to teach doctors, nurses, clergy and their own families* (40th Anniversary Edition). Oxon: Routledge.

Lawrence, V., Fossey, J., Ballard, C., Moniz-Cook, E., & Murray, J. (2012). Improving quality of life for people with dementia in care homes: Making psychosocial interventions work. *British Journal of Psychiatry, 201*(5), 344–351.

Lichtner, V., Dowding, D., Esterhuizen, P., Closs, S. J., Long, A. F., Corbett, A., & Briggs, M. (2014). Pain assessment for people with dementia: A systematic review of systematic reviews of pain assessment tools. *BMC Geriatrics, 14*(138). doi:10.1186/1471-2318-14-138

McCaffery, M. (1968). *Nursing practice theories related to cognition, bodily pain, and man-environment interactions.* Los Angeles: University of California Print Office.

Meier, D. E., Ahronheim, J. C., Morris, J., Beskin-lyons, S., & Morrison, R. S. (2001). High short-term mortality in hospitalized patients with advanced dementia: Lack of benefit of tube feeding. *Archives of Internal Medicine, 161*(4), 594–599.

Melis, R. J. F., Marengoni, A., Rizzuto, D., Teerenstra, S., Kivipelto, M., Angleman, S. B., & Fratiglioni, L. (2013). The influence of multimorbidity on clinical progression of dementia in a population-based cohort. *PLoS ONE, 8*(12), e84014. doi:10.1371/journal.pone.0084014

Melzack, R., & Torgerson, W. S. (1971). On the language of pain. *Anesthesiology, 34*(1), 50–59.

Mental Capacity Act. (2005). *Code of practice.* Department for Constitutional Affairs. London: TSO. Retrieved from www.legislation.gov.uk/ukpga/2005/9/pdfs/ukpgacop_20050009_en.pdf

Mitchell, S. L., Kiely, D. K., & Hamel, M. B. (2004). Dying with advanced dementia in the nursing Home. *Archives of Internal Medicine, 164*(3), 321–326.

Moran, J., & Avergun. A. (1997). Creating lasting change. *The TQM Magazine, 9*(2), 146–151.

Morrison, R. S., & Siu, A. L. (2000). A comparison of pain and its treatment in advanced dementia and cognitively intact patients with hip fractures. *Journal of Pain and Symptom Management, 19*(4), 240–248.

Murphy, J., Gray, C. M., & Cox, S. (2007). *Using "talking mats" to help people with dementia to communicate.* York: Joseph Rowntree Foundation.

National Council for Palliative Care. (2008). *Advance care planning: A guide for health and social care staff.* London: National Council for Palliative Care.

National Council for Palliative Care. (2009). *Out of the shadows: End of life care for people with dementia.* London: National Council for Palliative Care.

National Council for Palliative Care. (2015). *Palliative care explained*. Retrieved from www. ncpc.org.uk/palliative-care-explained

National Health Service England. (2015). *Enhanced service specifications: Facilitating timely diagnosis and support for people with dementia 2015/16*. Retrieved from www.england.nhs.uk/commissioning/wp-content/uploads/sites/12/2015/03/facilitate-tmly-diag-dementia.pdf

National Institute for Health and Care Excellence. (2010). *Dementia: Support in health and social care: Quality Standard 1*. London: NICE. Retrieved from www.nice.org.uk/guidance/qs1

National Institute for Health and Care Excellence. (2011). *End of life care for adults*. Quality Standard 13. London: NICE. Retrieved from www.nice.org.uk/guidance/qs13

National Institute for Health and Care Excellence. (2016). *Dementia: Supporting people with dementia and their careers in health and social care: Clinical guideline 42*. Retrieved from www. nice.org.uk/guidance/cg42?unlid=13608378720158241495

National Palliative and End of Life Care Partnership. (2015). *Ambitions for palliative and end of life care: A national framework for local action 2015–2020*. Retrieved from http://endoflife careambitions.org.uk/wp-content/uploads/2015/09/Ambitions-for-Palliative-and-End-of-Life-Care.pdf

Nolan, M., & Ryan, T. (2011). Family carers, palliative care and the end of life. In M. Gott & C. Ingleton (Eds.), *Living with ageing and dying: Palliative and end of life care for older people* (pp. 170–180). Oxford: Oxford University Press.

Office for National Statistics. (2015). *Statistical bulletin: Deaths registered in England and Wales (Series DR): 2015*. Retrieved from www.ons.gov.uk/peoplepopulationandcommunity/births deathsandmarriages/deaths/bulletins/deathsregisteredinenglandandwalesseriesdr/2015

Owen, J. E., Goode, K. T., & Haley, W. E. (2001). End of life care and reactions to death in African-American and white family caregivers of relatives with Alzheimer's disease. *OMEGA: Journal of Death and Dying, 43*(4), 349–361.

Oyebode, J. (2008). Grief and bereavement. In M. Downs & B. Bowers (Eds.), *Excellence in dementia care: Research into practice* (pp. 379–394). Maidenhead: Open University Press.

Pace, V., Treloar, A., & Scott, S. (Eds.). (2011). *Dementia: From advanced disease to bereavement*. Oxford: Oxford University Press.

Parkes, C. M. (1976). Determinants of outcome following bereavement. *OMEGA: Journal of Death and Dying, 6*(4), 303–323.

Porsteinsson, A. P., & Antonsdottir, I. M. (2015). Neuropsychiatric symptoms in dementia: A cause or consequence? *American Journal of Psychiatry, 172*(5), 410–411.

Regnard, C., Reynolds, J., Watson, B., Matthews, D., Gibson, L., & Clarke, C. (2007). Understanding distress in people with severe communication difficulties: Developing and assessing the Disability Distress Assessment Tool (DisDAT). *Journal Intellectual of Disability Research, 51*(4), 277–292.

Roberts, T., Nolet, K., & Gatecliffe, L. (2008). Leadership in dementia care. In M. Downs & B. Bowers (Eds.), *Excellence in dementia care: Research into practice* (pp. 455–475). Maidenhead: Open University Press.

Robinson, L., Dickinson, C., Clark, A., Hughes, J., & Exley, C. (2012). A qualitative study: Professionals' experiences of advance care planning in dementia and palliative care, "a good idea in theory but . . .". *Palliative Medicine, 27*(5), 401–408.

Royal College of Physicians, British Geriatrics Society, & British Pain Society. (2007). *The assessment of pain in older people: National guidelines*. Concise Guidance to Good Practice Series, No. 8. London: Royal College of Physicians.

Sampson, E. L., & Burns, A. (2013). Planning a personalised future with dementia: "The misleading simplicity of advance directives". *Palliative Medicine, 27*(5), 387–388.

Sampson, E. L., Burns, A., & Richards, M. (2011). Improving end-of-life care for people with dementia. *The British Journal of Psychiatry, 199*(5), 357–359.

Saunders, C. (1967). *The management of terminal illness.* London: Hospital Medicine Publications.

Scottish Government. (2000). *Adults with incapacity (Scotland) Act 2000.* Retrieved from www.legislation.gov.uk/asp/2000/4/contents

Scottish Government. (2015). *Strategic framework for action on palliative and end of life care.* Retrieved from www.gov.scot/Publications/2015/12/4053

Scottish Government. (2016). *Proposal for Scotland's National Dementia Strategy 2016–19.* Retrieved from www.gov.scot/Resource/0049/00497716.pdf

Shanley, C., Russell, C., Middleton, H., & Simpson-Young, V. (2011). Living through end-stage dementia: The experiences and expressed needs of family carers. *Dementia, 10*(3), 325–340.

Simard, J., & Volicer, L. (2010). Effects of Namaste care on residents who do not benefit from usual activities. *American Journal of Alzheimer's Disease and Other Dementias, 25*(1), 46–50.

Skills for Health, Health Education England and Skills for Care. (2015). *Dementia core skills education and training framework.* Retrieved from www.skillsforhealth.org.uk/images/projects/dementia/Dementia%20Core%20Skills%20Education%20and%20Training%20Framework.pdf?s=cw1

Snow, A. L., O'Malley, K. J., Cody, M., Kunik, M. E., Ashton, C. M., Beck, C., . . . Novy, D. (2004). A conceptual model of pain assessment for non-communicative persons with dementia. *The Gerontologist, 44*(6), 807–817.

Social Care Institute for Excellence. (2009). *Dementia: Positive communication.* Retrieved from www.scie.org.uk/dementia/e-learning/7-positive-communication.asp

Sommerlad, A., Manela, M., Cooper, C., Rapaport, P., & Livingston, G. (2014). START (Strategies for RelaTives) coping strategy for family carers of adults with dementia: Qualitative study of participants' views about the intervention. *BMJ Open 2014, 4*(6), 1–9. doi:10.1136/bmjopen-2014-005273

Stacpoole, M., Hockley, J., Thompsell, A., Simard, J., & Volicer, L. (2014). The Namaste Care programme can reduce behavioural symptoms in care home residents with advanced dementia. *International Journal of Geriatric Psychiatry, 30*(7), 702–707.

Stephan, B., & Brayne, C. (2008). Prevalence and projections of dementia. In M. Downs & B. Bowers (Eds.), *Excellence in dementia care: Research into practice* (pp. 9–34). Maidenhead: Open University Press.

Summersall, J., & Wight, S. (2004). When it's difficult to swallow: The role of the speech therapist. *Nursing and Residential Care, 6*(11), 550–553.

van der Steen, J., Radbruch, L., Hertogh, C. M. P. M., de Boer, M. E., Hughes, J. C., Larkin, P., . . . European Association for Palliative Care. (2014). White paper defining optimal palliative care in older people with dementia: A Delphi study and recommendations from the European Association for Palliative Care. *Palliative Medicine, 28*(3), 197–209.

Warden, V., Hurley, A. C., & Volicer, V. (2003). Development and psychometric evaluation of the Pain Assessment in Advanced Dementia (PAINAD) Scale. *Journal of the American Medical Directors Association, 4*(9), 9–15.

Welsh Assembly. (2011). *National Dementia Vision for Wales.* Retrieved from http://gov.wales/docs/dhss/publications/110302dementiaen.pdf

Welsh Government. (2017). *Palliative and End of Life Care Delivery Plan.* Retrieved from http://gov.wales/docs/dhss/publications/170327end-of-lifeen.pdf

Winter, L., & Parks, S. M. (2008). Family discord and proxy decision makers' end-of-life treatment decisions. *Journal of Palliative Medicine, 11*(8), 1109–1114.

World Health Organisation. (2012). *Dementia: A public health priority*. Retrieved from http://apps.who.int/iris/bitstream/10665/75263/1/9789241564458_eng.pdf?ua=1

Wynne, C. F., Ling, S. M., & Remsberg, R. (2000). Comparison of pain assessment instruments in cognitively intact and cognitively impaired nursing home residents. *Geriatric Nursing, 21*(1), 20–23.

Xie, J., Brayne, C., Matthews, F. E., & Medical Research Council Cognitive Function and Ageing Study Collaborators. (2008). Survival times in people with dementia: Analysis from population based cohort study with 14 year follow-up. *British Medical Journal, 336*(7638), 258–262. doi:10.1136/bmj.39433.616678.25

Zarit, S. H., & Zarit, J. M. (2008). Flexibility and change: The fundamentals for families coping with dementia. In M. Downs & B. Bowers (Eds.), *Excellence in dementia care: Research into practice* (pp. 85–102). Maidenhead: Open University Press.

Zwakhalen, S. M., Hamers, J. P., & Berger, M. P. (2006). The psychometric quality and clinical usefulness of three pain assessment tools for elderly people with dementia. *Pain, 126*(1–3), 210–220.

Section 2

Social and cultural contexts, including ethics, bereavement, and policy issues

Chapter 5

Ethical issues in palliative and end-of-life care

Anne Halli-Tierney, Amy Albright, Deanna Dragan, Megan Lippe, and Rebecca S. Allen

Introduction to ethical behaviour in psychology and medicine

Palliative care is a team-based approach to care focused on: 1) improving the quality of life for individuals facing serious or life-limiting illness and their care partners; 2) preventing and relieving suffering by means of early identification; 3) providing thorough, culturally sensitive assessment and treatment of physical, psychosocial, and spiritual problems; and 4) providing bereavement care (Kelley & Morrison, 2015; National Consensus Project [NCP] for Quality Palliative Care, 2013). A patient approaching the end of life is faced with many challenges, and among these is the need to achieve a "good" or "desired" death. Depending on the knowledge base, beliefs, and culture of the individual and family involved, this may take many forms, and sometimes the treatment choices and other actions at end of life for one individual may press the limits of what is considered ethical behaviour among healthcare providers.

As deaths from chronic and debilitating diseases become more common with an increasing lifespan, patients and providers must explore relatively new venues of care. Some care education and provision, while beneficial to the patients' quality of life, may require ethical exploration for providers and family members. Whenever ethical issues arise, healthcare providers are required to respond in accordance with state, national, professional, and organizational guidelines. Codes of Ethics serve as foundational, profession-specific guidelines to which providers must adhere. Code of Ethics statements for psychology (American Psychological Association, 2017), medicine (American Medical Association, 2016a), and nursing (American Nurses Association, 2015), among those of other disciplines, dictate how each profession is to address these dilemmas. Analogous codes are available to professionals in other countries. Each provider must be well versed in the guidelines associated with their practice to ensure they address ethical issues properly. Common ethical dilemmas faced by interprofessional members of palliative care teams may involve any of the following issues: 1) patient autonomy versus providers' beneficent responsibility, 2) provider beneficence versus nonmaleficence, and 3) justice, or providing equal access to palliative and end-of-life treatments for diverse individuals (American Medical Association, 2016a; American Nurses Association, 2015; Bush, Allen, Heck, & Moye, 2015; Bush, Allen, & Molinari, 2017).

This chapter deals with ethical issues that may arise at end of life and how patients, caregivers, and healthcare providers can determine the best course of action to provide compassionate, ethical care. Capacity to engage in shared decision-making between patients and providers will be discussed throughout the chapter, as well as health literacy as a determinant of decision-making. Ethical issues that take place in different healthcare settings will be explored, as well as international variations on what makes a "good death." Finally, ways that providers can work to increase awareness and improve quality of ethical practices will be described.

Case example

Joe, a 74-year-old man with a history of pancreatic cancer with metastases to the lungs, is brought into the emergency room unresponsive and in acute respiratory distress. He has been receiving hospice care, but his daughter requests that he be placed on life support and undergo extensive diagnostic testing. She reports she has never spoken with her father about his wishes regarding life support. The patient's son is the healthcare proxy, but no one has been able to reach him. As the healthcare provider, you have serious reservations about placing this patient on mechanical ventilation. Given his clinical presentation, his prognosis is poor even with intervention. You question how much the daughter understands about her father's condition. Other members of the healthcare team are on hand and ready to place the patient on mechanical ventilation.

Questions

1   As a medical provider, how might you address this ethical dilemma? What specific steps would you want to take first to help the patient and his family, and what are your main concerns? How might this differ depending on the provider's primary discipline?

2   If you were a behavioural health provider such as a psychologist or social worker, how might your expertise help your team and the patient's daughter in this situation?

Situation specific ethical issues in end-of-life care

Even if people have given thought to what they consider a "good death," they may not have discussed this with loved ones and, near the end of life, family members may have differing opinions about what is best for a patient. Furthermore, even when advance care planning discussions are completed, they might be held long before the end of life, and values, circumstances, and the will to live may change (Chochinov, Tataryn, Clinch, & Dudgeon, 1999). These differences of opinion within families and the potential for evolving treatment preferences within patients based on their changing medical circumstances may create ethical dilemmas for providers similar to the situation described in the case example. To address the end-of-life needs of the rapidly growing population of adults reaching increasingly older age and dying slowly with chronic conditions, the Institute of Medicine's (2015) *Dying in America; Improving Quality and Honoring Individual Preferences at End of Life* delineated some of the issues that patients and families may face when approaching death. Their recommendations aimed to educate the public about the dying process and the need for a patient-centred care plan to help establish parameters for each individual's "good" death. Among these are recommendations for patient-centred, family-oriented care, clear clinician-patient communication, advance care planning, and professional development to help train providers in the delivery of quality end-of-life care.

Questions of capacity to make autonomous medical decisions may arise among patients with advanced chronic illness and, in combination with a potentially fluctuating will to live and diverse family opinions about the best treatment options, may complicate best practice treatment provision by palliative care teams. Determining capacity among individuals with diminished cognitive ability may involve several disciplines, including medicine, psychiatry, and psychology. These disciplines vary in their skill set, complementing one another in comprehensive capacity evaluations. Psychologists, for example, consider within their professional skill set cognitive and emotional assessment and team-based communication in addition to comprehensive clinical interviewing. Thus, psychologists as interprofessional team members may help the team discuss ethical principles across disciplines and assist in determining patient understanding and goals of care. Physicians bring as their skill set an ability to determine whether impairment in capacity is due to an organic cause, to treat medical issues that may affect cognition and decision-making, and to serve as treatment provider and patient educator about disease processes at end of life. Psychiatry can act as a bridge between medicine and psychology, and can help both with identifying and treating medical causes of illness as well as providing psychosocial support for patients needing to make end-of-life decisions. Overall, behavioural health providers across disciplines and across treatment settings may assist family members in understanding and processing the risks and benefits of their care decisions.

Notably, ethical issues faced by providers may differ based on the location where a patient is receiving care. The issues may differ due to the acuity of the patient's condition or regulations that dictate a particular delivery of care that might not be in line with a given profession's ethical practices. Such locations might include acute care, such as a hospital setting, a long-term care setting such as assisted living or skilled nursing facility, or in a palliative care or hospice unit. Some location-specific potential ethical issues are considered below.

Hospital/Acute Care: Most acute care takes place in a hospital setting, where ethical issues most likely stem from the need for urgent care and the ambiguity surrounding whether someone is able to make informed decisions regarding treatment plans. Some specific ethical issues within this setting include:

1 Patient autonomy vs. beneficence within the context of a new terminal diagnosis or disappointing test findings. Ethical issues arise when family members do not want patients to know about the severity of their disease due to a fear that patients will "give up." This can be an issue in the outpatient setting as well, but acute care settings are often where new diseases and worsening prognoses unfold quickly. In these cases, the urgent need to relay information and make care decisions can cause family members concern about information disclosure. This issue can be compounded when a diagnosis of dementia or delirium exists and there is a question of the patient's capacity to understand information and make informed decisions. In addition, as discussed later in the chapter, it is the norm in some cultures for family members to withhold negative health information from a patient, and providers must determine how to respect the patient's right to information as well as the norms of the culture to which the patient and family belong.

2 Establishing end-of-life wishes in an urgent manner. In certain emergency cases, decisions must be made about provision or termination of care without much time for discussion and patient education about the options. In this case the patient's right to informed consent (and thus autonomy and informed and shared decision-making) may be threatened through lack of information and the traditional patriarchal provision of medical care, in which the physician as expert makes care decisions that the patient is expected to follow without question.

3 Determining wishes for end-of-life care in acute settings where patients may quickly become unable to consent to medical care and often have not established a healthcare proxy. In these situations, a proxy decision-maker must be established, and this decision needs to take into account the laws and regulations of the state where the patient is being cared for, as well as the best approximation of the patient's wishes and the patient's best interest.

Nursing Home/Long-Term Care Facility: As of 2009, approximately 28% of older adults live their last days in a long-term care facility (Teno et al. 2013). Their placement in such a facility is often a consequence of an inability

Ethical issues 95

to attend to one or more of their basic activities of daily living, and the prevalence of cognitive impairment is high in long-term care settings. These findings, along with the need of administrators to comply with strict guidelines for care, may lead to the following ethical issues.

1   Hiding medications in food following patient refusal to take medication. This issue speaks to the conflict between beneficence (staff wanting patient to get adequate treatment) and patient autonomy (patient being able to refuse care). The questionable decision-making capacity of the nursing home resident and the potentially conflicting wishes of a proxy decision-maker may complicate staff's provision of quality palliative care. As noted by Hung and colleagues, the covert administration of medications is fraught with ethical implications for the providers and for family members who may either be ignorant of the practice or who may feel that they should approve of such a practice to provide care for their loved one (Hung, McNiel, & Binder, 2012).
2   Honouring advance directives to withhold nutrition/hydration at the end of life. If a resident has executed advance directives to withhold nutrition but is unable at the time to express his or her wishes, and if the state allows, a proxy decision-maker might wish to provide food or hydration against the expressed wishes of the patient within the advance directive (Bükki, Unterpaul, Nübling, Jox, & Lorenzl, 2014).
3   Promoting feeding tubes for quality parameters at end of life. Long-term care facilities have regulations on skin health and weight loss and are often caught between providing compassionate, patient-centred care and meeting required quality standards. Indeed, a study of end-of-life preferences for patients in long-term care showed that nursing home placement itself was a risk factor for discordance with adherence to patient care desires (Biola, Sloane, Williams, Daaleman, & Zimmerman, 2010). Arguments for placing feeding tubes in patients with dementia in order to decrease weight loss to meet "quality care" mandates again involve the struggle between patient autonomy and nonmalificence (not providing unnecessary care) versus administrator need to meet quality parameters for all patients (justice).

Palliative Care Unit/Hospice Facility: The hospice or palliative care unit or freestanding facility may be the most overt place where end-of-life ethical issues occur, as these are healthcare venues that are less understood by the general public and because death is often imminent in these settings. Issues seen here are usually more focused on the acute dying process and whether a patient has the autonomy to direct care that may hasten death (thus, patient autonomy versus physician nonmalificence). Ethical issues include:

1   Palliative sedation: this may be achieved either to relieve a patient of pain or to reduce agitation that may affect the patient or family. The sedation

comes at the cost of reducing meaningful interaction with loved ones and may also hasten death through decreased respiratory drive, although with judicious use of medication this is not often the case. This dual action of treating pain or anxiety and yet suppressing respiratory drive is frequently referred to as "double effect" in the literature.

2   Physician aid in dying: this issue stems from the patient's desire to have his or her own say in the timing of death. It has been debated whether physicians should be complicit in the prescription of medications that can be used to shorten life, even if they are not the ones themselves administering the medications. Indeed, in their 2016 code of medical ethics, the American Medical Association states that both physician–assisted death and euthanasia are "fundamentally incompatible with the physician's role as healer, would be difficult or impossible to control, and would pose serious societal risks" (AMA Code of Medical Ethics, Chapter 5, 2016b). Recently, the American Psychological Association reaffirmed their position to maintain neutrality on assisted death in order to best assist all clients in their decision-making process regarding this issue (www.apa.org/pi/aging/programs/eol/index. aspx).

3   Euthanasia: this issue takes physician aid in dying a step further and places the physician as the actor in actively ending a patient's life. It further illustrates the conflict between patient autonomy (deciding when one's life should end) and physician nonmaleficence as well as beneficence (as abiding by the "do no harm" rule may actually cause some harm to the patient through suppression of their autonomy).

Shared and informed decision-making: the role of professionals and patients

Health and palliative care literacy definitions

Health literacy, or "the cognitive and social skills which determine the motivation and ability of individuals to gain access to, understand, and use information in ways which promote and maintain good health" (Nutbeam, 1998), is an essential component of an individual's ability to process and utilize health information. High health literacy is positively correlated with treatment adherence (Miller, 2016), which may lead to a wide variety of improved health outcomes, including participation in informed and shared decision-making. Knowledge of a patient's health literacy levels may have ramifications for ethical practice, as a patient's ability to understand health information has an impact on the medical decision-making process. For example, patients with low health literacy may require more guidance from healthcare providers (Livaudais, Franco, Fei, & Bickell, 2013), as they may not fully understand information relating to diagnosis and treatment. Care must be taken to ensure that patients are truly receiving desired care, particularly at the end of life.

When assessing health literacy, palliative care literacy is a further component to consider. Patients with inadequate palliative care literacy may lack sufficient understanding of what palliative care entails, which creates a potential ethical dilemma regarding justice if patients are unable to access beneficial or needed services. More adults are familiar with the term "hospice" compared to the term "palliative care" (Cruz-Oliver et al., 2016), but general knowledge of even hospice in the United States remains quite low (Cagle et al., 2016). For example, more than half of a diverse sample of adults within the United States were not aware that hospice could not provide curative treatment to patients, and misconceptions may also exist at the provider level (Gawande, 2016). These misconceptions complicate the ethical provision of quality end-of-life care within interprofessional teams wherein team members may have varying levels of palliative care literacy themselves, as well as varying knowledge of family members' palliative care literacy.

While health literacy has been consistently linked to education level (Paasche-Orlow, Parker, Gazmararian, Nielsen-Bohlman, & Rudd, 2005), providers should not assume that high levels of education correspond to high levels of palliative care literacy. For example, in a highly educated sample of Non-Hispanic Whites and Latino adults in which over 90% of participants had at least some college, general knowledge of hospice remained low (Kreling, Selsky, Perret-Gentil, Huerta, & Mandelblatt, 2010). Misconceptions were higher in Latino participants, indicating that cultural disparities exist independently of education level. Racial disparities in utilization of palliative care are well-documented (Payne, 2016). For example, African American individuals have been shown to utilize hospice at a lower rate than their Non-Hispanic White counterparts. This constitutes an ethical dilemma, as these disparities can result in lack of desired care or unnecessarily prolonged treatment near the end of life.

Informed and shared decision-making

In medical decision-making, several distinct models have emerged in which the patient has varying amounts of responsibility in making healthcare related decisions (Emanuel & Emanuel, 1992). Under the more traditional paternalist model, the physician acts as an expert who is uniquely suited to making decisions based on experience gained through training and practice. In this case, the physician guides the patient towards making the decision that the physician deems best, with little input from the patient necessary. Patients with low or inadequate health literacy are particularly at risk of falling into a paternalistic model of decision-making by default (Safiya, Geiser, Jacob Arriola, & Kripalani, 2009).

In contrast, under the informative or consumer model, the physician provides the patient with all of the information that the patient needs to make an informed decision (Emanuel & Emanuel, 1992). In this case, the patient has ultimate authority, and he or she makes the final decision based on what is learned from the physician. While this allows the patient to have a high degree of autonomy, it also requires the patient to understand what can often be highly complicated medical information (Sudore, Schillinger, Knight, & Fried, 2010). Additionally, not all patients have the health literacy or palliative care literacy levels necessary to make a truly informed decision (Smith, Dixon, Trevena, Nutbeam, & McCaffery, 2009). As an additional complication, the ready availability of medical information on the internet, regardless of factuality, may increase patient inclination to view the patient-physician relationship under consumerist terms (Wald, Dube, & Anthony, 2007). This tension could elicit ethical dilemmas for healthcare providers when uninformed or misinformed patients or families express an autonomous wish that conflicts with known best medical practice.

Rather than simply informed decision-making, as described by the consumer model, shared decision-making may be more adaptable to the unique circumstances of healthcare teams (Legare et al., 2011), which include the patient, family members, and medical professionals. As a process, shared decision-making allows all involved to contribute to the well-being of the patient, and this shared decision-making among the patient and the healthcare team may maximize enactment of both patient autonomy and healthcare provider beneficent responsibility (Barry & Edgman-Levitan, 2012). Through this shared and patient-centered communication, medical decision-making, including decisions regarding the end of life and advance care planning, can take place on an individual basis. This allows both providers and patients to communicate their ideas and expectations, while still taking cultural and individual patient values and goals into account (Blanch-Hartigan et al., 2016), maximizing both autonomy and beneficence. Professionally diverse teams may be more successful when there is an expectation of shared decision-making and collaboration among all involved (Legare et al., 2011). While shared decision-making is often regarded as ideal within Western healthcare, involved parties may not always be in agreement about future treatment. In these cases, the wishes of the patient should be deferred to whenever possible, as this allows for the retention of autonomy.

Patients who prefer to engage in shared decision-making tend to have a great deal of trust in their physician; this trust is built through the physician gaining individual knowledge regarding the patient's unique circumstances and care preferences (Eliott & Olver, 2010). Shared decision-making also allows patients to have their desired level of autonomous control (Hoffman et al., 2014), as they can collaborate with providers to a varying extent based on their preferences and knowledge of the topic under discussion. However, shared decision-making may be difficult for some patients because of low health literacy levels, cultural norms or physician behaviours, and individuals in this situation may defer to the wishes of their physician, regardless of their true desires (Muscat et al., 2016). In such situations, no clear "gold standard" decision-maker is likely to emerge; instead, optimal collaborative decision-making may require compromise, as well

Ethical issues 99

as a willingness to hear and accept choices and preferences of the other, even and especially when such choices are different than those we may make for ourselves.

Lack of shared decision-making may also have repercussions in situations in which family members are required to use substituted judgement when making decisions for incapacitated relatives (Hirschman, Kapo, & Karlawish, 2006). Previous research has demonstrated that, in some situations involving hypothetical medical scenarios, substituted judgements may be concordant in only 58% of cases (Bravo, Sene, & Arcand, 2017). This discordance may create an ethical dilemma for family members and healthcare professionals who are attempting to make the best care decision possible (Dunn et al., 2013), particularly in the case of limited information.

While the models described by Emanuel and Emanuel (1992) can include all aspects of medical decision-making, end-of-life decisions may include additional complications. For example, end-of-life discussions may be difficult for patients and their families to initiate due to discomfort or fear of "giving up" (Gawande, 2016), and these conversations may be postponed until an imminent decision is necessary (Bailey et al., 2012). This again requires that patients be able to understand and contemplate complicated or hypothetical medical scenarios (Sudore et al., 2010), which frequently requires assistance and guidance from healthcare professionals. In addition, it may be difficult to make decisions regarding care for the future self (van Wijmen, Pasman, Widdershoven, & Onwuteaka-Philipsen, 2014), particularly as health status and treatment preference change. Despite receiving guidance from providers, almost half of patients express uncertainty regarding advance care planning decisions they have made, and this uncertainty may be higher in ethnic minorities than in Non-Hispanic White individuals (Sudore et al., 2010). Not surprisingly, patients with limited health and palliative care literacy may require additional assistance to express their autonomous treatment wishes.

When conducting serial end-of-life discussions over multiple occasions, the provider should be responsive to the patient's need to end the conversation if it becomes too difficult (Barnes, Jones, Tookman, & King, 2007). It is important to remember that healthcare providers bring their own experiences and biases with end-of-life care to discussions with patients and their families (Ho, Jameson, & Pavlish, 2016). This creates the risk of the provider failing to take the values and wishes of the patient into account, or simply avoiding end-of-life discussions (Weiner & Cole, 2004), both of which may constitute ethical lapses and potentially prevent the patient from receiving desired care. When patients are able to have these discussions with their providers and/or family members, they are less likely to experience unwanted medical interventions (Mack, Weeks, Wright, Block, & Prigerson, 2010). This includes lower rates of mechanical ventilation, resuscitation, and ICU admissions, as well as improved quality of life and lower rates of bereavement complications for caregivers following patient death (Wright et al., 2008).

Ethical implications of patient education

Decisions relating to end-of-life care may be difficult for all involved, and physicians frequently report discomfort related to these discussions (Enzinger, Zhang, Weeks, & Prigerson, 2014). Patient education regarding advance care planning is highly important, particularly as many patients feel that it is the duty of the physician to initiate end-of-life conversations (Hajizadeh, Uhler, & Perez Figueroa, 2014). Despite this preference, multiple studies (Bailey et al., 2012; Levin et al., 2008) have demonstrated that a large percentage of do-not-resuscitate (DNR) orders are signed within 48 hours of death. This indicates that many patients do not discuss advance directives with their healthcare providers until the end of life is imminent. This is an important ethical gap to address, as earlier discussions about palliative care options lead to fewer unnecessary medical interventions and improved quality of life (Greer, Jackson, Meier, & Temel, 2013). Advance directives may be discussed by multiple members of the healthcare team, including physicians, nurses, and behavioural health professionals.

When considering patient education, it is often important to include family members or friends given potentially fluctuating decisional capacity among patients. Patients whose family members were involved in end-of-life care were more likely to have discussed palliative care with their healthcare providers, in addition to experiencing higher quality of life prior to death (Sudore, Casarett, Smith, Richardson, & Ersek, 2014). Emphasis on quality of life is often crucial to terminally ill patients, and focus on and respect for this patient desire is an important aspect of ethical practice. Healthcare providers may need to consider whether patient or family wishes are being expressed; might a family member's desires unduly influence a patient's stated preferences? Communication with the patient is essential to determining his or her desired balance between maintaining autonomy (e.g., possibly pursuing or possibly declining aggressive treatment options), adequate palliation, and quality of life; the ultimate decision may be a difficult one for all involved. By providing training to increase collaborative decision-making in cancer patients, their families, and oncologists, Hoerger and colleagues (2013) were able to demonstrate significant improvements in communication between all parties. This has the potential to allow treatment to become more patient centered. Individuals with low health literacy have more uncertainty regarding end-of-life decision-making (Volandes, Barry, Chang, & Paasche-Orlow, 2010) and may require more guidance and education from providers. In such cases, patient education may allow individuals to receive desired care at the end of life that is consistent with personal goals.

Unwanted medical interventions at the end of life may cause physical and psychological distress in patients and their families (Mack et al., 2010), making this a crucial area of communication related to ethical practice. While patient education typically involves discussions regarding advance directives and future plans, healthcare providers may be able to play a unique role in preparation for these difficult discussions and decisions. Rather than asking healthy patients to envision care preferences in future hypothetical scenarios, healthcare providers can work with patients to help prepare them to make these plans after diagnosis (Sudore & Fried, 2010). If the possibility of changing circumstances and high levels of stress are explained in advance, patients may anticipate having to face these decisions in the future. This allows them to begin thinking of their values and goals, but still allows for the possibility of needing to adapt based on unanticipated circumstances. This also encourages the patient to begin discussing possibilities with family members, who may be involved in later decision-making processes. This potentially reduces possible effects of response shift, in which patients may adjust standards regarding acceptable quality of life when faced with deteriorating health (Elliott, Gessert, Larson, & Russ, 2014). If patients are aware that their advance care plans can be adjusted, they may have an easier time initiating this conversation with unfamiliar care providers (Sudore & Fried, 2010). Emotional states, such as "numbness" related to diagnosis or prognosis, may impair a patient's ability to participate in end-of-life decisions (Maciejewski & Prigerson, 2015). This issue may again be alleviated if a patient is aware of these complications prior to needing to make decisions in a moment of medical crisis.

What to do when patients autonomously choose not to be involved

Patients may vary in the level of autonomy that they desire. As patients have the right to be highly involved in their medical care, they also have the right to defer to the physician's expertise. Collaboration cannot be forced, and situations in which the patient does not seek shared decision-making may arise. For example, in a study involving Australian patients with terminal cancer, Eliott and Olver (2010) examined preferences for the desired role of the physician when making DNR decisions. Results demonstrated that their desires regarding shared decision-making were highly variable. Several patients believed that the doctor should have a paternalistic role based on their greater medical training and experience, while others believed that the doctor was an untrustworthy figure who did not have the personal knowledge of the patient and family that was necessary for such an important decision. While shared decision-making may be viewed as ideal by many within the medical community, respecting patient autonomy also includes respecting the right of the patient not to prepare advance directives or be involved in advance care planning.

If patients are not involved in their care due to low or inadequate health or palliative care literacy, steps should be taken to ensure that they are truly choosing to cede autonomy rather than simply feeling overwhelmed. Patients with low health or palliative care literacy frequently do not ask as many questions as those with high health literacy (Aboumatar, Carson, Beach, Roter, & Cooper, 2013; Katz, Jacobson, Veledar, & Kripalani, 2007), and healthcare providers may benefit from ascertaining the health literacy or palliative care literacy levels of their patients. A variety of quick screeners such as the Newest Vital Sigh (Weiss et al., 2005) or brief questions developed by Chew and colleagues (2004) may be utilized to ascertain health literacy levels in an outpatient setting. However, there is some controversy regarding the ethics of routine screening of patients for health literacy levels, as it has been suggested that doing so may cause patients to become stigmatized or alienated (Paasche-Orlow & Wolf, 2008). One possible solution is to use screeners without high face validity, as these measures do not appear to induce feelings of shame or inadequacy in patients with low health literacy (VanGeest, Welch, & Weiner, 2010). Additionally, measures of palliative care literacy are still under development (Kozlov, Carpenter, & Rodebaugh, 2017) and not widely available or utilized.

In a diverse sample of older adults living in San Francisco, approximately 20% of participants expressed a preference for their physician to make final decisions regarding end-of-life care (Chiu, Feuz, McMahan, Miao, & Sudore, 2016). Overall, adults in this study who chose not to make their own decisions indicated that they were satisfied with their communication with their healthcare provider, illustrating that such an arrangement does not arise solely due to lack of discussion or personal relationship. However, if patients choose to cede authority to the physician, the provider should still inform the patient of decisions that have been made. This presents the opportunity for the patient to comprehend and discuss the desirability of their future care, including situations such as full code or DNR orders. As with all end-of-life conversations (Barnes et al., 2007), this should be an ongoing process.

If the patient chooses to alter these orders at any point, their decisions in these cases should be respected. This introduces a further ethical dilemma for providers, as time constraints may prohibit asking patients about their future preferences during every interaction. In addition, it may create an unnecessary burden for patients to reiterate preferences continuously (Beecham et al., 2017). However, unwanted medical interventions may significantly increase physical and mental distress (Mack et al., 2010), and desired interventions may change drastically over the course of treatment (Schubart et al., 2015). If healthcare providers emphasize the changing nature of care preferences, this may allow patients the freedom to inform their physician of any desired changes autonomously (Sudore & Fried, 2010). While patients will ideally be able to address and discuss changes with their providers, a variety of barriers, such as low health or palliative care literacy, may prevent this from occurring. Currently, it is recommended that preferences in individuals with terminal illnesses be assessed following a change in medical condition or every six to twelve months (Beecham et al., 2017).

International variation

From an international perspective, the nature of end-of-life care and discussions – and the ethical implications that arise from them – can vary between different cultural groups. As global immigration increases, providers may be increasingly called upon to treat patients from a variety of cultural backgrounds. While a model of shared decision-making may be viewed as ideal within Western societies (Legare et al., 2011), this may not be the preferred method of decision-making within all cultures (Hawley & Morris, 2017; Romain & Sprung, 2014). There is no universal standard of what makes a "good death," and there are cultural disparities regarding how involved patients, families, and communities would like to be in the end-of-life process (Zaman, Inbadas, Whitelaw, & Clark, 2017).

In certain populations, spiritual or religious beliefs may be of particular importance in how a patient determines when to seek care and how to pursue treatment, and providers should evaluate end-of-life preferences on a case-by-case basis. While some may view religiosity as a barrier to end-of-life care and treatment, collaboration between healthcare providers and spiritual leaders may allow physicians to provide better support to patients (Payne, 2016). If this is desired by the patient, inclusion of spirituality is within the guidelines of ethical practice. Being able to draw comfort and support from religious or spiritual beliefs may be linked to improved well-being in patients with terminal illnesses, such as cancer (Lopez-Sierra & Rodriguez-Sanchez, 2015).

As another example, physicians of different cultures may have different values regarding the sharing of prognostic information with patients and their families, influencing the autonomy-beneficence ethical balance. For instance, the majority of Japanese physicians reported that it is more appropriate to inform the family of the patient of a terminal diagnosis before informing the patient (Ruhnke et al., 2000). This is in direct contrast to American physicians surveyed in the same study, but the concept that it is the right of the family to convey or withhold prognostic information is also found in other cultural groups (Ni & Alraek, 2017). For example, Latino families are more likely than Non-Hispanic White families to believe that it is necessary to shield the patient from news of a terminal diagnosis (Kreling et al., 2010), and they may be more reluctant to discuss end-of-life care and decisions with a physician. In contrast, a study of Korean adults with terminal cancer found that patients who were aware of their prognosis were more likely to make their own care decisions, even if there was discordance between their wishes and those of family members (Ahn et al., 2013). This creates an ethical dilemma for the provider, as it is necessary to respect both cultural values and the autonomy of the patient. This may be addressed by discussing disclosure preferences with the patient, allowing the provider to ascertain whether they wish to be informed of prognostic information. In cases of conflict, the patient should be allowed to retain autonomy if they have the legal capacity to make medical decisions. Ultimately, it is important to remember that differences may also be observed within groups; thus, care must be taken to ascertain the preferences of each individual, rather than making assumptions based on factors such as age, ethnicity, or race in order for providers to follow ethical guidelines.

Immigrants may be particularly at risk for low health literacy (Gele, Pettersen, Torheim, & Kumar, 2016). As a further complication, language differences may create an additional barrier independent of the health literacy levels of the patient (Sudore et al., 2009). Interventions that target increased integration within the community (Gele et al., 2016), such as acquisition of language and employment skills, may help reduce health disparities found in immigrant populations. In the United States, Latino immigrants may be particularly at risk of experiencing medical disparities related to health literacy (Calvo, 2016), and further work is needed to address palliative care inequalities.

When considering end-of-life discussions from an international perspective, a common theme that emerges is a desire for a level of respect and trust between the patient, family members, and the healthcare team (Bosma, Apland, & Kazanjian, 2010). Individuals from different cultures have different expectations regarding the role that physicians and family members will play in end-of-life care, but a willingness to be accommodating and respectful of cultural values is an integral part of shared decision-making. For example, members of the Maori people of New Zealand have expressed a desire to incorporate traditional Maori practices such as songs and prayers into end-of-life care to create a more personalized care plan to adequately address patient end-of-life needs (Oetzel, Simpson, Berryman, & Reddy, 2015).

Death with dignity: international definitions

Perhaps no other ethical dilemma receives greater attention than the participation of healthcare providers in hastening the death of a patient at the competent, autonomous behest of the patient. Terminology regarding hastening the end of life may vary, and terms such as physician-assisted death (PAD), physician-assisted suicide, euthanasia, and death with dignity are frequently used. There is a great deal of controversy surrounding terminology, particularly as terms such as "suicide" have cultural or religious implications (Chochinov, 2016; Miccinesi et al., 2005). There may also be legal connotations associated with choice of terminology, as "euthanasia" may refer to the active ending of a patient's life by a medical professional (Emanuel, Onwuteaka-Philipsen, Urwin, & Cohen, 2016). This is an important distinction, as several jurisdictions, including several U.S. states and Switzerland, protect PAD but not euthanasia. Other countries, such as Belgium (Chambaere et al., 2010), allow euthanasia in circumstances where the patient is not able to provide direct consent (e.g., dementia) and involve consultation from family members. Unless otherwise indicated, we will be using the term PAD.

In 1997, Oregon became the first North American jurisdiction to legalize PAD through the Oregon Death with Dignity Act (Death with Dignity, 2017). Within the United States, PAD is currently legal in the states of California, Colorado, Oregon, Vermont, and Washington. As of February 20, 2017, the District of Columbia also has a legal statute in effect allowing for PAD (Death with Dignity Act of, 2015). While Montana does not have specific legislation that allows PAD, physicians who provide hastened death to terminally ill patients cannot be prosecuted under the Rights of the Terminally Ill Act (*Baxter v. Montana*, 2009). In addition to the named states, multiple other jurisdictions will be hearing bills regarding PAD in 2017. Currently, all U.S. states that allow PAD require that the patient be at least 18 years of age, be terminally ill, and possess the legal capacity to make medical decisions (Emanuel et al., 2016).

In Quebec, PAD was first legalized in 2014, although national legislation applying to all Canadian provinces went into effect in June 2016 (*Carter v. Canada*, 2015). Similar to the United States, Canadian patients who choose PAD must be consenting adults of at least 18 years of age with an "irremediable" illness that causes "suffering." As the legalization of PAD in Canada is relatively recent, there is some question regarding what exactly is meant by the legislative terminology (Chochinov, 2016) and some have noted a lack of a plan for comprehensive data collection (Emanuel et al., 2016). This may create ethical dilemmas for health professionals practising in Canada, as they may be called upon to make judgements regarding the suffering of individual patients (Duffy, 2015). As with all cases of patients requesting PAD, respect for autonomy will need to be balanced with protection of individual rights.

Within Europe, Belgium and Luxembourg have legally allowed both PAD and euthanasia since 2002 and 2009, respectively (Emanuel et al., 2016). Both countries require that the patient be experiencing severe physical or mental suffering, and individuals in Luxembourg must be at least 18 years of age. In contrast, children in Belgium under the age of 18 have been able to seek PAD since 2014, with the first reported incidence of this occurring in 2016 (Narayan, 2016). Unlike adults, children must have received a diagnosis of a terminal illness to seek PAD (Emanuel et al., 2016). Life-ending treatment, most typically through opioid administration, may be performed without the express consent of the patient, which is usually due to coma or advanced dementia (Chambaere et al., 2010). However, it should be noted that euthanasia is frequently withheld from patients with dementia despite previous requests, as it can be both ethically and legally difficult to make end-of-life decisions in these circumstances (Chambaere, Cohen, Robijn, Bailey, & Deliens, 2015).

Unlike Belgium and Luxembourg, Switzerland protects only the right to seek PAD, with euthanasia expressly prohibited (Emanuel et al., 2016). Switzerland has recognized the legal right to assist others in suicide since 1942, as long as no criminal motive, such as the desire for financial gain, is involved. This assistance may take the form of delivering a prescription or mixing a lethal dosage of medication, and several private organizations are available to help facilitate this process (Ziegler & Bosshard, 2007). In contrast to other jurisdictions, Switzerland does not require individuals to provide a medical reason for desiring PAD, although research has shown that pain related to medical conditions is frequently cited (Fischer et al., 2009). Switzerland also does not have a residency requirement, and individuals may travel to Switzerland to seek PAD (Fischer et al., 2008).

Both PAD and euthanasia have been protected by law in the Netherlands since 2002 (Emanuel et al., 2016). In contrast to North American jurisdictions, Dutch patients between the ages of 12 and 17 may choose PAD with parental agreement and consultation (Dyer, White, & Garcia Rada, 2015). Patients with neurocognitive degeneration are also eligible for PAD if they prepared advance directives indicating this choice when legally competent (Menzel & Steinbock, 2013). Additionally, physicians may provide euthanasia to newborn infants to end "unbearable suffering" when there is no likelihood of improvement (Verhagen & Sauer, 2005). The majority of these cases reported to the Dutch government in recent years have involved severe spina bifida. Prior to providing PAD, the attending physician must consult with an independent assessor and, finally, report the patient's subsequent death to a governmental committee (Dyer et al., 2015).

Finally, Colombia is the only country outside of Europe or North America that currently protects the legal status of PAD (Emanuel et al., 2016). Although the Colombian Supreme Court ruled in 1997 that euthanasia was legal, guidelines were not established until 2015 (Dyer et al., 2015). Requests for PAD must be reviewed by an independent committee, which includes a psychiatrist. Patients must be at least 18 years of age, and they must be terminally ill to receive euthanasia.

Interventions to improve ethical education and practice

As this chapter has detailed, there are numerous ethical issues that arise across end-of-life care settings. In response, professionals have outlined a number of ways to improve practice to prevent and effectively manage these ethical concerns. This section will briefly discuss interventions that have been developed to address the following factors involved in end-of-life care: care provider education, interdisciplinary team (IDT) meetings, and the inclusion of family members in IDT meetings. It is important to note that another chapter in this book reviews additional interventions, from a broader scope, that have been developed to improve communication and decision-making in the context of serious illness. For a more comprehensive review of the interventions available, see Chapter 2 in this volume.

Competencies and guidelines for education

Increasing one's awareness of the potential ethical issues that may arise in end-of-life care and discussions is a useful first step to managing their effects. Frequently, awareness is gained through educational modules and ethical scenarios presented during professional training. Technological advances have prompted innovation concerning training modules and how they are delivered. An international, interprofessional team of scholars collaborated to create a healthcare ethics casebook to be available as an interactive web-based training opportunity that encourages the practitioner to engage in reflection on ethical challenges (Moses, Berlinger, Dunn, Gusmano, & Chin, 2015). The casebook is not solely focused on end-of-life care situations, but many of the cases address end-of-life decision-making challenges from a healthcare professional's point of view. While this casebook is specific to the healthcare context of Singapore, the authors note its global availability as useful for cross-cultural learning that reinforces the complex interaction between culture and healthcare decisions. (Moses et al., 2015). The authors describe anecdotal support for the casebook from local physicians. For example, junior level professionals noted appreciating the complexity of the cases in the casebook because it simulates real situations more closely (Moses et al., 2015). Additionally, exposure to this casebook may increase a clinician's awareness of their own gaps in understanding and prompt self-directed learning.

Similarly, researchers have found encouraging results evaluating the effectiveness of educational modules delivered to community nurses over a six-month period using a distance-learning approach (Wheeler, Anstey, Lewis, Jeynes, & Way, 2014). The results demonstrated this intervention's utility to increase the nurses' knowledge of palliative and end-of-life care, as well as their confidence with these domains of care (Wheeler et al., 2014). The ability to reflect real world clinical situations was identified as a major strength of this training material, which coincides with the noted strength of the casebook. Both examples illustrate positive utilizations of technology, but within the research on palliative and end-of-life care there are studies that find it challenging to incorporate technology into practice. For example, a mixed methods study conducted in Scotland found significant barriers to the use of technology to educate practitioners on identifying patients for palliative care services using the Electronic Palliative Care Summary (Mason et al., 2015). In an evaluation of the Electronic Palliative Care Summary, respondents indicated a lack of trust that the technology will work as it is supposed to due to problems with its user-friendliness (Mason et al., 2015).

Using technology to address training goals can have positive outcomes, but there is still room for innovation to improve professional utilization of technology. The user-friendliness and realistic portrayal of clinical situations are important aspects of training materials that should be evaluated and improved upon. Also, training materials should not be created with a "one size fits all" approach. It is important to recognize that one method of training may be well received by one discipline but not all disciplines. For example, a research study highlighted how disciplines fundamentally differ in their needs for education on ethical dilemmas due to their varying levels of interactions with patients (Bollig, Schmidt, Rosland, & Heller, 2015). The study suggests that tailoring training materials and approaches to target the most common ethical dilemmas per discipline may increase their effectiveness and user-friendliness. Education and training of professionals are critical steps in developing a foundational understanding of the best practices for managing ethical dilemmas, but there are additional ways to proactively manage ethical dilemmas.

Foundational principles are similar across profession-specific and palliative care-specific guidelines, such as the provision of competent care, respect for human rights, and practising within the law; however, palliative care-specific guidelines address unique ethical considerations for individuals with severe illness. One primary document governing the management of palliative care ethical issues for all healthcare professional is the *Clinical Practice Guidelines for Quality Palliative Care* (NCP, 2013). The document includes three ethics-specific guidelines, including: 1) providing person-centred care consistent with best practice standards, 2) identifying and addressing ethical issues within this vulnerable population, and 3) practising within legal and practice boundaries (NCP, 2013, pp. 32–34). Internationally, the European Association for Palliative Care website (www.eapcnet.eu/Themes/Resources/Ethics.aspx) makes available published white papers and position statements regarding various ethical issues, such as advance care planning, sedation, and physician-assisted death (2015).

Healthcare providers require prelicensure education to ensure they are knowledgeable about their Codes of Ethics and competent to address ethical issues when caring for all patients, including those receiving palliative care. Each profession determines educational competencies for providing palliative care in accordance with respective scopes of practice, such as within medicine (Hospice and Palliative Medicine Competencies Project Work Group, 2009) and nursing (American Association of Colleges of Nursing, 2016). The European Association for Palliative Care has published palliative care competencies for all healthcare providers that focus on addressing patient needs across bio-psycho-social domains, working within interprofessional teams to meet patient needs and goals of care, and continuing professional development (Gamondi, Larkin, & Payne, 2013). Currently, there is a marked deficit in specific palliative care standards for behavioural and mental health providers. Educators should consider these competencies as they design instructional interventions, integrating ethical issues throughout the curriculum.

Practitioners must also be educated on how to work in interprofessional teams to achieve the goals of palliative care. Core competencies for interprofessional teamwork should guide education, specifically within four key domains: 1) values/ethics for interprofessional practice; 2) roles/responsibilities; 3) interprofessional communication; and 4) teams and teamwork (Interprofessional Education Collaborative, 2016). Interventions catered to ethics education for interprofessional teams include ethics courses (Lennon-Dearing, Lowry, Ross, & Dyer, 2009) and case studies (Wilhelm, Poirier, Otsuka, & Wagner, 2014). These interventions help foster interprofessional collaboration and enhance students' abilities to work within teams.

IDT meetings

Ethical issues that unfold in interprofessional team meetings are another set of circumstances with the potential for improvement. IDT meetings serve an integral role in creating comprehensive care plans. Interventions targeting providers' abilities to make effective use of these meetings have three potential impacts on ethical issues in end-of-life care. First, interventions to improve IDT meetings could proactively minimize the frequency of ethical issues through better team communication. Second, these interventions could better prepare providers for addressing ethical issues as they arise. Further, by encouraging more open communication about ethical concerns among team members and increasing the attention given to these concerns, there could be an increase in the reporting of problematic situations during IDT meetings. There are federal regulations in place that require IDT meetings, but this does not ensure that the goal of a collaborative team process is always being met (Wittenberg-Lyles, Oliver, Demiris, & Regehr, 2010). Thus, careful evaluation of how to improve one's own IDT meetings can be a beneficial step in proactively addressing ethical concerns. Research on interprofessional care teams has been ongoing for more than four decades (Fulmer, 2016). This research has outlined some notions of what constitutes an effective IDT, but there are still many questions about which professionals need to be involved in the care planning per case. Fulmer (2016) highlighted the importance of providers' communication skills, having clearly defined roles and responsibilities for each provider, and using teamwork to address the patient's and family's preferences for care.

Family involvement in IDT meetings

As indicated in the criteria summarized by Fulmer (2016), the patient's and the family's well-being is important, yet, family caregivers' roles in care planning meetings received little attention until recently (Washington, Parker Oliver, Gage, Albright, & Demiris, 2016). Research continues to demonstrate positive improvements to the shared decision-making process by including the patient and family caregivers in the process. For example, interprofessional team care has been shown to have an impact on symptom management, length of hospital stays, financial burden of care, the amount of time patients spend at home, patient and family satisfaction with care, and the ability to fulfill patients' preferences for where they want to die (Hearn & Higginson, 1998; Wittenberg-Lyles et al., 2010). The inclusion of family members and patients in the care planning process simultaneously elicits improved ethical practice and increased logistical challenges. Planning for integrating family members and patients into IDT meetings is a necessary step. As noted by Washington and colleagues (2016), bringing family caregivers to the IDT meetings does not automatically invite their participation as collaborators in the decision-making process. Additionally, there is some research to support the logical conclusion that, by including family members and patients in the IDT meetings, the communication patterns of the professionals are altered (Wittenberg-Lyles et al., 2010).

Recent research studies have begun to outline beneficial practices related to fostering collaborative communication. Washington and colleagues (2016) suggest hospice providers use several strategies to facilitate effective integration of family members into the IDT meetings. They argue that ethical practice can still be achieved by following Legare and Witteman's (2013) conceptualization of shared decision-making involving only three factors: that the providers and care recipient "recognize the need for a decision, understand the best available evidence, and take into account the provider's guidance and the care recipient's preferences and values" (Legare & Witteman, 2013; Washington et al., 2016, p. 277). They highlight the importance of meeting with the caregivers outside of the IDT meetings to provide information and offer emotional support. Also, they suggest training interprofessional team members on effective communication strategies and identifying one team member to be the facilitator of the meetings (Washington et al., 2016). Lastly, they evaluated the effectiveness of videoconferencing tools to address the logistical challenges of family member participation in IDT meetings. The study supports videoconferencing as a useful tool, but requires effort from IDT members to ensure the caregivers feel capable of participating and not just observing.

An ethical consideration for providers in the inclusion of family members in IDT meetings is that these individuals may represent their own treatment wishes as opposed to their patient's treatment wishes. Kozlov, Reid, and Carpenter (2017) evaluated the effectiveness of a brief educational intervention including a brief video and an information page about palliative care targeting laypersons' knowledge of palliative care. The results of this study suggest that improving the layperson's understanding of palliative care may make them more prepared for participation in shared decision-making. While more evidence is needed, this is a promising approach that may be influential in alleviating some of the barriers faced when attempting to integrate patients and family members into IDT meetings.

Overall, new interventions targeting ethical clinical practice in end-of-life care settings are being developed and there is a push to find more evidence for the interventions that have already been developed. Moreover, interventions related to ethics rely on improved education and training for the varied disciplines working in palliative care. Further, these interventions are utilizing technological advances to increase their effectiveness. Researchers posit new suggestions for evaluating the effectiveness of the IDT meetings in these settings and are challenging the assumptions of who should be involved in the IDT meetings. Numerous strategies for improving ethical practice in palliative and end-of-life care settings have been identified, and more research evidence for these strategies is needed.

Conclusion

This chapter has considered ethical dilemmas faced by members of interprofessional palliative care teams as they attempt to weigh considerations of patient autonomy, beneficent responsibility, nonmaleficence, and justice. These ethical issues become apparent across various healthcare settings and situations and often involve a patient's diminished decision-making capacity and treatment wishes that differ from the treatment wishes presented by the family. Providers in various settings may confront different practice guidelines that influence their ethical decisions. Issues including health and palliative care literacy influence the extent to which patients and family members may effectively participate in informed and shared decision-making.

Education of patients and families regarding palliative care and recurring advance planning discussions may improve providers' ability to initiate and manage patient-centered treatment planning effectively. Additionally, cultural variation in a patient's desire for involvement in autonomous treatment decisions at the end of life must be considered by providers. The cultural and ethical appropriateness of not involving the patient in decision-making when this is not in accord with cultural context can complicate palliative care providers' ethical practice decisions. International and national variations surrounding the legal practice of physician-assisted death, particularly among patients with diminished capacity for decision-making, continue to gain public, practice, and policy attention.

Within the circumstances near the end of life, providers may find their own personal beliefs at odds with the treatment preferences of their patients and, thus, ethical considerations become paramount. Educational interventions to improve providers' knowledge and the incorporation of patients and families into IDT meetings offer exciting new avenues to improve ethical interprofessional palliative care practice but require further investigation. As the world population ages, ethical considerations in the interprofessional delivery of palliative care will continue to evolve and professional organizations will refine their practice guidelines in accordance with new knowledge.

Case example

Juliette, an 84-year-old patient with late-stage dementia, currently resides in a nursing home. She has an advance directive, executed ten years prior to her dementia diagnosis, that states that she would not want any artificial hydration or nutrition. Her advance directive also names her daughter as healthcare proxy and states that the daughter has the right to make decisions that may be different from those stated in the directive if medical circumstances have changed and the daughter believes a different treatment option is in the patient's best interest. The patient has ceased eating due to her dementia, and the administrator of the nursing home is strongly suggesting to the attending physician that a percutaneous gastrostomy (PEG) tube be placed, as he is concerned about weight loss, which is a quality measure on which the nursing home is evaluated. The daughter agrees that her mother said frequently that she wanted "no tubes" but is also pressuring the physician to order the PEG tube because "we can't let Mom starve to death." The physician is aware that in end-stage dementia, PEG tubes do not reduce mortality, do not reduce aspiration events, and come with their own side effects from placement and maintenance. Furthermore, the physician knows that cessation of eating in end-stage dementia is a natural course of the disease, and the patient does not sense hunger at this time. Thus, the physician faces an ethical dilemma putting her at odds with the patient's proxy and the nursing home administration.

Questions

1   What are the ethical issues facing the physician in the above scenario?
2   How does the physician reconcile the needs and wishes of the patient with the concerns of the other interested parties (administrator and POA)?
3   How would assessment of health literacy, responsiveness to cultural cues, and use of interprofessional teams aid the healthcare providers with determining the most ethical solution to this issue?

References

Aboumatar, H. J., Carson, K. A., Beach, M. C., Roter, D. L., & Cooper, L. A. (2013). The impact of health literacy on desire for participation in healthcare, medical visit communication, and patient reported outcomes among patients with hypertension. *Journal of General Internal Medicine, 28*(11), 1469–1476.

Ahn, E., Shin, D. W., Choi, J. Y., Kang, J., Kim, D. K., Kim, H., . . . Cho, B. (2013). The impact of awareness of terminal illness on quality of death and care decision making: A prospective nationwide survey of bereaved family members of advanced cancer patients. *Psycho-Oncology, 22*(12), 2771–2778.

American Association of Colleges of Nursing. (2016). *CARES: Competencies and recommendations for educating undergraduate nursing students: Preparing nurses to care for the seriously ill and their families.* Retrieved from www.aacn.nche.edu/elnec/New-Palliative-Care-Competencies.pdf

American Medical Association. (2016a, June). *Code of medical ethics* [Electronic version]. Retrieved from www.ama-assn.org/about-us/code-medical-ethics

American Medical Association. (2016b, June). *Code of medical ethics chapter 5: Opinions on caring for patients at the end of life*. Retrieved from www.ama-assn.org/sites/default/files/media-browser/code-of-medical-ethics-chapter-5.pdf

American Nurses Association. (2015). *Code of ethics for nurses with interpretive statement* (3rd ed.). Washington, DC: American Nurses Association.

American Psychological Association. (2017, January 1). *Ethical principles of psychologists and code of conduct, including 2010 and 2016 amendments* [Electronic version]. Retrieved from www.apa.org/ethics/code/

Bailey, F. A., Allen, R. S., Williams, B. R., Goode, P. S., Granstaff, S., Redden, D. T., & Burgio, K. L. (2012). Do-not-resuscitate orders in the last days of life. *Journal of Palliative Medicine, 15*(7), 751–759.

Barnes, K., Jones, L., Tookman, A., & King, M. (2007). Acceptability of an advance care planning interview schedule: A focus group study. *Palliative Medicine, 21*, 23–28.

Barry, M. J., & Edgman-Levitan, S. (2012). Shared decision making: The pinnacle of patient-centered care. *The New England Journal of Medicine, 366*, 780–781.

Baxter v. Montana, 354 Mont. 234 (Montana Supreme Court, 2009).

Beecham, E., Oostendorp, L., Crocker, J., Kelly, P., Dinsdale, A., Hemsley, J., . . . Bluebond-Langner, M. (2017). Keeping all options open: Parents' approaches to advance care planning. *Health Expectations, 20*(4), 675–684.

Biola, H., Sloane, P. D., Williams, C. S., Daaleman, T. P., & Zimmerman, S. (2010). Preferences versus practice: Life-sustaining treatments in last months of life in long-term care. *Journal of the American Medical Directors Association, 11*(1), 42–51. http://doi.org/10.1016/j.jamda.2009.07.005

Blanch-Hartigan, D., Chawla, N., Moser, R. P., Finney Rutten, L. J., Hesse, B. W., & Arora, N. K. (2016). Trends in cancer survivors' experience of patient-centered communication: Results from the Health Information National Trends Survey (HINTS). *Journal of Cancer Survivorship, 10*(6), 1067–1077.

Bollig, G., Schmidt, G., Rosland, J. H., & Heller, A. (2015). Ethical challenges in nursing homes: Sstaff's opinions and experiences with systematic ethics meetings with participation of residents' relatives. *Scandinavian Journal of Caring Sciences, 29*(4), 810–823. doi:10.1111/scs.12213

Bosma, H., Apland, L., & Kazanjian, A. (2010). Cultural conceptualizations of hospice palliative care: More similarities than differences. *Palliative Medicine, 24*(5), 510–522.

Bravo, G., Sene, M., & Arcand, M. (2017). Surrogate inaccuracy in predicting older adults' desire for life-sustaining interventions in the event of decisional incapacity: Is it due in part to erroneous quality-of-life assessments? *International Psychogeriatrics, 29*(7), 1061–1068.

Bükki, J., Unterpaul, T., Nübling, G., Jox, R. J., & Lorenzl, S. (2014). Decision making at the end of life: Cancer patients' and their caregivers' views on artificial nutrition and hydration. *Supportive Care in Cancer, 22*(12), 3287–3299.

Bush, S. S., Allen, R. S., Heck, A. L., & Moye, J. (2015). Ethical issues in geropsychology: Clinical and forensic perspectives. *Psychological Injury and Law, 8*(4), 348–356.

Bush, S. S., Allen, R. S., & Molinari, V. (2017). *Ethical practice in geropsychology*. Washington, DC: American Psychological Association. ISBN: 978-1-4338-2626-9

Cagle, J. G., Van Dussen, D. J., Culler, K. L., Carrion, I., Hong, S., Guralnik, J., & Zimmerman, S. (2016). Knowledge about hospice: Exploring misconceptions, attitudes, and preferences for care. *American Journal of Hospice & Palliative Medicine, 33*(1), 27–33.

Calvo, R. (2016). Health literacy and quality of care among Latino immigrants in the United States. *Health & Social Work, 41*(1), 44–51.

Carter v. Canada (Attorney General), 2015 SCC 5 (Supreme Court of Canada, 2015).

Chambaere, K., Bilsen, J., Cohen, J., Onwuteaka-Philipsen, B. D., Mortier, F., & Deliens, L. (2010). Physician-assisted deaths under the euthanasia law in Belgium: A population-based survey. *CMAJ: Canadian Medical Association Journal, 182*(9), 895–901.

Chambaere, K., Cohen, J., Robijn, L., Bailey, S. K., & Deliens, L. (2015). End-of-life decisions in individuals dying with dementia in Belgium. *Journal of the American Geriatrics Society, 63*(2), 290–296.

Chew, L. D., Bradley, K. A., & Boyko, E. J. (2004). Brief questions to identify patients with inadequate health literacy. *Family Medicine, 38*(8), 588–594.

Chiu, C., Feuz, M. A., McMahan, R. D., Miao, Y., & Sudore, R. L. (2016). "Doctor, make my decisions": Decision control preferences, advance care planning, and satisfaction with communication among diverse older adults. *Journal of Pain and Symptom Management, 51*(1), 33–40.

Chochinov, H. M. (2016). Physician-assisted death in Canada. *JAMA, 315*(3), 253–254.

Chochinov, H. M., Tataryn, D., Clinch, J. J., & Dudgeon, D. (1999). Will to live in the terminally ill. *Lancet, 354*(9181), 816–819.

Cruz-Oliver, D. M., Malmstrom, T. K., Fernandez, N., Parikh, M., Garcia, J., & Sanchez-Reilly, S. (2016). Education intervention "caregivers like me" for Latino family caregivers improved attitudes toward professional assistance at end-of-life care. *American Journal of Hospice & Palliative Medicine, 33*(6), 527–536.

Death with Dignity. (2017). *Take action.* Retrieved from www.deathwithdignity.org/take-action/Death with Dignity Act of 2015. B21–0038.

Duffy, O. A. (2015). The Supreme Court of Canada ruling on physician-assisted death: Implications for psychiatry in Canada. *Canadian Journal of Psychiatry, 60*(12), 591–596.

Dunn, L. B., Fisher, S. R., Hantke, M., Appelbaum, P. S., Dohan, D., Young, J. P., & Roberts, L. W. (2013). "Thinking about it for somebody else": Alzheimer's disease research and proxy decision makers' translation of ethical principles into practice. *The American Journal of Geriatric Psychiatry, 21*(4), 337–345.

Dyer, O., White, C., & Garcia Rada, A. (2015). Assisted dying: Law and practice around the world. *BMJ, 351*, h4481.

Eliott, J. A., & Olver, I. (2010). Dying cancer patients talk about physician and patient roles in DNR decision making. *Health Expectations, 14*, 147–158.

Elliott, B. A., Gessert, C. E., Larson, P. M., & Russ, T. E. (2014). Shifting responses in quality of life: People living with dialysis. *Quality of Life Research, 23*(5), 1497–1504.

Emanuel, E. J., & Emanuel, L. L. (1992). Four models of the physician-patient relationship. *JAMA, 267*(16), 2221–2226.

Emanuel, E. J., Onwuteaka-Philipsen, B. D., Urwin, J. W., & Cohen, J. (2016). Attitudes and practices of euthanasia and physician-assisted suicide in the United States, Canada, and Europe. *JAMA, 316*(1), 79–90.

Enzinger, A. C., Zhang, B., Weeks, J. C., & Prigerson, H. G. (2014). Clinical trial participation as part of end-of-life cancer care: Associations with medical care and quality of life near death. *Journal of Pain and Symptom Management, 47*(6), 1078–1090.

European Association for Palliative Care. (2015, April 16). *Ethics.* Retrieved from www.eapcnet.eu/Themes/Ethics.aspx

Fischer, S., Huber, C. A., Furter, M., Imhof, L., Imhof, R. M., Schwarzenegger, C., . . . Bosshard, G. (2009). Reasons why people in Switzerland seek assisted suicide: The view of patients and physicians. *Swiss Medical Weekly, 139*(23–24), 333–338.

Fischer, S., Huber, C. A., Imhof, L., Imhof, R. M., Furter, M., Ziegler, S. J., & Bosshard, G. (2008). Suicide assisted by two Swiss right-to-die organisations. *Journal of Medical Ethics, 34*(11), 810–814.

Fulmer, T. (2016). Effective interdisciplinary teams: Do we really know how to build them? *Generations, 40*(1), 64–70.

Gamondi, C., Larkin, P., & Payne, S. (2013). Core competencies in palliative care: An EAPC white paper on palliative care education: Part 2. *European Journal of Palliative Care, 20*(3), 140–145.

Gawande, A. (2016). Quantity and quality of life duties of care in life-limiting illness. *Journal of the American Medical Association, 315*(3), 267–269.

Gele, A. A., Pettersen, K. S., Torheim, L. E., & Kumar, B. (2016). Health literacy: The missing link in improving the health of Somali immigrant women in Oslo. *BMC Public Health, 16*, 1–9.

Greer, J. A., Jackson, V. A., Meier, D. E., & Temel, J. S. (2013). Early integration of palliative care services with standard oncology care for patients with advanced cancer. *CA: A Cancer Journal for Clinicians, 63*(5), 349–363.

Hajizadeh, N., Uhler, L. M., & Perez Figueroa, R. E. (2014). Understanding patients' and doctors' attitudes about shared decision making for advance care planning. *Health Expectations, 18*(6), 2054–2065.

Hawley, S. T., & Morris, A. M. (2017). Cultural challenges to engaging patients in shared decision making. *Patient Education and Counseling, 100*(1), 18–24.

Hearn, J., & Higginson, I. J. (1998). Do specialist palliative care teams improve outcomes for cancer patients? A systematic literature review. *Palliative Medicine, 12*(5), 317–332.

Hirschman, K. B., Kapo, J. M., & Karlawish, J. H. T. (2006). Why doesn't a family member of a person with advanced dementia use a substituted judgment when making a decision for that person? *The American Journal of Geriatric Psychiatry, 14*(8), 659–667.

Ho, A., Jameson, K., & Pavlish, C. (2016). An exploratory study of interprofessional collaboration in end-of-life decision-making beyond palliative care settings. *Journal of Interprofessional Care, 30*(6), 795–803.

Hoerger, M., Epstein, R. M., Winters, P. C., Fiscella, K., Duberstein, P. R., Gramling, R., . . . Kravitz, R. L. (2013). Values and options in cancer care (VOICE): Study design and rationale for a patient-centered communication and decision-making intervention for physicians, patients with advanced cancer, and their caregivers. *BMC Cancer, 13*, 188.

Hoffman, T. C., Legare, F., Simmons, M. B., McNamara, K., McCaffery, K., Trevena, L. J., . . . Del Mar, C. B. (2014). Shared decision making: What do clinicians need to know and why should they bother? *The Medical Journal of Australia, 201*(1), 35–39.

Hospice and Palliative Medicine Competencies Project Work Group. (2009). *Hospice and palliative medicine core competencies.* Retrieved from http://aahpm.org/uploads/education/competencies/Competencies%20v.%202.3.pdf

Hung, E. K., McNiel, D. E., & Binder, R. L. (2012). Cover medication in psychiatric emergencies: Is it ever ethically permissible? *The Journal of the American Academy of Psychiatry and the Law, 40*(2), 239–245.

Institute of Medicine. (2015). *Dying in America: Improving quality and honoring individual preferences near the end of life.* Washington, DC: National Academies Press.

Interprofessional Education Collaborative. (2016). *Core competencies for interprofessional collaborative practice: 2016 update.* Washington, DC: Interprofessional Education Collaborative.

Katz, M. G., Jacobson, T. A., Veledar, E., & Kripalani, S. (2007). Patient literacy and question-asking behavior during the medical encounter: A mixed-methods analysis. *Journal of General Internal Medicine, 22*(6), 782–786.

Kelley, A. S., & Morrison, R. S. (2015). Palliative care for the seriously ill. *New England Journal of Medicine, 373*(8), 747–755.

Kozlov, E., Carpenter, B. D., & Rodebaugh, T. (2017). Development and validation of the Palliative Care Knowledge Scale (PaCKS). *Palliative & Supportive Care, 15*(5), 524–534.

Kozlov, E., Reid, M. C., & Carpenter, B. D. (2017). Improving patient knowledge of palliative care: A randomized controlled intervention study. *Patient Education and Counseling, 100*(5), 1007–1011.

Kreling, B., Selsky, C., Perret-Gentil, M., Huerta, E. E., & Mandelblatt, J. S. (2010). "The worst thing about hospice is that they talk about death": Contrasting hospice decisions and experience among immigrant Central and South American Latinos with US-born white, non-Latino cancer caregivers. *Palliative Medicine, 24*(4), 427–434.

Legare, F., Stacey, D., Gagnon, S., Dunn, S., Pluye, P., Frosch, D., . . . Graham, I. D. (2011). Validating a conceptual model for an inter-professional approach to shared decision making: A mixed methods study. *Journal of Evaluation in Clinical Practice, 17*(4), 554–564.

Legare, F., & Witteman, H. O. (2013). Shared decision making: Examining key elements and barriers to adoption into routine clinical practice. *Health Affect, 32*(2), 276–284.

Lennon-Dearing, R., Lowry, L., Ross, C., & Dyer, A. (2009). An interprofessional course in bioethics: Training for real-world dilemmas. *Journal of Interprofessional Care, 23*(6), 574–585. doi:10.3109/13561820902921621

Levin, T. T., Li, Y., Weiner, J. S., Lewis, F., Bartell, A., Piercy, J., & Kissane, D. W. (2008). How do-not-resuscitate orders are utilized in cancer patients: Timing relative to death and communication-training implications. *Palliative & Supportive Care, 6*(4), 341–348.

Livaudais, J. C., Franco, R., Fei, K., & Bickell, N. A. (2013). Breast cancer treatment decision-making: Are we asking too much of patients? *Journal of General Internal Medicine, 28*(5), 630–636.

Lopez-Sierra, H. E., & Rodriguez-Sanchez, J. (2015). The supportive roles of religion and spirituality in end-of-life and palliative care of patients with cancer in a culturally diverse context: A literature review. *Current Opinion in Supportive and Palliative Care, 9*(1), 87–95.

Maciejewski, P. K., & Prigerson, H. G. (2015). Emotional numbness modifies the effect of end-of-life discussions on end-of-life care. *Journal of Pain and Symptom Management, 45*(5), 841–847.

Mack, J. W., Weeks, J. C., Wright, A. A., Block, S. D., & Prigerson, H. G. (2010). End-of-life discussions, goal attainment, and distress at the end of life: Predictors and outcomes of receipt of care consistent with preferences. *Journal of Clinical Oncology, 28*(7), 1203–1208.

Mason, B., Buckingham, S., Finucane, A., Hutchison, P., Kendall, M., McCutcheon, H., . . . Murray, S. A. (2015). Improving primary palliative care in Scotland: Lessons from a mixed methods study. *BMC Family Practice, 16*(176), 1–8. doi:10.1186/s12875-015-0391-x

Menzel, P. T., & Steinbock, B. (2013). Advance directives, dementia, and physician-assisted death. *Journal of Law, Medicine & Ethics, 41*(2), 484–500.

Miccinesi, G., Fischer, S., Paci, E., Onwuteaka-Philipsen, B. D., Cartwright, C., van der Heide, A., . . . Mortier, F. (2005). Physicians' attitudes towards end-of-life decisions: A comparison between seven countries. *Social Science & Medicine, 60*, 1961–1974.

Miller, T. A. (2016). Health literacy and adherence to medical treatment in chronic and acute illness: A meta-analysis. *Patient Education and Counseling, 99*(7), 1079–1086.

Moses, J., Berlinger, N., Dunn, M. C., Gusmano, M. K., & Chin, J. J. (2015). Bioethics casebook 2.0: Using web-based design and tools to promote ethical reflection and practice in health care. *Hastings Center Report, 45*(6), 19–25. doi:10.1002/hast.514

Ethical issues 117

Muscat, D. M., Shepherd, H. L., Morony, S., Smith, S. K., Dhillon, H. M., Trevena, L., . . . McCaffery, K. (2016). Can adults with low literacy understand shared decision making questions? A qualitative investigation. *Patient Education and Counseling, 99*(11), 1796–1802.

Narayan, C. (2016, September 17). First child dies by euthanasia in Belgium. *CNN*. Retrieved from www.cnn.com/2016/09/17/health/belgium-minor-euthanasia/

National Consensus Project (NCP) for Quality Palliative Care. (2013). *Clinical practice guidelines for quality palliative care* (3rd ed.). Retrieved February 16, 2017, from www.nationalconsensus project.org/Guidelines_Download2.aspx

Ni, Y. H., & Alraek, T. (2017). What circumstances lead to non-disclosure of cancer-related information in China? A qualitative study. *Supportive Care in Cancer, 25*(3), 811–816.

Nutbeam, D. (1998). Health promotion glossary. *Health Promotion International, 13*(4), 349–364.

Oetzel, J. G., Simpson, M., Berryman, K., & Reddy, R. (2015). Differences in ideal communication behaviours during end-of-life care for Maori carers/patients and palliative care workers. *Palliative Medicine, 29*(8), 764–766.

Paasche-Orlow, M. K., Parker, R. M., Gazmararian, J. A., Nielsen-Bohlman, L. T., & Rudd, R. R. (2005). The prevalence of limited health literacy. *Journal of General Internal Medicine, 20*(2), 175–184.

Paasche-Orlow, M. K., & Wolf, M. S. (2008). Evidence does not support clinical screening of literacy. *Journal of General Internal Medicine, 23*(1), 100–102.

Payne, R. (2016). Racially associated disparities in hospice and palliative care access: Acknowledging the facts while addressing the opportunities to improve. *Journal of Palliative Medicine, 19*(2), 131–133.

Romain, M., & Sprung, C. L. (2014). End-of-life practices in the Intensive Care Unit: The importance of geography, religion, religious affiliation, and culture. *Rambam Maimonides Medical Journal, 5*(1), e0003.

Ruhnke, G. W., Wilson, S. R., Akamatsu, T., Kinoue, T., Takashima, Y., Goldstein, M. K., . . . Raffin, T. A. (2000). Ethical decision making and patient autonomy: A comparison of physicians and patients in Japan and the United States. *Chest, 118*(4), 1172–1182.

Safiya, A. A., Geiser, H. R., Jacob Arriola, K. R., & Kripalani, S. (2009). Health literacy and control in the medical encounter: A mixed-methods analysis. *Journal of the National Medical Association, 101*(7), 677–683.

Schubart, J. R., Green, M. J., Van Scoy, L. J., Lehman, E., Farace, E., Gusani, N. J., & Levi, B. H. (2015). Advanced cancer and end-of-life preferences: Curative intent surgery versus noncurative intent treatment. *Journal of Palliative Medicine, 18*(12), 1015–1018.

Smith, S. K., Dixon, A., Trevena, L., Nutbeam, D., & McCaffery, K. J. (2009). Exploring patient involvement in healthcare decision making across different education and functional health literacy groups. *Social Science & Medicine, 69*, 1805–1812.

Sudore, R. L., Casarett, D., Smith, D., Richardson, D. M., & Ersek, M. (2014). Family involvement at the end-of-life and receipt of quality care. *Journal of Pain and Symptom Management, 48*(6), 1108–1116.

Sudore, R. L., Landefeld, C. S., Perez-Stable, E. J., Bibbins-Domingo, K., Williams, B. A., & Schillinger, D. (2009). Unraveling the relationship between literacy, language proficiency, and patient-physician communication. *Patient Education and Counseling, 75*(3), 398–402.

Sudore, R. L., & Fried, T. R. (2010). Redefining the "planning" in advance care planning: Preparing for end-of-life decision making. *Annals of Internal Medicine, 153*(4), 256–261.

Sudore, R. L., Schillinger, D., Knight, S. J., & Fried, T. R. (2010). Uncertainty about advance care planning treatment preferences among diverse older adults. *Journal of Health Communication, 15*, 159–171.

Teno, J. M., Gozalo, P. L., Bynum, J. P., Leland, N. E., Miller, S. C., Morden, N. E., . . . Mor, V. (2013). Change in end-of-life care for Medicare beneficiaries: Site of death, place of care, and health care transitions in 2000, 2005, and 2009. *JAMA: The Journal of the American Medical Association, 309*(5), 470–477. http://doi.org/10.1001/jama.2012.207624

VanGeest, J. B., Welch, V. L., & Weiner, S. J. (2010). Patients' perceptions of screening for health literacy: Reactions to the Newest Vital Sign. *Journal of Health Communication, 15*(4), 402–412.

van Wijmen, M. P. S., Pasman, H. R. W., Widdershoven, G. A. M., & Onwuteaka-Philipsen, B. D. (2014). Motivations, aims and communication around advance directives: A mixed-methods study into the perspective of their owners and the influence of a current illness. *Patient Education and Counseling, 95*(3), 393–399.

Verhagen, E., & Sauer, P. J. J. (2005). The Groningen Protocol: Euthanasia in severely ill newborns. *New England Journal of Medicine, 352*(10), 959–962.

Volandes, A. E., Barry, M. J., Chang, Y., & Paasche-Orlow, M. K. (2010). Improving medical decision making at the end of life with video images. *Medical Decision Making, 30*(1), 29–34.

Wald, H. S., Dube, C. E., & Anthony, D. C. (2007). Untangling the Web: The impact of internet use on health care and the physician-patient relationship. *Patient Education and Counseling, 68*(3), 218–224.

Washington, K. T., Parker Oliver, D., Gage, L. A., Albright, D. L., & Demiris, G. (2016). A multimethod analysis of shared decision-making in hospice interdisciplinary team meetings including family caregivers. *Palliative Medicine, 30*(3), 270–278. doi:10.1177/0269216315601545

Weiner, J. S., & Cole, S. A. (2004). Three principles to improve clinician communication for advance care planning: Overcoming emotional, cognitive, and skill barriers. *Journal of Palliative Medicine, 7*(6), 817–829.

Weiss, B. D., Mays, M. Z., Martz, W., Castro, K. M., DeWalt, D. A., Pignone, M. P., . . . Hale, F. A. (2005). Quick assessment of health literacy in primary care: The newest vital sign. *Annals of Family Medicine, 3*(6), 514–522.

Wheeler, C., Anstey, S., Lewis, M., Jeynes, K., & Way, H. (2014). The effect of education on community nursing practice in improving the patient: Carer experience at the end of life. *British Journal of Community Nursing, 19*(6), 284–290.

Wilhelm, M., Poirier, T., Otsuka, A., & Wagner, S. (2014). Interprofessional ethics learning between schools of pharmacy and dental medicine. *Journal of Interprofessional Care, 28*(5), 478–480. doi:10.3109/13561820.2014.911722

Wittenberg-Lyles, E., Oliver, D., Demiris, G., & Regehr, K. (2010). Interdisciplinary collaboration in hospice team meetings. *Journal of Interprofessional Care, 24*(3), 264–273. doi:10.3109/13561820903163421

Wright, A. A., Zhang, B., Ray, A., Mack, J. W., Trice, E., Balboni, T., . . . Prigerson, H. G. (2008). Associations between end-of-life discussions, patient mental health, medical care near death, and caregiver bereavement adjustment. *JAMA, 300*(14), 1665–1673.

Zaman, S., Inbadas, H., Whitelaw, A., & Clark, D. (2017). Common or multiple futures for end of life care around the world? Ideas from the "waiting room of history". *Social Science & Medicine, 172*, 72–79.

Ziegler, S. J., & Bosshard, G. (2007). Role of non-governmental organisations in physician assisted suicide. *British Medical Journal, 334*(7588), 295–298.

Chapter 6

Diversity in family bereavement

Lee H. Matthews, Janet R. Matthews, Shiva Akula, Laura Phillips, and Keisha D. Carden

Why might providers such as psychologists, physicians, counselors, and social workers want to know about family bereavement issues? What role does diversity, broadly defined, play in this process for the individual, the family, and the provider? Why should mental health and healthcare workers care about diversity in bereavement and grief experiences? Perhaps a simplistic answer is that as professionals, regardless of our discipline, we are bound by legal and ethical obligations to provide equitable care to our increasingly diverse patients, as well as civil and criminal laws that govern all people. Yet another, perhaps more nuanced, answer is that individuals are influenced by a myriad of factors including cultural, religious, ethnic, and familial traditions, and that these factors play large, if often unnoticed, roles in the human experience of bereavement and loss.

In the past few decades, psychologists have become more involved in end-of-life and bereavement counseling with patients and family members, as well as bereavement therapy (Haley, Larson, Kasl-Godley, Neimeyer, & Kwilosz, 2003). The term *bereavement counseling* is typically used to refer to the process of helping mourners with normal grief reactions work though the task of grieving, which may be accomplished in group or individual settings. In contrast, the term *bereavement therapy* is typically used to describe interventions for people with more serious grief reactions and often aims to help them identify and solve problems in separating from the person who has died. Several factors have contributed to such expanding roles for providers. One of these factors is psychologists' training in both assessment and behavioral-based intervention for a variety of chronic illnesses such as HIV/AIDS (see chapter 7), neurological disorders, cancer (see chapter 4), and dementia (see chapter 9). Psychologists' ability to use psychotherapy with both patients and family members, including techniques such as pain management and relaxation training, provides another set of services that may not be available from other healthcare providers. Another area for psychologists is in research into various aspects and cultural expressions of grief and bereavement practices across diverse populations. Psychologists also have a role in providing education and training to other professionals and the public on topics such as effective coping methods, the difference between normative grief and clinical depression, and advance directives and living wills.

Involvement in local, state, and national advocacy for policy change in the provision of services regarding death and dying is another role in which psychologists have become more involved (Nydegger, 2008).

In this chapter, the descriptions of the bereavement processes across religions, cultures, subcultures, and diverse groups are necessarily brief. Each of the traditions outlined here could easily be an entire chapter. We have organized this chapter according to terms and definitions, issues related to informing patients and families about patients' illness, and providing services to underserved populations. We consider how, as providers, we may learn from our patients about bereavement issues. Vignettes illustrate these topics and are followed by questions for further consideration by the reader. In addition, beliefs that seem to transcend any specific religious or cultural group, but apply across groups, are addressed. Due to space limitations, our discussion is generally limited to groups within the United States. We hope that these descriptions, vignettes, and questions will encourage the reader to review the referenced material, as well as other information on the diverse topic of family bereavement.

A final note is worth mentioning. In order to provide an overview of the diversity of bereavement customs, information in this chapter is labeled by group affiliations (e.g., Buddhists, Irish-Americans). Although this grouping is useful for organizing the chapter, it is both artificial and incomplete and neglects the great diversity within these groups and the intersectionality of individual characteristics (see Chapter 6) that affect bereavement practices. We recognize that outright and encourage readers to bear in mind that much of the nuance inherent in the individual differences of our clients, especially related to grief and bereavement practices, is not practicably captured in a few dozen pages in a text. Thus, we hope that this chapter serves as an introduction to the diversity of customs in which humans engage, and that providers take upon themselves the responsibility to understand the preferences and needs of their individual clients. Above all, approaching diverse others with a sense of humility and respect, whether related to bereavement or other topics, is our primary role as culturally competent providers.

Terms and definitions

There are several terms that are used to signify the process, emotions, and social expressions of family and friends at the death of someone close to them. These terms include *bereavement* (the loss), *grief* (the responses to the loss), and *mourning* (the social expression of grief). Historically, the term bereavement was generally used to describe the objective state of having suffered a loss due to death of someone who is important to you, including the length of time to adjust to and recover from the loss. Bereavement can be arbitrarily divided into the following stages: preparing for the loss, at death, funeral and/or wake, burial, and remembrance. This chapter focuses on various aspects of these stages. There is no "normal" time period for bereavement. While some traditions of the mourning process may suggest timelines for activities, it may take months or even years to come to terms with the loss. As an example, the fifth edition of the *Diagnostic and Statistical Manual of Mental Disorders* (DSM-5) removed the bereavement exclusion for diagnosing depressive disorders, in part to remove the implication that bereavement lasts only a few months (American Psychiatric Association, 2013). For the purpose of this chapter, bereavement is defined as occurring from the time of death, as well as the time after the loss during which grief is experienced and mourning occurs.

Grief refers to the personal experience of loss and is a normal reaction to death. It is the subjective feelings and affect that are precipitated by loss or that occur with anticipatory loss. Experiences of grief may include various behavioral, emotional, physical, psychological, social, and spiritual reactions to the interpretation of the loss. These intense feelings and physical symptoms are how the entire person – mind, body, and spirit – copes with the loss (Doka, 2016).

Behavioral reactions of grief may include problems eating or sleeping. Crying is very common. Withdrawal from activities and social contacts may be present. An increased or excessive use of alcohol or drugs may occur. Thus, questions should be asked about such use so that appropriate intervention is provided. Some individuals try not to talk about the deceased around other people in the belief that it will help them feel more comfortable, while others need to keep retelling the story of the loved one's death.

Emotional responses are varied and may include sadness, relief, feeling numb, or being angry. The anger may be directed at the deceased for "leaving," the healthcare team, the situation, or one's religious faith/deity. In fact, for some bereaved, the effects of grief may result in a perceived "spiritual crisis," wherein an individual may challenge his or her beliefs, question the meaning of life, ask why the death happened, and what meaning was in the death. Feelings of guilt are another common response, usually related to something the person felt that they did not do to help the deceased, or something they did that they regret. Anxiety, frustration, and worry are also normal and common emotions. Emotions may occur in waves, with someone feeling relatively calm at one moment, then suddenly depressed, anxious, or angry the next, especially in the first few days or weeks.

In addition to these behavioral and emotional reactions, bereaved individuals may also experience physical and psychological symptoms. Exhaustion, disrupted sleep, somatic aches/pains (e.g., headaches, chest pain, arm pain), changes in eating patterns (e.g., overeating, lack of appetite), indigestion, and muscle symptoms (e.g., trembling, tightness) are not uncommon. Psychological or cognitive responses may include disturbing dreams or dreams of the deceased. Some people think that they hear or see the deceased person in the house. Cognitive symptoms, such as difficulty in concentration or slowed thinking processes, may also occur. For example, it is not uncommon for bereaved individuals to have memory lapses or an inability to make decisions. The emotional and physical symptoms of grief may make the person feel that they are "going crazy."

Mourning refers to the processes of how an individual, family, community, or culture attempts to handle the loss, resolve the grief, integrate the experience into daily life, and keep living in recovery from the loss (American Psychological Association, 2016). Mourning is, thus, the social expression of grief, including rituals and behavior, expected by those in the community. Examples of mourning may be seen in the manner in which the funeral service is held. It may be reflected in an expected withdrawal from social events or work. Mourning may involve the wearing of certain color clothing or hanging black bunting or some other symbol outside the home to acknowledge the loss. There may be prescribed periods of engagement in religious rituals. Specific mourning traditions may even specify what emotions are appropriate. For example, crying is a common reaction to pain or loss and is often associated with grief. However, if the crying or the manner of crying occurs because of cultural expectations, it may be considered mourning. Thus, the same behavior can be an indication of different aspects of bereavement. Such examples of behaviors and practices that would seem "typical" at a funeral are as diverse as the cultures and religions involved. For example, crying at the time of death, immediately after death and during funerals, is considered disruptive by Tibetan Buddhists while other cultures, including Latino Catholics, consider crying to be a sign of respect.

The goal then for psychologists and other mental health workers is to help those who are bereaved and mourning to resolve their grief in a "healthy" manner. As a provider, to do this work effectively means having flexibility for the concept of "healthy," which fits not only general standards of mental health practice but also the religion, culture, and personal situation of the individual. Thus, there are many ways that individuals may grieve in a healthy way. Some people focus on experiencing the feelings and processing those emotions by themselves or with other people. Other individuals involve themselves in adaptive activities such as returning to work and participating in social interactions. Regardless of the approach taken, "healthy" bereavement is characterized by having the person accept the loss on physical, emotional, mental, and spiritual levels in a time frame that feels acceptable to them and allows them to continue in their life unimpeded by the loss. It involves eventually resuming life interests, activities, goals, and forming new bonds with others. It requires obtaining some resolution to those mental questions of how and why the loss occurred and acceptance of ways to move forward with life. Finally, healthy bereavement may involve regaining or growing a faith in something that may not be understood, based on one's religious or spiritual beliefs (Kleespies, 2004).

Anticipatory grief and illness decisions

Another area in which cultural factors may play a role, especially in first- and second-generation citizens of the United States, is with regard to communication of "bad news." In many areas of the world it is not uncommon to conceal the severity of a diagnosis or the patient's status from the patient or the family. Revealing such information would be considered impolite, disrespectful, or in some way even harmful. Such beliefs may prevent patients from entering hospice care or hinder communication with the family regarding a patient's status in hospice (Giger, Davidhizar, & Fordham, 2006).

For example, in many Asian-American subcultures, it is perceived as unnecessarily cruel to inform a patient directly of a cancer diagnosis. Although perhaps not as widespread, in certain other ethnic groups with European backgrounds such as Bosnian-Americans and Italian-Americans, individuals can perceive direct disclosure of death or illness as, at minimum, disrespectful (Yeo & Hikuyeda, 2000). This viewpoint also applies to some Muslim-Americans, where discussions about end-of-life care should involve both a religious leader and an appointed male family member.

Other cultures, such as Filipino-American and some Native Americans emphasize that words should be carefully chosen because, once spoken, they may become a reality. One example is concern over the process of discussing diagnosis. There is a commonly held Navajo belief that speaking should be done in a positive manner and that negative words and thoughts about health become self-fulfilling. (Devi, 2011). Researchers have noted that about half of their Navajo family members would not discuss advance directives or certain treatments as such communications might be seen as harmful to the patient (Giger et al., 2006; Zager & Yancy, 2011,).

Some Filipino-Americans may not want a family member to know they are dying, either for fear of loss of hope or a religious belief that only God can determine when life ends. Also, older generations of Filipino-Americans tend to believe in divine healing, that they are being tested by God, and that miracles could happen; thus, these individuals often do not consider palliative care as a treatment option. In the Korean-American culture, only about 21% of the elderly discuss issues such as bereavement preferences (Ko, Roe, & Higgins, 2013). If in hospice care, for Asian-American Catholics, as for most Roman Catholics, requesting a priest to give the Sacrament of Anointing of the Sick is often a part of the end-of-life process and the beginning of bereavement. In addition, some families will hold nightly prayers with the patient. Cultural and generational differences within Filipino-American families may create conflict when a young person with a terminal illness considers palliative or hospice care, as older family members may be opposed to such placements (Ciria-Cruz, 2013).

Across cultures and ethnic groups, there are some patients who may prefer not to know the severity of their medical status. They have an autonomous right not to know such information; however, other factors may be involved. One of these factors is biomedical ethics, especially the principle of *autonomy*, which is often relevant to the right of a patient to choose or refuse treatment independently. However, not informing the patient of a change in medical treatment may result in either a unilateral decision by the provider or the lack of opportunity for the patient to make an informed decision about such treatment. In addition, federal law regarding informing patients of their status and other legal considerations may need to be considered. Thus, ongoing decision-making may be more difficult for health and mental health staff when related to end-of-life care (Beauchamp & Childress, 2013). Regardless of their personal views on informing the patient, providers need to consider such preferences when discussing life expectancy and prognosis with both the patient and the family.

Case example

Judge Lee Baker was an 89-year-old retired judge in a nursing home with an advance directive that instructed against artificial nutrition, in addition to a do-not-resuscitate order and several other specific instructions regarding pain medications, antibiotics, and other procedures. He had decided earlier that as he became more ill, he did not want to be informed of the severity of his medical status. Thus, in consultation with one of his sons, Robert, who was also an attorney, Judge Baker and Robert had arranged for a Durable Power of Attorney (POA). Another son, John, who was a politician living in another state, came to the nursing home over a weekend. At John's insistence, and via consultation from a physician brought to the facility by John, a PEG (percutaneous endoscopic gastrostomy) feeding tube was placed. When the situation was revealed to the patient's other son, Robert, another copy of the POA with the advance directive was brought to the nursing home with a request for the nursing home to remove the PEG tube and stop artificial feeding. Shortly thereafter, Judge Baker was transferred to a hospice facility.

Questions

1   In addition to the issue of autonomy, what roles might a psychologist have with regard to the family preferences about issues of prognosis and palliative care and the family dynamics in this case?
2   What ethical dilemmas arise for hospice staff regarding Judge Baker's documented wishes, the POA held by Robert, and potential future visits or actions taken by Judge Baker's son, John?
3   What role might a psychologist have in bereavement counseling following the death of Judge Baker? What issues may come up for Robert? For John?

Bereavement rituals

Rituals are a significant, and often comforting, part of the bereavement process for many individuals. Norton and Francesca (2014) have suggested that rituals done before, at the time of, and following any significant life event can both help with the outcome of the event, as well as help relieve negative feelings. Rituals may be based on structured religious beliefs or tradition, or more informal norms established by friends, family, and culture. In many rituals, the underlying principle is to restore or regain a sense of control, as well as facilitate coping. For example, consider a woman whose husband recently died. Her bereavement practices include spending at least an hour a day in prayer for him. This structured time allows her to feel a sense of control over her frequent thoughts of her husband at other times of day and also provides her with a sense of comfort.

The concept of some type of transition of the spirit at the time of death also gives rise to various rituals. These may include not touching the body for some hours, taking care of the body and burying it relatively quickly, or not having a burial for several days. For some Chinese-Americans, there is a belief that the spirit returns to the home seven days after death. In some Orthodox Christian churches, after death, a candle is lit. This ritual is repeated for 40 days, as some traditions say that the soul roams the earth for 40 days, as Jesus did in the wilderness (Orthodox Christian Resource Center, 2016).

Most religions and cultures have rituals regarding the color of clothing to be worn to funerals. However, the color varies widely. In many protestant religions in the United States of America, the color to wear is black. In many Asian cultures and religions, the color to be worn is white. Romani-Americans wear red and white, as do many people whose families came from African nations. For many Asian Indian-Americans, brown is the color of mourning. Egyptians wear the color yellow for mourning, while Korean-Americans often follow a family ritual of wearing blue, and those from Brazilian ancestry wear purple. In a similar manner, some Thai-Americans follow a tradition of wearing purple when mourning the loss of a spouse (Taylor, 2000).

Other racial or cultural beliefs have an impact on the mourning practices of various minority groups in the United States of America. For example, to native Hawaiians, music, prayer, and chanting will restore the balance of mind, body, and spirit. It is also a way of displaying respect for a dying elder, so extended family and friends will gather in the patient's room to tell stories, pray, and play music. Black clothing is not to be worn, either when visiting the patient or at the funeral; instead, bright-colored clothing is worn. Leis may be worn at a funeral or memorial service, as leis symbolize appreciation, love, and respect (Braun & Nichols, 1997). A relatively new tradition is to plant a Koa tree in remembrance, as the word, Koa, means brave, bold, fearless, or warrior (Kepler, 1998).

Traditions that transcend groups

Some bereavement traditions are not limited to a specific religious, cultural, or ethnic group. An example involves the covering of mirrors. In Victorian

England and the Antebellum South, mirrors were covered so that mourners would not see how they looked and so could mourn peacefully. Another aspect of covering the mirror was because people believed that if the dying person looked in a mirror while taking their last breath, the soul would be trapped in the mirror for all eternity instead of going to heaven. The practice can be traced to African American, Belgian, German, Greek, Irish, English, Scottish, Jewish, and Hindu traditions, but for different reasons. In the Jewish tradition, it was based on not facing a mirror during prayer. In several of the other groups, there were beliefs that either the next person to see the reflection of the deceased would die, or to avoid bad luck (Lobar, Youngblut, & Brooten, 2006). Regardless of the origins, especially in the South, the covering of any mirror in the dying patient's room has become part of many families' heritage. The stopping of a clock at the time of death is another tradition that seems to exist across cultural groups, but often with different beliefs for the practice (Brasch & Brasch, 2014).

The removal of a body with the feet going out the door first is a tradition in several cultures. This practice may involve the body's removal from the house, religious building, or funeral home. Various groups within Christianity, Hinduism, and Native Americans have this practice, but based on different beliefs. In some families from central Europe, the belief is to prevent the spirit from looking back into the house and beckoning another member of the family into death. In families with Scottish traditions, it is so the soul cannot find its way back home. Some Filipino-Americans believe that, if the deceased is taken out of the house head first, the spirit of the person will not leave the home (Superstitious Dictionary, 2014).

Another tradition involves the funeral procession from the church or funeral home to the gravesite. While most states have enacted laws regarding right-of-way for the procession, another historic practice was for all the vehicles to have their headlights on. In the past 20 years, this practice has changed, with federal law requiring "running lights" on all vehicles, which are illuminated when the vehicle is driven during the daytime. Today, the practice (and law) in many locations is for each vehicle to have on the "emergency flashers" (Matthiesen, Wickert, & Lehrer, 2013). However, especially in the southeastern US, two aspects of this tradition are still preserved: every vehicle in the procession would turn on their headlights to "light the way" to heaven, and cars traveling in the opposite direction on two lane roadways pull off on the side of the road to show respect for the deceased.

Underserved populations

Racial, ethnic, and cultural minorities

In the United States, although ethnic minorities compose about one-third of the population, ethnic disparities in access to bereavement services have been identified. Such disparities are also experienced by cultural, racial, religious, socioeconomic, and rural minorities. There are a multitude of reasons for such disparities. These include lack of awareness of services for bereavement, mistrust of institutions or of healthcare systems, lack of cultural fit between Western interventions and non-Western cultural conceptions of healing and illness, a general stigma associated with bereavement services that may be viewed as mental health services, and language barriers (Greer, 2005; McGuire & Miranda, 2008). For example, hospice bereavement coordinators have indicated that language and cultural barriers were challenges when communicating, offering, and delivering bereavement services to Hispanic individuals (Arriaza, Martin, & Csikai, 2011).

Individuals who identify as LGBTQ

For lesbian, gay, bisexual, transgender, and/or queer (LGBTQ) individuals in the United States, in addition to problems related to discrimination and social attitudes during their lives, they and their healthcare advocates, partners, or family often have to deal with legal complications regarding end-of-life decisions, estate planning, funeral arrangements, and burial (DeBernardo, 2015). It is still rare for LGBTQ individuals to have their lives and deaths honored appropriately. Even in recent years and with legalization of same-sex marriages, many same-sex couples find, upon one partner's death, that the other partner has no recognized rights regarding issues such as funeral arrangements. For example, LGBTQ individuals had funerals canceled when someone in the church learned that the deceased was gay or lesbian (Zinn, 2013). Transgender individuals, even with gender changes and legal name changes, have been buried with their birth names and gender. Other areas where a partner may have no rights involve finances (such as spousal benefits under some retirement policies) and retention of the deceased partner's personal possessions (Movement Advancement Project, 2010). Other examples include refusal to give communion to LGBTQ persons at parents' funerals and denial of death or survivor benefits, such as veteran's spousal benefits from the Department of Defense and the Department of Veterans Affairs, depending on the state in which the couple was married (American Civil Liberties Union, 2016). Care providers need to be aware of these potential situations that can intensify the grief process.

Case example

John and David had lived together for years. They owned some separate and some joint assets, had a joint mortgage, and ran a successful business, although they were not married. David's family supported their relationship, but John's family refused to acknowledge the couple. When John died suddenly after only a few days in his local hospice,

David found he had no rights. John's family of origin took his body back to his home state, arranged the funeral, and removed any mention of David from the memorial service or online postings, took his possessions from the home, claimed assets from John's bank account, and asked David to pay for the transport of John's body and the funeral (Zinn, 2013). David called the social worker from the hospice facility, with whom he and John had met jointly for a short time while he was on the unit, and expressed his feelings of grief not only over the loss of his partner, but over what felt like an erasure of the entire history of their relationship by John's family.

Questions

1   What role conflicts might occur among the family, religious leaders, and the social worker?
2   What role might a psychologist or social worker have in discussing with LGBTQ clients these possible legal issues before and after death?
3   As a mental health provider in this scenario, how might you address providing support to David? What concerns would you have, if any, about overstepping boundaries?

Religious beliefs at and after death

There are fundamental differences in religious views related to the philosophical concepts of reincarnation and resurrection. These two concepts are also tied to religious views that include faith in one supreme God, or religious views based on multiple gods or deities. We will briefly explore these concepts as they relate to various diverse beliefs and bereavement rituals (Snyder, 1984).

Many religions, especially those of the Asian or Indian subcontinent, sometimes referred to as "Eastern," such as Hinduism, Buddhism, Jainism and Sikhism, teach *reincarnation*, sometimes referred to as "transmigration of souls" or "rebirth." The concept is that some part of a living being starts a new life, either in the physical body of another person or an animal, after each biological death. While these religions teach some form of immortality and a future life, this does not involve the belief that the same person will ever be seen again (Snyder, 1984). In contrast, resurrection involves a bodily rebirth of each individual person. This concept is common to the three largest world religions: Christianity, Judaism, and Islam. Each of these three religions includes faith in one supreme

God who created the universe. Orthodox Judaism retains a belief in bodily resurrection, whereas Reform Judaism has focused more on the concept of the immortality of the soul (Jacobs, 2002). The Christian idea of resurrection is a transformation of a body into an immortal form of existence. The body that dies is the same one that is risen. In Islamic teachings, people will be resurrected into their original physical bodies from their graves by Allah. He will then judge them by their deeds on earth. Those people who have done good deeds and been obedient to Allah will be awarded happiness in Paradise. Those people who had been rebellious to Allah and had spent their lives in evil deeds will be punished in Hell (Smith & Haddad, 2002).

Religious beliefs at and after death

Buddhism

Buddhism has diverse schools and belief systems. However, most Buddhists believe in reincarnation and see death as a transition to the next incarnation, bringing the soul closer to *nirvana*, a state of absolute bliss. For Buddhists, the color of clothing worn around critically ill patients is important. Red is the color of luck, but white is associated with mourning and bad luck. Buddhism, with its emphasis on having a clear mind to obtain spiritual meaning, may have an impact on preferences for pain management and palliative sedation. Medical staff may need to be aware of not only the physical management, but also the patient's focus on full mental awareness, so that controlling anxiety, pain, and restlessness ensures a calm state at the time of death. Such calmness may involve practices such as chanting or meditation, rather than medication. For those of the Buddhist faith, a person's life is predetermined, so taking extraordinary measures to prolonging life is not consistent with their belief system. Near death, the family may want a monk to pray at the bedside to assist the person for a peaceful journey to the next life (Braun, Beyth, Ford, & McCullough, 2008). In Buddhist traditions, the spirit is still present for several hours after the last breath (regardless of vital signs), so not touching the body may be part of the family's belief in the transition of the soul to a new life. This belief may present issues to medical staff regarding removal of the body, if they are not aware of this perspective on death (Lobar et al., 2006).

Because of reincarnation beliefs, Buddhist funerals are to be celebrations, marking the soul's ascent from the body. During the funeral, it is traditional for attendees to bow before the casket, then sit on the floor quietly during meditation, but otherwise not participate in other rituals, which are reserved for family members. There may be chants or comments by family members, often focused on the transitional nature of life. During the viewing of the body, guests offer condolences to the family, bowing in front of the casket to honor the fleeting nature of life. The person may be buried or cremated. Following burial, family and friends may visit the burial site or give offerings to the local temple (Harvey, 1990).

Hinduism

In Hinduism, death is not the final end but another path in a long journey of the soul, through many animals and people. Generally, Hindus believe that life and death are part of the concept of *samsara* or rebirth. However, this is not the final state, but a step to reach a transcendent state of salvation or *moksha*. Even within a specific religion, many different traditions and practices may be grouped together. For example, in Hindu tradition, cremation is part of the end of life and traditionally occurs within 24 hours of death so that the soul can be released to find a new body. However, cremation is surrounded by elaborate rituals that start usually within an hour of a person's death. These include the family washing the body, placing flowers around the person's neck, and often holding a brief wake. Open expression of grief is allowed. The day after the cremation, the eldest male relative will collect the ashes. Historically, the ashes were placed in the Ganges River. Today, other rivers may be used, but there are also agencies that will arrange shipment to India. The period of mourning generally lasts from 10 to 40 days, although the average is around 13 days. One year after death, a memorial and meal is hosted by the eldest male in the family (Bhaskarananda, 2002).

Christianity

Christians believe that Jesus was the Son of God, whose coming as the Messiah was foretold in the Old Testament of the Bible (Woodhead, 2014). However, within Christianity, there are many differences in worship traditions, interpretations of the meaning of scripture, organization of structure, and leadership of churches. The largest groups of Christians in the United States are members of the Church of Jesus Christ of Latter-day Saints, Orthodox Catholic, Protestant, and Roman Catholic churches (Olson, 2016).

The Church of Jesus Christ of Latter-day Saints

The Church of Jesus Christ of Latter-day Saints (Mormonism) is the fourth largest Christian denomination in the United States (Linder, 2012). Mormons teach that scriptural statements on the unity of the Father, the Son, and the Holy Ghost represent oneness of purpose, not of substance. They believe that life does not begin with birth nor end with death. At the time of death, there is the separation of the physical body from the spirit body. At death, the soul goes to the spirit world to receive instruction and to be cleansed, because when the person dies, they are not ready to enter heaven immediately. The physical and spiritual bodies are later reunited in resurrection (Packer, 2008).

Case example

Jayden Christensen, a few weeks before his death in hospice, met with a funeral director to plan the details of his funeral. Jayden preferred burial to cremation because internment in the earth symbolizes the return of dust to dust. As a Mormon, he believed in a *pre-mortal life*, that at the time of death, he would reside in that world as a spirit, at least for a time. Eventually, the body and spirit would be reunited, never to be separated again. The second day after his death, he was dressed in his temple clothing, a white long-sleeved shirt, white pants, a white tie, and white socks and shoes. He had received them as a young man as he went out as a missionary. He was dressed by two men from his local *Ward* (congregation). There was a gathering of family, friends, and church members at the funeral home. The next day, the funeral was held at the family's Ward, led by a Bishop. A hymn and prayer were said to thank the Heavenly Father for his life and for comfort to the family. Several family and friends talked of his virtues and contributions to the community. Then there was a final prayer and hymn. Mourners were ushered past the open coffin. Then there was a procession to the cemetery that involved a prayer, reading from Psalms and a song at the gravesite. A luncheon, called a *mercy meal*, and traditionally consisting of ham or turkey, *funeral potatoes* (a potato casserole), Jell-O salad, rolls, and cake for dessert, was served in the Ward and additional stories were shared about Jayden's life (Millet, 1999).

Questions

1   How might you as a clinician discuss with a Mormon family their idea of Heaven having many dwellings and different levels of blessings to facilitate the grieving process?
2   How does Mormon teaching regarding the idea of the spirit body going to a spirit world before going to Heaven influence what you might say at a funeral to support the family?

Orthodox Catholic church

Orthodox Catholic (Eastern Orthodox Catholic) churches form a group of 14 independent but connected groups, often regional or national in nature, such as the Russian, Greek, and Cyprus Orthodox churches. Like some older Roman

Catholic traditions, Orthodox Christians believe in a purgatory type period – in this case, that the soul at death is temporarily separated from the body and lingers on Earth for 40 days. Then the soul is directed to heaven or hell. This latter belief is in contrast to the Roman Catholic view, according to which, if the soul goes to purgatory, at some point, it will go to heaven. Traditionally, the funeral is either the day after death or on the third day after death. Special prayers are said on the third, seventh, and ninth day after death (depending on the regional church) but almost all have a special observance 40 days after death at the gravesite. Often there are additional prayer days at 3, 6, 9, or 12 months afterwards (Greek Orthodox Archdiocese of America, 2016).

Protestantism

Church groups that are identified as Protestant may include African Methodist, Anglican, Assembly of God, Baptist, Church of Christ, Church of God, Episcopalian, Lutheran, Methodist, Methodist Episcopal, United Methodist, Presbyterian, various Pentecostal organizations, and the United Church of Christ. Commonly held views by most Protestant religions include that Jesus of Nazareth was the Son of God; the doctrine of justification by faith alone (which may include demonstration of such faith by good or holy works in most protestant traditions); that the Bible is the ultimate authority in matters of both morals and faith, although groups vary widely in how closely they follow Scripture; and that there is a priesthood of all believers. In most Protestant denominations, the belief that forgiveness cannot be earned, but is granted by God, puts the focus on salvation through the saving grace of Jesus. This belief means that, during a funeral, there may be little mention of the deceased's activities in the church (HealthCare Chaplaincy, 2009). Most Protestant funerals take place within a week after death. There is a time for visitation, the funeral service, and a service at the gravesite. Funeral services may be held in church or in the funeral home. Funeral practices may vary by denomination and from person to person, but often include readings from the Bible by family members or the clergy. Hymns are frequently sung. A eulogy or recollections about the life of the deceased by family members and friends is often a component of the service. Some families have a final viewing before the start of the funeral service, others prior to the start of the service. The form of internment or choice of cremation also varies. A procession to the burial site is common, as well as an organized prayer or prayers at the grave. A gathering or a meal after the funeral may occur. In general, Protestant Christianity does not have a prescribed amount of time for formal mourning.

Roman Catholic

Roman Catholics believe in the immortality of the soul, and that upon death, the person will be judged and go to Heaven, Hell, or Purgatory, but that in

Purgatory, after a period of purification from sins, God will give the person a place in Heaven. In contrast to some Protestant beliefs that declared faith alone (*sola fide*) will admit a person to Heaven, Roman Catholics believe that a person must be baptized and remain in a state of grace (without mortal sin) to go to Heaven. Thus, most Catholics believe that salvation is based on an individual's faith and works while on earth and the state of their soul at the time of death (Morris, 2003). Following death, the funeral rites include a wake and a funeral liturgy at a Mass celebrating the life of the deceased, followed by a graveside burial. A reception, usually involving a meal, is held in the home of the deceased or the home of a relative, and there may be several pictures of the deceased in different rooms so the mourners can share stories and memories, to share grief and help bereavement (Lobar et al., 2006).

Seventh Day Adventists

Seventh Day Adventists view death as an unconscious state (a "sleep" or "soul sleep"). They believe that when Christ appears, those who believe will be awakened and go to heaven with God. Near the end of life, either a minister or elder will come to the patient and family. Flowers may be sent to the family, except for arrival on Saturday, as that is the Adventists' Sabbath. The funeral usually resembles many other Protestant services, with music, prayer, sermon, scripture readings, and benediction. Dark clothing is to be worn, with no jewelry. Because the Seventh Day Adventists do not believe that the deceased will immediately go to heaven, comments such as "he is in heaven" should not be used. At the gravesite, traditionally flower petals are placed on the casket (Clark, 2015).

Islam

In Islamic tradition, there is often a strong preference that care should be given by same-sex staff. When death is imminent, by tradition, the person should be placed on their right side, facing the city of Mecca; if not possible, then the person should be on their back with the face and soles of the feet facing Mecca (i.e., to the Southeast in the United States). Grief at the death of a beloved person is normal, and weeping for the dead (by males or females) is acceptable, but without loud bewailing or actions. Burial customs may vary, but the preference is for internment as soon as possible after death. A traditional prayer, usually said at daily worship, is used with additional prayers during the funeral. Muslims believe in the existence of the soul after death and the resurrection of the body. In traditional Islamic faith, the body should touch the soil when buried. Therefore, some cemeteries remove part of the bottom of the casket at the time of burial, but not for the funeral service to comply with the law (Athar, 2000). The period for mourning for a close relative is three days. For a woman whose husband has died, the prescribed period is four months and 10 days.

Judaism

In Judaism, death is viewed as a natural part of life. There are many branches of Judaism, from Orthodox Judaism with its emphasis on the belief that the *Torah* contains the actual words of God, to Reform Judaism with its emphasis on adaptation of Jewish law to reflect reason and a focus on moral laws adapted to modern society. Thus, these branches may have different interpretations of how bereavement and grieving may be expressed. Across these branches, however, traditions associated with bereavement serve two functions: to honor the dead and to provide comfort to the living. After death, the body is covered with a linen shroud. The body is never displayed. Mourners traditionally make a tear in outer clothing either before or immediately after a funeral: on the left side (over the heart) for parents, and on the right side for children, spouses and siblings. Non-orthodox Jews may make a tear in a small black ribbon pinned to the lapel, rather than tearing clothing. The funeral is within three days of death. Sections of the *Torah* are read, such as Psalms, which reflect the deceased's life. One of the most common is Psalm 23: The Lord Is My Shepherd. The Memorial Prayer is also said. In Orthodox Judaism caskets are not required. If a casket must be used, according to Jewish Law, the casket must be made of wood and completely free of any metal. Depending on state burial ordinances, holes will be drilled in the bottom, or a liner placed in the casket, with soil on top of the liner and under the body so the deceased may touch the earth (Lamm, 2000).

After the burial, a simple meal is prepared and given only to the family. The meal includes hard-boiled eggs (as a symbol of life) and bread (symbolizing simple foods). Part of the mourning tradition is *sitting shiva* (for seven days) in the home, with family and other mourners receiving visitors, who bring food. Conversations are about the deceased and the giving of traditional blessings or wishes. For 30 days, mourners are prohibited from attending a festive religious meal or marrying. A common practice is for a group to study the *Mishnah* (a written part of the Jewish oral tradition) in memory of the deceased. If the deceased was a parent, formal mourning lasts 12 months. The *Kaddish*, a prayer in Aramaic praising God, is traditionally said daily for that time by a son of the deceased. Yearly, family members observe the anniversary of the death, and mourners light a candle, which burns for 24 hours. A tombstone is placed after the burial, most often on the one-year anniversary, with a reading of Psalms and a saying of the Kaddish. Some communities place small stones on the gravesite or on top of the tombstone once it is erected. Explanations for the practice vary, but one possible origin is a belief that leaving a permanent reminder to the deceased shows that you came to pay your respects (Lamm, 2000).

Sikhism

Sikhism is an Asian-Indian religion and focuses on a path of discipline of meditating on God's name, earning a living by honest means, sharing good fortunes with the needy, and selfless service to humanity. There is only one God for

Sikhs, and he has no form but many names. Sikhs believe that the development of moral character is obtained through humility, generosity, and self-reliance. Sikhism teaches that all people, regardless of race, religion, or sex are equal in the eye of God. As such, it teaches that women have full equality with men; thus, they may participate in any Sikh ceremony. Like Hindus, Sikhs believe in reincarnation and karma. Human life is the gift of the Divine, and death is a return to the Divine source. The soul is a part of God, and it yearns for reunion with the Supreme Being. Since death is an act of God, no crying is permitted immediately before or at the time of death (Labun & Emblen, 2007).

Case example

Arman Singh, who was Sikh, was in hospice. His first name means "Desire or Wish" (an attribute of God). His last name Singh means "a Lion" and is a title, to eliminate discrimination based on the "family name" (which denotes a specific caste) and also reinforces that all humans are equal under God. Prior to entering hospice, he had requested that, as much as possible, he be attended by male staff, a common request for Sikhs. On entering hospice, he had four of the five "K's," religious symbols or articles of faith worn at all times. Arman would not allow his hair (Kesh) to be cut; as such, he always wore a Dastar (Turban); he carried a wooden comb (Kangha), wore a steel bracelet (Kara) and white cotton shorts worn as underwear (Kachha), while entrusting his ceremonial sword (Kirpan) to a male relative. Near his end of life, he was unable to wear his turban, so a surgical cap was worn. The turban was given to a family member, after he instructed hospice staff that it should never be placed with his shoes. He often requested a recording of sacred music at his bedside. Prior to his admission, Arman had requested to have a Sikh Granthi recite Gurbani (writing of the Gurus) and prayers. During his stay in hospice, Arman made funeral and cremation arrangements, in consultation with his family. At the time of his death, family members consoled themselves with the recitation of sacred hymns. Almost immediately after his death, the body was washed by the family and dressed in clean clothing, prior to being moved to the funeral home for cremation.

Questions

1   How might a psychologist working with Arman need to consider his specific end-of-life needs?

2 How might health professionals alter their routine to honor his request for all male staff?
3 If no male staff member is available for a specific role, how should this situation be discussed with him and what are some possible alternatives to be considered?

Racial and cultural beliefs

African Americans

In African American families, bereavement issues intersect with economic status, faith beliefs, family dynamics, and family traditions. More than half of all African American families across the United States are members of historically Black churches. In the South, 68% of African Americans belong to historically Black church denominations (Waters, 2001). These include the African Methodist Episcopal Church, the African Methodist Episcopal Zion Church, the Christian Methodist Episcopal Church, the Church of God in Christ, National Baptist Convention of America, the National Baptist Convention, USA, and the Progressive National Baptist Association (Linder, 2012). Such churches tend to interpret Bible scripture as the literal word of God. Not only family members, but also close friends and church members, are expected to attend to the person near death and afterwards at the funeral service, or in some traditions a wake. The concept of a wake, which historically might go on for several days, was designed to meet several needs; foremost, the wake provided an opportunity to get all extended family to the funeral, as well as being a demonstration of the financial success of the deceased. There may be discussions with the person near the end of life by family members to discuss the "Homegoing" service or celebration. This term represents the religious idea that the deceased is "going home" to heaven and to glory, to be with the Lord (Smith, 2010).

Clothing for men during the service has been, traditionally, a dark suit and black tie, with a black band in the hat or worn on the sleeve. Women traditionally wear black dresses or a suit with pants or skirt. It is traditional to have a procession to the gravesite and, afterwards, away from the site (Waters, 2001). Perhaps the ultimate expression of these traditions are the jazz funerals of New Orleans, generally linked to West African traditions of celebrating the passage of an acclaimed elder, or as part of rituals as transformative journeys. Such funeral processions involve jazz bands playing dirges as they follow the body to the cemetery and then breaking into upbeat parade music after burial, as they return home to celebrate the deceased person's Homegoing. A frequent activity following the funeral is the post-burial home visitation, also known as the bereavement meal or the repast (Gaudet, 2000).

Asian-Americans

Asian-Americans come from diverse cultural and religious backgrounds in Asia and the Indian subcontinent. Asian-Americans are classified according to the U.S. Census (Hoeffel, Rastogi, Kim, & Shahid, 2012) as including Chinese, Filipino, Asian Indian, Vietnamese, Japanese, Korean and Other Asians. The largest Asian-American groups are Chinese-Americans, Filipino-Americans, and Asian-Indians, followed by Vietnamese-Americans, Korean-Americans and Japanese-Americans (Humes, Jones, & Ramirez, 2011). As expected from such a diverse group, Asian-Americans follow a variety of religions, with Buddhism, Hinduism, Confucianism, Taoism, and Christianity being the most often practiced. Given their many traditions, funeral, burial, and bereavement practice may vary widely. For example, to show respect for an elder, open casket viewings are used in some religions with a burial, as in Confucianism. In other religions, such as Buddhism (discussed earlier), cremation is the usual practice. However, perhaps guided by the common value across Asian-American cultures of loyalty to and respect for elders, many religions appear to have some bereavement practices in common. The family usually makes funeral arrangements together. Decisions such as the funeral route, place of internment, and grave marker are led by the family elders. Many Asian-American groups will burn incense at the funeral or burial ceremony. Most groups have a tradition of feeding the guests who attended the funeral and of keeping a picture and other mementos in the home as a type of shrine (Disaster and Community Crisis Center at the University of Missouri, 2014).

German-Americans

Burial and bereavement customs of German-Americans are shaped by the region of Germany from which the family originated. One burial custom is related to grave markers and memorials. Frequent images include females in mourning, angels, or drapery. Earlier markers included symbols or *hex signs*, such as stars, rosettes, and other shapes, to ward off evil spirits. Such hex signs can even be seen today outside of cemeteries, painted on the side of barns (Bushkofsky & Satterlee, 2008). Following death, especially in states with a high percentage of members German-Americans who belong to the Evangelical Lutheran Church in America, such as North Dakota, South Dakota, Minnesota, Wisconsin, and Nebraska, the protocol for the burial is in the *Lutheran Book of Worship* (Augsburg Fortress, 1978). Such a service would likely include a procession of the coffin into the church, the liturgy, scriptural readings from the Old and New Testaments, the Apostle's Creed, the Lord's Prayer, and a sermon.

Hmong

The Hmong, an ethnic group that perhaps had its roots in China, spread to Thailand, Vietnam, and Laos. This culture later split into several groups; among the two largest are the Hmong and Mong. Following the Vietnam War, immigration of Hmong into the United States started. The culture has animistic beliefs, which share basic ideas with the concept of reincarnation and differ in the belief that the soul can take on multiple forms, including human, plant, ghost, or that of inanimate objects, such as boulders. Hmong also believe that the soul can exist outside the body, so sickness is a sign that the person has "lost" their soul and rituals must be practiced to recover it (Gerdner, Cha, Yang, & Tripp-Reimer, 2007). Such rituals may require a sacrifice, such as a chicken, to replace the "lost soul." At the time of death, a small towel is used to wipe the individual's face in an up and down motion three times.

The Hmong traditionally set the burial day based on the lunar calendar. However, the current practice is that most funerals are abbreviated to three days, with the initial day beginning on Friday and lasting until Monday, as the burial day. The family typically purchases a whole slaughtered cow and there is cooking all day and night, the making of rice, with music played on wind instruments and drums (Thao, 2006). There may be over 20 "funeral directors," the people responsible for preparing the food, providing counseling to the family, chanting songs, playing music, and collecting monetary gifts from those visiting the family. On the night before the burial date, four funeral directors and the descendant counselor prepare a table to initiate the blessing process. With music playing and drum beating, the directors set up a table in front of the casket to partake in the singing of blessings. During the funeral procession, the path to the burial site is marked by turns and stops, to try to confuse evil spirits so they don't follow the deceased. Before the burial, everyone sings a final ceremonial song to let the deceased's soul know it's time to begin their journey to the afterlife. After the burial, there is a burning of incense and symbolic paper money and stones are put around the grave. There is then a mourning period for 13 days. During this time, family members pay their respects to their deceased loved one. On the last day, they perform one last ritual for the deceased before the deceased begins the journey to the afterlife (Her, 2005).

Irish-American

In Irish-American families, both Catholics and Protestants, the traditional sequence after death is a *wake*, funeral, and burial. The wake historically was named as the time between death and the burial. Traditionally, the wake is held in the home of the deceased after death but before burial, with the deceased lying in the house or a room in or near the church. The funeral often includes an open casket. This is also the custom in Appalachia, mostly of families of Scotch-Irish ancestry. Usually, curtains in the windows are closed. Mirrors are covered and clocks are covered or turned to face the walls. The wake lasts two or three days, with family or friends watching over the body, as someone needs to be awake and to have light in the room where the deceased is lying. Today, the wake may last only one day and be at another location. It has become a

Diversity in family bereavement 139

celebration of the deceased, rather than watching over the person. Given the celebratory nature, music, food (including Irish wake cakes) and drink (Irish whiskey and beer) are common parts of a wake (Rogak, 2013). Those gathered will tell stories and relate memories about the deceased, both happy and sad, and may include professional mourners, hired to cry, wail, and recite poetry. Currently, the funeral is held in either a church or funeral home. For Catholics, the funeral is most often held in church and includes a funeral Mass. On the one-month anniversary of the wake, a "month's mind" is held in church to celebrate the life, and at the end of the year, a Mass is held.

Italian-American

For Italian-American families, the bereavement sequence involves the "laying out" of the deceased body for a viewing in the funeral home, then moving to the church with last rites, vigils, funeral liturgies, and a Mass. The funeral may include an open casket, so that viewers may kiss the cheek or forehead of the departed. Then the mourners move on to the burial, often using pallbearers from the family or close friends. After the service at the gravesite, a reception either at the family home or on church property is commonly held (United States Conference of Catholic Bishops, 2016).

Historically, there was a belief that a person's soul might not leave the world, and thus certain rituals were performed to aid in transition to eternal life. Both traditionally and today, part of these rituals center on the type and placement of floral arrangements, which have symbolic meaning. Typical themes included a half-moon with a star (for the soul to go between them to heaven), a stopped clock (set to the time of death), and gates of heaven (to guide the soul to heaven). Another older tradition was not to talk of the deceased after the reception until after a mourning period had passed (Mathias, 2016).

Latino-American

"Latino" is a term that refers not to a population from a specific country, but rather to a variety of cultures and a diversity of religious practices. For example, there are at least 21 countries, including Spain, Mexico, Argentina, Chile, Peru, Cuba, Dominican Republic, and Equatorial Guinea, where Spanish is the only or one of the official languages of the country. Statistically, Roman Catholicism is the predominant religion of Latinos, but *Cristiana* (Protestant Evangelical practices) are also present in the culture. Estimates of hospice utilization in the Latino population in the United States are less than 10 percent, according to the National Hospice and Palliative Care Organization (Saccomano & Abbatiello, 2014). In some families, this is due to a belief that the spirit may be lost if the person dies in a hospital or hospice rather than at home.

Rituals and prayer are a common part of the end-of-life process but may vary based on the family's country of origin and religious identification. Special rosaries or amulets may be used by family members. Some individuals want candles burning 24 hours a day (electric candles can be used), and other families may want to display pictures of specific saints. For example, St. Joseph is associated with aiding the dying, Our Lady of Lourdes with healing of bodily illness, and St. Peregrine as the patron saint of cancer patients. Some families may want to honor the deceased by washing the body immediately after death. Because grieving is considered by many Latinos to be part of life, consultation with social workers or psychologists may not feel comfortable, as these disciplines often have associations with mental illness. Displays of strong emotions are often not part of the anticipatory stages of bereavement, but such displays and crying at the time of death by family members are considered a sign of respect. A *novena*, or period of praying the rosary, is usually held the night before the funeral and burial. The older tradition was to carry out the novena for nine days, but frequently in current culture it is fewer days. The Last Rites involve administering the Eucharist (Holy Communion) to a dying person.

Native Americans

Native Americans (in Canada the term used to describe these groups of people is *First Nations*) belong to many diverse tribes (*nations*), each with unique traditions, customs, and beliefs about life and death. A view that is common to most Native Americans is a belief in "The Great Spirit" as the deity that shaped the universe and all that is in it. Along with this belief is a respect for "Mother Earth," that all things in nature are interconnected, and that, with death, one's biological material is recycled and becomes a part of the oneness of all of nature. Within nations, individuals and families may interpret these beliefs differently. In typical hospice settings, patients are often encouraged to talk directly about death and dying. However, such discussions may be uncomfortable for many Native Americans. As an adjustment, some hospices develop indirect statements that address issues such as advance directives.

Although diverse, there are commonalities in Native American death rituals. Modern day Native Americans may incorporate ancient death rituals, handed down from their ancestors, in a modern funeral service. Death in most tribes is believed to be a journey to the spirit world, a parallel plane of existence. Another common belief among most Native American tribes is the focus on helping the deceased be comfortable or being protected in the afterlife. Death rituals include placing food, weapons, jewelry, tools, or pots in the casket or within the burial site for the use of the deceased during the journey and in the spirit world (Pass, 2009). The Ojibwa (Ojibway, Ojibwe) or Chippewa (Chippeway) nation have a ritual on the death of a child that involves cutting the child's hair and making a small doll. The mother of the deceased carries this "doll of sorrow" for a year as part of the bereavement process (Cacciatore, 2009). Navajo rituals reflect other beliefs. Family members do not express grief openly or touch the body. There is a cleansing ritual but no burial for four days. In many

Diversity in family bereavement 141

tribes, there is a belief that the spirit of the person never dies. For this reason, many Navajo never completely close the coffin to allow the spirit to be released. In addition, no footprints may be in or around the grave. This must be done so the spirit guide will not take the wrong spirit (Brokenleg & Middleton, 1993).

For the Lakota (Sioux) nation, as for other tribes, life is a great gift, but death is a natural happening, regardless of the person's accomplishments. Following burial, there is a four-day journey to the spirit world, so food is often placed in the casket. Funeral practices incorporate Lakota spirituality with Christian traditions, so families invite a medicine man or spiritual leader, as well as clergy, to lead the service. During the funeral, often hanging behind the deceased's open casket, a star quilt is displayed. The funeral is the time for family and friends to share memories of the deceased, based on several Lakota values. One of these is the value of kinship (both to the family and to the rest of the community), and children from a young age attend many funerals of family, friends, and neighbors. Other Lakota values are those of bravery, generosity, and wisdom. On the memorial anniversary of the burial, it is customary to give away possessions of the deceased (Pass, 2009).

Case example

Nathan Iron Cloud was part of the Lakota (Sioux) nation and was 65 years old when he died in hospice after a short illness. He grew up on tribal land. However, he spent much of his life in the city. He completed technical school and became a small aircraft mechanic. He enjoyed collecting model aircraft, especially famous fighter planes. Near death, he said he wanted traditional tribal burial rituals, because of his beliefs in the oneness of all of nature, the sky, trees, animals, and humans.

Nathan's wake lasted 24 hours with family and friends playing a drum and chanting. The wake was held in the tribal community center. During the funeral, family and friends shared memories of Nathan, based on Lakota values. They spoke of ways in which Nathan had a positive impact on each of them and the world. As Nathan's casket was closed and family carried it to the gravesite, the mourners started to sing and wail. His children led the other people present in filling the grave. The family then fed the over 100 people present, while the community told stories of Nathan Iron Cloud's life. As part of the bereavement process, an anniversary event was held one year later. Family and friends again gathered at the community center. The family showed slides of Nathan's life, and his eldest son spoke about how the community had helped the

142   Lee H. Matthews et al.

family in the past year. The family then individually handed out dozens of the model warplanes from Nathan's collection.

Questions

1   How does the Native American concept of "oneness with all of nature" compare to other belief systems regarding interactions with animals? How would you use this concept in bereavement counseling?
2   How does the concept of a parallel spiritual world compare to either resurrection or reincarnation beliefs?
3   How might the Lakota concept of a four-day spiritual journey be compared to the Catholic concept of Purgatory?

Romani-Americans

The Romani (or Roma) are a traditionally nomadic ethnic group. Having migrated all over the world, they are often referred to pejoratively as *gypsies*. Many Romani in the United States of America are Roman Catholic but also hold other, more mystical views. Because many Romani believe that good and evil spirits are always around, charms and spoken spells may be used to protect an ill person. Tears and crying and chanting will intensify as the person nears death, so hospice staff may need a plan for this increased sound level in order to respect the wishes of the Romani and of other patients and families on the unit.

The dying person of Romani background must leave this life in a happy state, to avoid returning as an evil spirit to haunt the living. Thus, at the time of death, mourners may ask for forgiveness for any bad behavior, in the belief that if past misdeeds are not resolved the deceased will become an evil spirit. Candles (or electric candles) are lit to guide the deceased person to the afterlife. Death is considered "impure," so family members do not touch the deceased, but employ an outsider. Objects or food may be buried with the person (to help in the journey to the afterlife) and other possessions broken or sold to non-Romani individuals. At some funerals, mourners may toss coins into the burial plot as the coffin is lowered in the belief that the coins are for payment into Heaven. Each relative announces the end of their period of mourning by a special meal throughout the year after death. Some Romani hold to an older tradition not to mention the name of the deceased, for fear that they might return to haunt the living. Thus, an infant is not named after the deceased relative. Instead, the family may spell the name differently or use a nickname (Steller, White, Barron, Gerzevitz, & Morse, 2010).

Conclusions and implications for providers

The process of bereavement (the loss), grief (the normal responses to the loss), and mourning (the social expression of grief), must be confronted by all of us. Regardless of our racial, ethnic, and faith communities, all cultures and subcultures have rituals, parts of funerals, burials, and remembrance processes to help us work through the loss with support and love of our relatives, friends, and wider community. Helping a client with bereavement involves helping the person in examining relational, circumstantial, historical, personality, and social factors facilitating or inhibiting the grief process.

Bereavement is influenced by a number of factors. Most providers think to ask about age of the deceased, religious beliefs, and cultural background. These can provide some information about how to intervene sensitively, for example, not making a comment at a Mormon funeral that the deceased is in heaven as it is inconsistent with the Mormon belief that the soul spends some time in preparation for entering heaven in a spirit world. Other factors influencing bereavement include the premorbid functioning of the bereaved in areas such as physical health, emotional or mental health, personality style, and cognitive functioning. The quality of the relationship with the deceased is another important factor. Were there conflicts in the relationship? Was the deceased estranged from the bereaved and what were the circumstances leading to that separation? Stressors on the bereaved related to illness and death should be investigated. These stressors might involve the deceased's length of illness, the amount and type of care given by the bereaved, and whether or not the death was slow and anticipated or rapid and unexpected. Other stressors may be present based on the many roles or activities of the deceased and bereaved in multiple areas, such as financial, home care, or planning for travel. For example, if the deceased handled financial matters, the bereaved may be reminded of loss repeatedly as they take on this new role, or may struggle to adjust to the new responsibility.

Psychologist William Worden, in his four-task grief model, conceptualized overarching goals that providers aim to help our clients to obtain. One task for the bereaved is to learn to accept the reality of the loss. Another goal is to develop the ability to adapt and work through grief and its impact on physical, emotional, mental, and spiritual functioning by expressing and accepting each of those aspects of grief as normal. Learning to adjust to an environment where the deceased is no longer present is another goal and often involves having to deal with new tasks, take on new responsibilities, and develop new skills. A fourth and final goal is to have some connection with the deceased as the bereaved moves forward with a new life (Worden, 2008).

In addition to the goals outlined by Worden, some clients, based on religious or spiritual affiliation, may take on the task of regaining or growing in their faith following loss. This may involve helping clients challenge distortions and maladaptive beliefs of events related to the death, which may have a negative impact on their healing process. Areas that might be addressed range from specific questions, such as why the loss occurred, to existential questions, for example, what is the meaning of life and death.

Clients also need to "relocate" the deceased emotionally and mentally in memory and move forward with life. For a time, this may be difficult, as they may continue enacting rituals that they used to do with their loved one. Behaviors such as making or putting out an extra cup of coffee or going home with the thought of telling the loved one that you have met an old friend may be common, especially early in the bereavement process. The client may have "flashbacks" to an event or conversations from the past, as if the loved one were still present. Eventually, the normative process of grief will subside, and the client will move forward, perhaps developing a new circle of friends, moving, changing jobs, and giving up old or acquiring new activities. Though life will be forever changed, and grief never totally absent, life regains shape again.

The passage of time and life events will always have an impact on bereavement. Significant dates of importance to the bereaved may include birthdays, anniversaries, holidays, and the anniversary of the death, and can continue to act as reminders of loss. At the same time, future happy moments, such as a child's high school or college graduation, may be tinged with the wish that the deceased were alive to share the joy. There is really no "typical' process of bereavement. Funeral, burial, and mourning practices are determined by many factors including religious, racial, and cultural associations, and family traditions. They are also influenced by the personal characteristics of the bereaved. Even within the category of individuals identified as "religious," there is great diversity. This includes differences between monotheistic religions, such as Christianity, Judaism, and Islam, and religions with a multitude of gods, such as Hinduism and some branches of Buddhism and Confucianism, not to mention differences in more specific beliefs such as reincarnation or resurrection. Despite differences, many people return to the same basic questions after the death of a loved one, such as: What is the meaning of life? What are the reasons for pain and suffering? How do I make sense of loss in the context of my larger understanding of the world?

Regardless of the categories that divide us, the reality of death and loss touches each person. In our own ways, and within the frameworks that make sense to us, we attempt to make sense of such loss, and deal with death, sometimes aided by customs and traditions unique to our identities.

References

American Civil Liberties Union. (2016). *Military spousal benefits*. Retrieved from www.aclu. org/files/pdfs/lgbt/legal-guidance/Post-DOMA_MilitarySpousalBenefits _v3.pdf

American Psychiatric Association. (2013). *Diagnostic and statistical manual of mental disorders* (5th ed.). Washington, DC: Author.

American Psychological Association. (2016). *Grief: Coping with the loss of your loved one* (Psychology Help Center). Retrieved from www.apa.org/helpcenter/grief.aspx

Diversity in family bereavement 145

Arriaza, P., Martin, S. S., & Csikai, E. L. (2011). An assessment of hospice bereavement programs for Hispanics. *Journal of Social Work in End-of-Life & Palliative Care*, 7(2–3), 121–138.

Athar, S. (2000). *Health concerns for believers: Contemporary issues.* Chicago: Kazi Publication.

Augsburg Fortress. (1978). *The Lutheran book of worship* (PEW ed.). Minneapolis, MN: Augsburg Fortress.

Beauchamp, T., & Childress, J. (2013). *Principles of biomedical ethics* (6th ed.). New York: Oxford University Press.

Bhaskarananda, S. (2002). *The essentials of Hinduism: A comprehensive overview of the world's oldest religion.* Seattle, WA: Viveka Press.

Brasch, R., & Brasch, L. (2014). *How did it begin?: The origins of our curious customs and superstitions.* New York: MJF Books.

Braun, K. L., & Nichols, R. (1997). Death and dying in four Asian American cultures: A descriptive study. *Death Studies, 21*(4), 327–359.

Braun, U., Beyth, R., Ford, M., & McCullough, L. (2008). Voices of African American, Caucasian, and Hispanic surrogates on the burdens of end-of-life decision making. *Journal of General Internal Medicine, 23*(30), 267–274.

Brokenleg, M., & Middleton, D. (1993). Native Americans: Adapting, yet retaining. In D. P. Irish, K. F. Lundquist, & V. J. Nelsen (Eds.), *Ethnic variations in dying, death and grief: Diversity in universality* (pp. 101–112). Washington, DC: Taylor & Francis.

Bushkofsky, D., & Satterlee, C. (2008). *Using Evangelical Lutheran worship: The Christian life, baptism and life passages.* Minneapolis: Augsburg Fortress.

Cacciatore, J. (2009). Appropriate bereavement practice after the death of a Native American child. *Families in Society, 90*(1), 46–50.

Ciria-Cruz, R. (2013, September 25). *At life's end Filipino care decisions rely on God, family and home.* Retrieved from http://newamericamedia.org/2013/09/at-lifes-end-filipino-care-decisions-rely-on-god-family-home.php

Clark, D. L. (2015). *The truth about the law of God.* Scott Valley, CA: CreateSpace Publishing.

DeBernardo, F. (2015, July 19). *Another gay person is denied communion at a parent's funeral* [Web log post]. Retrieved from https://newwaysministryblog.wordpress.com/2015/07/19/another-gay-man-is-denied-communion-at-a-parents-funeral/

Devi, S. (2011). Native American health left out in the cold. *Lancet, 377*(9776), 1481–1482.

Disaster and Community Crisis Center at the University of Missouri. (2014). *Cultural guidelines for working with families who have experienced sudden and unexpected death.* Retrieved from http://tdc.missouri.edu/doc/culture_guide_unexpected_death_dcc.pdf

Doka, K. J. (2016). *Grief is a journey: Finding your path through loss.* New York, NY: Atria Books.

Gaudet, M. (2000). Cultural Catholicism in Cajun-Creole Louisiana. *Louisiana Folklore Miscellany, 15*, 3–20.

Gerdner, L. A., Cha, D., Yang, D., & Tripp-Reimer, T. (2007, May). The circle of life: End-of-life care and death rituals for Hmong-American elders. *Journal of Gerontological Nursing, 33*(5), 20–29.

Giger, J., Davidhizar, R., & Fordham, P. (2006). Multi-cultural and multi-ethnic considerations and advanced directives: Developing cultural competency. *Journal of Cultural Diversity, 13*(1), 3–9.

Greek Orthodox Archdiocese of America. (2016). *The Greek Orthodox Archdiocese of American.* Retrieved from https://edit.goarch.org

Greer, T. M. (2005). Interventions for bridging the gaps in minority health. In L. VandeCreek & J. B. Allen (Eds.), *Innovations in clinical practice: Focus on health and wellness* (pp. 145–158). Sarasota, FL: Professional Resource Press.

Haley, W., Larson, D., Kasl-Godley, J., Neimeyer, R., & Kwilosz, D. (2003). Roles for psychologists in end-of-life care: Emerging models of practice. *Professional Psychology: Research and Practice, 34*(6), 626–633.

Harvey, P. (1990). *An introduction to Buddhism: Teachings, history and practices.* Cambridge: Cambridge University Press.

HealthCare Chaplaincy. (2009). *A dictionary of patients' spiritual & cultural values for health care professionals.* Retrieved from www.healthcarechaplaincy.org/userimages/doc/Cultural%20 Dictionary.pdf

Her, V. K. (2005). Hmong cosmology: Proposed model, preliminary insights. *Hmong Studies Journal,* (6), 1–25. Retrieved September 10, 2017, from http://hmongstudies.org/ HerHSJ6.pdf

Hoeffel, E. M., Rastogi, S., Kim, M. O., & Shahid, H. (2012, March). The Asian population: 2010. *2010 Census Briefs.* Retrieved from www.census.gov/population/race

Humes, K. R., Jones, N. A., & Ramirez, R. R. (2011, March). *Overview of race and Hispanic origin: 2010.* Washington, DC: U. S. Census Bureau.

Jacobs, L. (2002). *Jewish resurrection of the dead* [Web log site]. Retrieved from www.myjewish learning.com/article/jewish-resurrection-of-the-dead/

Kepler, A. K. (1998). *Hawaiian heritage plants* (Rev. ed.). Honolulu, HA: University of Hawaii Press.

Kleespies, P. (2004). *Life and death decisions: Psychological and ethical considerations in end-of-life care.* Washington, DC: American Psychological Association.

Ko, E., Roe, S., & Higgins, D. (2013). Do older Korean immigrants engage in end-of-life communications? *Educational Gerontology, 39*(8), 613–622.

Labun, E., & Emblen, J. D. (2007). Spirituality and health in punjabi Sikh. *Journal of Holistic Nursing, 25*(3), 141–148.

Lamm, M. (2000). *The Jewish way in death and mourning, revised and expanded.* Middle Village, NY: Jonathan David Publishers.

Linder, E. W. (2012). *2012 yearbook of American and Canadian churches.* Washington, DC: National Council of Churches.

Lobar, S. L., Youngblut, J. M., & Brooten, D. (2006). Cross-cultural beliefs, ceremonies and rituals surrounding death of a loved one. *Pediatric Nursing, 32*(1), 44–50.

Mathias, E. (2016, September). *The Italian-American funeral: Persistence through change.* Retrieved from www.italianancestry.com/mathias/

Matthiesen, B. W., Wickert, G. L., & Lehrer, S. C. (2013). *Funeral procession traffic laws in all 50 states.* Retrieved from www.mwl-law.com/wp-content/uploads/2013/03/Subro-and-funeral-procession-laws-chart-00143368.pdf

McGuire, T. G., & Miranda, J. (2008). New evidence regarding racial and ethnic disparities in mental health: Policy implications. *Health Affairs, 27,* 393–403.

Millet, R. L. (1999). *Life after death: Insights from Latter-Day revelation.* Salt Lake City, UT: Deseret Book Co.

Morris, J. P. (2003). *What Catholics believe: Exploring our faith today.* New London, CT: Twenty-Third Publications.

Movement Advancement Project. (2010). *Improving the lives of LGBT older adults: Issue briefs.* Retrieved from http://lgbtmap.org/improving-the-lives-of-lgbt-older-adults-issue-briefs

Norton, M. I., & Francesca, G. (2014). Rituals alleviate grieving for loved ones, lovers and lotteries. *Journal of Experimental Psychology: General, 143*(1), 266–272.

Nydegger, R. (2008). Psychologists and hospice: Where we are and where we can be. *Professional Psychology: Research and Practice, 39*(4), 459–463.

Olson, R. E. (2016). *The mosaic of Christian belief* (2nd ed.). Downers Grove, IL: IVP Academic.

Orthodox Christian Resource Center. (2016, September). *What happens to the soul after death?* [Web log post]. Retrieved from http://theorthodoxchurch.info/blog/ocrc/2009/06/what-happens-to-the-soul-after-death/

Packer, B. K. (2008). *Mine errand from the Lord: Selections from the sermons and writings of Boyd K. Packer.* Compiled by C. J. Williams. Salt Lake City, Ut: Deseret Book.

Pass, S. (2009). Teaching respect for diversity: The Oglala Lakota. *Social Studies, 100*(5), 212–217.

Rogak, L. (2013). *Death warmed over: Funeral food, rituals and customs from around the world.* Seattle, WA: Amazon Digital Service.

Saccomano, S., & Abbatiello, G. (2014). Cultural considerations at end of life. *Nurse Practationer, 39*(2), 24–39.

Smith, J. I., & Haddad, Y. Y. (2002). *The Islamic understanding of death and resurrection.* New York, NY: Oxford University Press.

Smith, S. E. (2010). *To serve the living: Funeral directors and the African American way of death.* Cambridge, MA: Belknap Press.

Snyder, J. (1984). *Reincarnation vs. resurrection.* Chicago, IL: Moody Press.

Steller, J., White, P., Barron, A. M., Gerzevitz, D., & Morse, A. (2010). Enhancing end of life with dignity: Characterizing hospice nursing in Romania. *International Journal of Palliative Care, 16*(9), 459–464.

Superstitious Dictionary. (2014, July 15). *Superstitions about the dead, dying, graves & cemeteries* [Web log post]. Retrieved from http://superstitiondictionary.com/superstitions-dead-dying-graves-cemeteries

Taylor, R. P. (2000). *Death and the afterlife: A cultural encyclopedia.* Santa Barbara, CA: ABC-CLIO.

Thao, Y. J. (2006). Culture and knowledge of the sacred instrument Qeej in the Mong-American community. *Asian Folklore Studies, 65*(2), 249–267. Retrieved September 10, 2017, from www.accessmylibrary.com/coms2/summary_0286-29239085_ITM

United States Conference of Catholic Bishops. (2016). *An overview of Catholic funeral rites.* Retrieved from www.usccb.org/prayer-and-worship/bereavement-and-funerals/overview-of-catholic-funeral-rites.cfm

Waters, C. M. (2001). Understanding and supporting African Americans' perspectives of end-of-life care planning and decision making. *Qualitative Health Research, 11*, 385–398.

Woodhead, L. (2014). *Christianity: A very short introduction* (2nd ed.). New York, NY: Oxford University Press.

Worden, W. (2008). *Grief counseling and grief therapy: A handbook for the mental health practitioner* (4th ed.). New York, NY: Springer Publishing Company.

Yeo, G., & Hikuyeda, N. (2000). Cultural issues in end-of-life decision making among Asians and Pacific Islanders in the United States. In K. Braun, J. H. Pietsch, & P. L. Blanchette (Eds.), *Cultural issues in end-of-life decision making* (pp. 101–125). Thousand Oaks, CA: Sage.

Zager, B. S., & Yancy, M. (2011). A call to improve practice concerning cultural sensitivity in advance directives: A review of the literature. *Worldviews on Evidence-Based Nursing*, (4), 202–211. Retrieved from http://onlinelibrary.wiley.com/journal/10.1111/(ISSN)1741-6787/homepage/ProductInformation.html

Zinn, K. (2013). *LGBT issues in the death of a partner or spouse.* Retrieved from www.heart2soul.com/lgbt-issues-spouse-dies-partner-death

Chapter 7

Policy and practice on psychosocial care in palliative care programs

Mai-Britt Guldin and Sheila Payne

Introduction

As research and knowledge about palliative and hospice care progresses, the centrality of psychological and psychosocial issues becomes increasingly evident. It is hard to imagine a more emotionally intense and psychologically demanding time than when a person's health is declining and the end of life is nearing. Suffering comes in many forms and emotional strain, grief, and psychosocial distress are common in individuals confronted with life-threatening illness and during palliative care. Symptom management and effective control of pain in palliative care include management of the pain and suffering based on physical as well as psychological, existential, social, and spiritual challenges. Symptom management of a psychological and social nature aims to address mental health problems, minimize suffering, enhance quality of life, and is generally called "psychosocial care."

What is meant by psychosocial care? Definitions vary but all encompass psychological and emotional well-being of the patient and their family, which includes enhancing well-being, maintaining quality of life, and enabling an understanding of the condition and its likely consequences on social functioning and relationships. The British National Council for Palliative Care defines psychosocial care as being concerned with the psychological and emotional well-being of the patient and their family/carers, including issues of self-esteem, insight into an adaption to illness and its consequences, communication, social functioning, and relationships (Field, 2000). Hence, supportive measures and interventions in palliative care programs reach out to patients, their families, and caregivers, including their children. Supportive measures are applied during palliative care (in Europe this can also be delivered concurrently with potentially curative treatments) as well as during bereavement after the death of the patient. The remit to deliver psychosocial care has been developed by a range of different clinical practitioners and includes activities called supportive services, advance care planning, psychosocial support, psycho-oncology, family/caregiver support, bereavement services, and many other concepts.

In this chapter, the provision of psychosocial care is described within a palliative care framework. Psychosocial care is introduced and described, and a brief

Policy and practice on psychosocial care 149

outline of the development, organization, and achievements in psychosocial care within palliative care is provided. Psychosocial care is described based on selected theories and models, levels of support, clinical practice guidelines, and recommendations, as well as core curricula and professional roles. In Europe, psychosocial care is a term used in the literature to refer to both psychological and social care. However, there is generally a distinction between psychological care as delivered by psychologists and others with specific training in mental health care (Payne & Haines, 2002) and social care as delivered by social workers and those with specific expertise in palliative care (Hughes, Firth, & Oliviere, 2014, 2015). The goals and challenges of palliative care will be predominantly discussed in relation to examples of psychological interventions, research, and policy development, and major gaps in knowledge will be identified. Finally, key points and practice implications are summed up along with future demands and opportunities.

A brief history of the development of psychosocial care in palliative care

The maturing of palliative care philosophy and recognition of specialist professional roles within palliative care have been accompanied by the ongoing development of psychosocial care. As described in Chapter 1, the hospice movement was based on the philosophy of a holistic view of human nature, and the fundamental idea that not only physical but also social, psychological, spiritual, and existential suffering must be addressed. Colin Murray Parkes, a well renowned British psychiatrist, started working at St. Christopher's Hospice in 1967 with Cicely Saunders (Parkes, 2000). Parkes has described that it quickly became clear to him that few patients actually had clear-cut psychiatric illnesses such as depression and anxiety, and most would not live long enough to benefit from weekly psychotherapy or medication. A different approach was needed to help the patients and their families alleviate psychological, social, existential, and spiritual suffering in this setting. As few patients and families could consult a psychiatrist, Parkes and Saunders came up with an alternative approach which involved the whole staff and the interdisciplinary team. Social workers, faith workers, and, a little later, psychologists then became involved in psychological and existential symptom management and psychosocial care. While the addition of home care to inpatient hospice programs extended palliative care to the private homes of the patients and increased the length of stay in the patients' own home up until the point of death in accordance with most patients' wishes, it also considerably increased the strain and burden for the families (Parkes, 2000). This further emphasized the need for support for families, not just following bereavement (e.g., to address adverse grief reactions after the death) but in proactive approaches for families at risk of psychological distress during the illness trajectory. Hence, the groundwork for development of preventive care, support programs, bereavement programs, counseling, and treatment within palliative care was laid. Today psychosocial and psychological care is considered a core part of palliative care and an integrated part of the alleviation of common symptoms near the end of life.

Professional roles in psychosocial palliative care

From the onset of palliative care, it has been generally agreed that the fulfillment of a holistic approach to care called for interdisciplinary team work (Haugen, Nauck, & Caraceni, 2015). A widely used definition of an interdisciplinary healthcare team is "an identified collective in which members share common team goals and work interdependently in planning, problem-solving, decision-making, and implementing and evaluating team-related tasks" (Haugen et al., 2015, p. 139). Interdisciplinary teamwork is an essential component of palliative care; however, the role and training of psychologists and social workers vary from country to country. In some countries, such as Germany, psychologists are a fundamental part of the multi-professional team in palliative care settings, but in some parts of Europe, the employment of social workers rather than psychologists is more common. For example, in Denmark, specialist palliative care teams are regarded as multi-professional only if they contain at least five different professions with psychologists regarded as fundamental professionals in the team. In contrast, in the United States psychologists are not included in the list of providers who must be included in a hospice team.

Naturally, the roles of the team members are tightly linked to profession and professional identity. For example, social workers provide advice on social matters which may encompass access to financial support and welfare benefits, taking account of individual family dynamics, employment status, and housing concerns. In comparison, psychologists may focus on identifying distress or dysfunction in family relationships and using psychotherapeutic approaches to address these concerns. Furthermore, the professional roles and functions tend to vary by country in response to their professional training and with regard to the organization of national healthcare systems, as well as the general roles and availability of psychologists and social workers. Haugen and colleagues (2015) state in the *Handbook of Palliative Medicine* that definition of functions and role clarification are advantageous as role overlap might lead to competition or organizational difficulties as well as sub-optimal care for patients.

Case example

Paul, 72 years old, is a retired teacher who cared for his wife Shirley, 70 years old, for five weeks from her diagnosis of late stage pancreatic cancer to her death. They had been married for 45 years and had no children. After her diagnosis, she was given the choice of staying in

Policy and practice on psychosocial care 151

hospital or going home; however, there was minimal discussion about her place of care. Paul acknowledged that, despite their good relationship, they did not discuss Shirley's illness and approaching death. When she was discharged from hospital, a number of different support services were organized. Paul found it confusing to have so many different people coming to the house:[1]

> The first problem I found was in the first few days at home, it was almost as though people were inundating us, and I got a little bit exasperated with the community nurses; somebody'd want to come, with a big questionnaire to assess her needs. Then somebody from Marie Curie Cancer Care came, another questionnaire, and she went away. Then somebody from the hospice came and another one . . . and it went on like this and I thought, well what about the practical help, you know, when she gets iller, getting her to the toilet and getting her washed and things like that, which was at that stage what was worrying me more.

On the whole, Paul was satisfied with the services Shirley received, but on occasion when they needed help out of hours they had to wait for people to respond:

> The community nursing service I thought was quite good: it was pretty exhausting in that – I don't know if you're familiar with it – you phone and leave a message on an answer phone, you don't contact them directly, so you don't know how long they're going to be [. . .] You wait for them to [receive the message] then they'll turn up an hour and a half later maybe or something like that. So there was a fair amount of sleep deprivation.

What also made it harder for Paul was that Shirley did not want any of their friends to visit. Paul also had to take responsibility for Shirley's emotional support, which he found worrying:

> If she was in extreme distress I could always phone up and say that, you know, she's having problems, and they would do their best to come. Obviously the nurses had quite a lot of people to see as you would expect, so they would maybe phone me up and say 'Look, we're stuck here with a patient who's having problems,

> can you cope?', and sometimes you just had to cope on your own, you know.

Questions

1 Whose task is it to talk to the patient and family about social, relational, and emotional problems and assess severity of mental distress?
2 Which professional(s) in the interdisciplinary team is appropriately qualified to help with these problems?
3 What care and treatment models can be applied?
4 What national and local policies are required to ensure that psychosocial care is integrated with palliative care?

In reference to our case example, is it the specialist palliative care nurse, the social worker, the pastoral worker, or the psychologist who is best suited to talk with patients and families about distress, communication problems, or even familial conflicts? The provision of psychosocial care and psychological support is normally not just provided by social workers and psychologists. According to guidelines and supportive programs, all health workers have a role in contributing to psychosocial care by providing compassionate communication and recognizing that patients and their families have psychological and social needs (Gamondi, Larkin, & Payne, 2013). Arguably, the role boundaries and description of who provides psychological support tend to be less clearly defined than, for instance, the role boundaries in the prescription of medications, and therefore the professional roles in providing psychosocial care are subject to discussion and negotiation. However, it is assumed that practicing within competencies across disciplines is advantageous for care outcomes, and that clear definition of responsibilities and roles, as well as interdisciplinary conferences can be helpful in providing the highest quality care for patients and families. At the same time, the importance of having trained mental health professionals to address mental health conditions, significant suffering, and complex psychological issues should not be overlooked.

It is not known how many teams struggle with role definition and clarification as a result of the unclear boundaries of psychosocial work. Psychologists have worked on the definition of their roles and functions, which is reflected in the descriptions provided by national psychological associations such as the American Psychological Association and the British Psychological Society, considering that psychologists find this task professionally relevant and desirable.

The contribution of clinical psychology

During the last two decades, clinical psychologists have increasingly contributed to the care of patients with medical illnesses, including those with palliative care needs. The psychological literature previously focused mainly on newly diagnosed patients, coping with curative treatments, and rehabilitation within the field of psycho-oncology (Payne & Haines, 2002). Although in some countries the contribution of clinical psychology to palliative care might have emanated from psycho-oncology, the psychologists' role and functions in palliative care have often exceeded this. In Denmark, for instance, the role of clinical psychology is increasingly mentioned in local and national recommendations and guidelines on palliative and supportive care (National Recommendations for Palliative Care, 2011), whereas its role is not quite as specified in cancer care where nurse specialists and other professionals carry out much of the supportive care. At the same time, the scope of clinical psychology seems vast in light of the evidence of unmet psychological needs of patients with, for instance, heart failure, lung disease, and neurologic diseases, not to mention the needs of their families (Cathcart, 2010). However, for many of the individuals with these diagnoses the involvement of psychologists is not widely applied.

Until recently, the contribution of clinical psychology in palliative care has only rarely been described, but the literature on psychological assessment and intervention in palliative care is growing (Grant & Kalus, 2010; Kalus et al., 2008; Nydegger, 2008). A number of national and international guidelines and recommendations have been published on how to meet the psychological needs of patients and families (Clinical Standards, 2002; Department of Health and Children, 2001; National Institute for Clinical Excellence in England [NICE], 2004). These guidelines and recommendations have provided an initial framework for incorporating psychological care within palliative care. Yet, with growing utilization of services, more evidence-based guidelines are needed to raise the profile of both palliative care and psychosocial care and provide support for clinicians, especially in Eastern European countries where national policies on palliative care may not yet be in place.

EAPC Task Force on core competencies for psychologists

The NICE clinical standards on supportive care suggest that all palliative care professionals should apply basic psychological skills in their everyday practice to recognize psychological needs and to help patients and families alleviate psychological suffering, and they also encourage that patients with complex psychological needs should be referred to mental health professionals (NICE, 2004). While systematic data on the tasks, work settings, specific competences, and number of psychologists working in palliative care are limited, national surveys have been carried out in Spain, England, and the USA (Grant & Kalus, 2010; Lacasta Reverte et al., 2008; Nydegger, 2008) and by the European Association for

Palliative Care (EAPC), leaving little doubt of the central contribution of clinical psychologists to palliative care. Here, findings from the survey of the EAPC on psychologists' tasks will be described.

In 2009, a Task Force (an international time-limited working group) under the auspices of the EAPC undertook a survey of European psychologists working within palliative care to describe their work setting, main tasks, professional profiles, and educational opportunities. In total, 323 psychologists from 41 countries participated (Jünger, Eggenberger, Greenwood, & Payne, 2010). Responses reflected that the primary role of psychologists were clinical tasks such as consultation with patients and families, and team members; however, participants estimated that their major contribution to palliative care was raising awareness of psychological issues on death and dying among professionals such as physicians and nurses. The survey showed that the following tasks were undertaken by psychologists:

> First, psychologists complete clinical tasks such as consultations with patients and relatives associated with pending death, facilitating emotional expression, communication regarding needs, hopes, and belief as well as consulting with team members on psychological issues of supportive care. Second, psychologists conduct assessment for depression, anxiety, or adjustment disorders, as well as psychotherapeutic treatment for depression, anxiety, and adjustment disorders or other mental health problems. Third, psychologists communicate with relatives and families and provide support with issues on loss and grief. Fourth, psychologists assist in educating other professionals on psychological issues of palliative care (e.g., teaching professionals about normal reactions to death, dying, and loss as well as reactions that need treatment). Fifth, psychologists contribute their professional skills and perspectives to the multi-professional team. Activities may include raising awareness of a psychological perspective on loss, death and dying in the daily work of the team; and bringing specific expertise to interdisciplinary meetings (for example adding to their colleagues' understanding of different aspects of patients' pain and suffering). Finally, psychologists conduct research, program evaluation, policy making, and audit work.

This list is in accordance with the core competencies described by the British Psychological Society for psychologists in end-of-life care (Kalus et al., 2008). The American Psychological Association similarly identifies common roles for psychologists, which primarily include clinical roles in which psychologists treat individual patients. In addition, the American Psychological Association highlights that psychologists are involved in delivering education and training, research, and promoting policy development (American Psychological Association, 2005). The concordance in international role descriptions for psychologists is striking.

The majority of psychologists in the EAPC survey reported that psychologists play an important role in palliative care policy in their country. Out of 45 collective membership organizations, 11 had psychologists working with

Policy and practice on psychosocial care 155

research and policy making as board members in their national palliative care associations, and this number is likely to have increased since the survey. At the same time, the psychologists also responded that their specific contribution was not clearly defined, and their roles and functions were ambiguous and lacked distinction and definition compared with other professional groups. A major challenge was that the work of psychologists did not seem to be sufficiently respected or acknowledged. They also generally experienced a lack of recognition of psychological aspects of care by collaborating professionals (Jünger et al., 2010). In sum, surveys show that psychologists consider that they have an important role in palliative care. However, psychologists also report a range of organizational challenges as well as clinical problems with the limited time available for interventions for those with complex problems. The survey reflected that policy development to promote and formalize the contribution of clinical psychology was urgently needed.

Models for the provision of psychosocial care

Psychosocial care emerged initially as a response to dealing with psychiatric symptoms such as depression, anxiety, delirium, suicidal thoughts (or desire for hastened death), and grief-related complications. It is generally accepted that the strain of disease is multimodal and pain, physical symptom distress, and neurobiological changes are likely to influence psychological responses and vice versa (Mehnert, 2015). However, the final phase of life often also involves a great deal of psychological distress in regard to anxiety about dying, grief in response to losses, worries about dependency, powerlessness about what will happen to family members, and hopelessness about the future (Lloyd Williams, 2008). Hence, psychological distress can range from transient experiences of vulnerability, sadness, and loss of meaning, purpose, and connection with loved ones, to severe, and persistent symptoms of depression and anxiety, new in their onset or recurrence of episodes from earlier in life. Treatment may range from compassion and emotional support to structured, evidence-based interventions and medical attention. Bolstering of coping strategies, such as active and targeted attempts to cope with the disease and the impact it has on daily life, also play an important role in adjusting to the challenges of illness. Further, psychological and emotional suffering are likely to be multifactorial and vary according to disease progression, physical symptom burden, personal vulnerabilities, or even previous risk factors and mental health problems (Gao, Bennett, Stark, Murray, & Higginson, 2010). Consequently, in order to apply a multidisciplinary approach to the management of symptoms, the idea of regular, systematic assessment has gained broad acceptance.

Case examples from Spain and Denmark contexts

As the field of palliative care continues to develop, psychologists are faced with a number of challenges to ensure their skills and resources are effectively used. The following section offers two case examples from Spain and Denmark that highlight different responses to national demands. In both countries, specialist palliative care services were available to the majority of the population. In Spain, there was a recognition that specialist palliative care services tended to focus on physical symptom management with medical and nursing staff having less expertise in psychosocial care. In Denmark, the "Domus" project started as a research project in response to the demand for integrated palliative care and dying at home. Hence, psychological support for family caregivers and enhancing family communication was strengthened with this project.

The "La Caixa" Project in Spain offers an example of a comprehensive psychosocial support program developed over more than ten years for patients with advanced and terminal diseases, their families, and their clinical teams. The program is funded by a commercial bank as part of their commitment to social action. Designed after a qualitative assessment of the situation of palliative care services in Spain, the project identified a list of weak points to be addressed and improved, other than the implementation of more conventional palliative care services. The qualitative evaluation identified the unmet emotional support of patients and families, the lack of evaluation of psychosocial needs (including emotional and spiritual) which often resulted in lack of support, the poor development of bereavement services, and the lack of comprehensive programs to support palliative care professionals. The implementation of psychosocial activities within palliative care services in Spain was described as patchy and scarce. Most organizations did not have bereavement services, and many did not have psychologists or other psychotherapeutic professionals. Spiritual care was very rarely offered. There are now over 30 dedicated psychosocial and spiritual support teams, sharing the same documentation, evaluations tools, and regular training (Gómez-Batiste et al., 2011). These teams provide individual support to patients with measurable improvements in well-being and reduction in anxiety and insomnia.

In Denmark, the Domus project of specialized and multidisciplinary palliative care for patients with incurable cancer and their caregivers systematically offers psychological assessment and supportive dyadic intervention. Through early transition to palliative care, the model aims to enhance patients' chances of receiving care and dying at home. Integration of psychological support seeks to facilitate this goal by alleviating distress in patients and caregivers. Psychologists provide dyadic needs-based sessions based on existential – phenomenological therapy to patients and their caregivers. The intervention efficacy is currently being investigated. Enrollment in a randomized controlled trial and uptake of the psychological intervention indicate that it is acceptable to patient and caregivers and feasible. The strengths of the psychological intervention include its focus on dyads, psychological distress and existential concerns, interdisciplinary collaboration, and psychological interventions offered according to need. The scope of this psychological intervention can be significant, as it is systematically integrated into palliative care. The Domus trial will provide evidence of a novel model of multidisciplinary palliative care (von Heyman-Horan et al., 2017).

Standards of psychological care in palliative care contexts

NICE (2004) proposed a model of the provision of psychological care within palliative care contexts to ensure that cancer care services appropriately help people cope with life-threatening illness. The model was developed to ensure care planning that is responsive to patients' and families' unique needs at different stages of the disease, as well as taking indvidual vulnerabilities and risks into consideration. Assessment of needs and risks are recommended at key points during the disease trajectory and encompass physical, psychological, social, spiritual, and financial aspects while ensuring continuity in care and employment of and collaboration among the relevant professionals.

A four-tiered, or layered, model of care provision is recommended in the guidance, ranging from services applicable to all patients to services targeted at specific groups and needs. The approach seeks to make sure people get the help that is matched to their need, with an emphasis on building natural community and network supports. Furthermore, care provision is also tiered based on the professional group providing the care ranging from services provided by all professionals in palliative care to highly specialized services provided by mental health professionals. The underlying idea of the NICE model has been incorporated into clinical guidelines, including the evidence-based standards for bereavement care developed by Hall and colleagues in Australia (Hall, Hudson, & Boughey, 2012) . The guidance recommends that psychosocial and supportive care be provided in a targeted way and that people's strengths and resilience should be included in the assessment as well as the provision of care at four different levels. The four components or levels of psychosocial care were defined as follows.

Level 1

Level 1 states that all health and social care profesionals assess psychological needs and provide effective information, compassionate communication, and general psychological support. All professionals should be able to treat patients and families with kindness, dignity, and respect, as well as establish and maintain supportive relationships. Since services at this level could benefit all patients and families, these services have been referred to as "*Universal.*" Recommendations include physicians and nurses participating in both physical and psychological assessments, or physicians and nurses providing general emotional support for the family during routine medical discussions. Services at this level may also include all staff members explaining the importance of mobilizing resources and personal networks as recommended in the EAPC white paper on core competencies in general palliative care (Gamondi et al., 2013). Family and friends will also provide much of this support, with information being supplied by health and social care professionals providing day-to-day care to families.

Level 2

Level 2 sets out that health and social professionals, such as nurse specialists and social workers, providing this level of care should have additional expertise and be able to screen for psychological distress. Many (but not all) patients and families could benefit from services at this level. Professionals need to be able to distinguish levels of care and decide when significant psychological distress requires referral to specialist care. They should also master the provision of techniques such as psychoeducation and problem solving and provide support in acute situational crises. This could encompass psychoeducation by the social worker on the most common reactions to life-threatening illness or a dialogue assessing the need for additional support.

Level 3

Level 3 services are provided by trained and accredited professionals who should be able to screen for psychological distress and diagnose some types of psychopathology. At this level a differentiation of moderate versus severe reactions need to be assessed and referral to specialist care arranged when appropriate. Level 3 providers should master counseling and specific psychological interventions such as anxiety management and solution-focused therapy, delivered according to an explicit theoretical framework. These services have been termed "targetted" services and are provided for people who have particular risk factors because of aspects of their personal or social situation, or relating to the illness trajectory, or circumstances surrounding the death of the patient. These services could be provided by trained nurse specialist or mental health specialists by providing counseling and basic therapeutic interventions for distress or well-defined social or emotional challenges.

Level 4

Level 4 is provided by mental health specialists only, such as psychologists and psychiatrists, and is based on the diagnosis of psychopathology. The professionals working at this level need to be able to assess complex psychological problems, including personality disorders, mood disorders, and the interplay between medical and psychological diagnoses. They provide specialist psychological and psychiatric interventions such as psychotherapy, including cognitive behavioral therapy (CBT), for complex problems which might originate not only from the difficult situation but also from a general lack of personal resources or a history of psychological problems. These services have been referred to as *treatment by indication*, and only small proportions of patients or families require this level of psychotherapeutic intervention.

In sum, the NICE guidance provides a framework for the provision of psychosocial care which matches the needs of the patients and families and differentiates

Policy and practice on psychosocial care 159

the roles of the professionals.[2] Although there will always be a gray area between distinguished levels of care, this model allows for conceptualization of patient and family needs based on common language and well-defined criteria.

Models of assessment

Risk or needs assessment and the application of the appropriate level of support have been described in models of psychosocial care in palliative care. We describe two examples from the United Kingdom and Australia:

1   Guidance on improving supportive and palliative care for adults with cancer (NICE, 2004).
2   Bereavement support standards for specialist palliative care services (Hall et al., 2012).

Assessment instruments and interventions with potential benefits

This section describes assessment instruments with potential benefits, and interventions that have been tested and shown to have evidence of effect. Not many assessment instruments and interventions specific to palliative care contexts have undergone rigorous testing. However, we will provide an example of a clinical guideline on the management of depression as well as a systematic review of psychosocial interventions for family carers. We are unaware of well-established formal guidelines or reviews on the management of anxiety.

Psychological distress is determined by assessment via diagnostic instruments and interview, and therefore it is recommended that patients with significant levels of psychological distress should be assessed by the relevant health professionals to determine whether they meet diagnostic criteria for specific psychiatric illness before being referred to a mental health professional for subsequent treatment (Mehnert, 2015). In order for a comprehensive assessments of psychological support needs to take place, assessment can be provided on a regular basis throughout key points in the disease trajectory to patients as well as family members. A variety of screening tools are available to assist in evaluation of the nature, severity, and duration of psychological distress of patients (Vodermaier, Linden, & Siu, 2009) and for families (Hudson et al., 2010). Mental distress and disorders often represent premorbid conditions or distress that have their onset before the time of the diagnosis and can continue and worsen with progression of the disease. Therefore, assessment can also be based on a dialogue with the patient about psychological distress and their willingness to explore the nature of the distress is fundamental to palliative care. However, clinical practice shows that assessment and communication about psychological distress is in danger of being over looked and underprioritized by healthcare professionals (Gao et al., 2010). It is not known why this is, but it has been speculated that it might be due to the focus on physical symptoms, the lack of resources, or even insufficient knowledge and training (Lloyd Williams, 2008).

Alleviation of psychological distress is likely to be enhanced if professionals are adequately trained and supervised in communication and symptom management about emotional suffering, as has been argued by Lloyd Williams (2008). A range of screening tools have been reviewed and generally brief screening tools have been proposed as useful in palliative care, for instance the single-item screening: *Are you depressed?* (Mehnert, 2015). The National Comprehensive Cancer Network has proposed the distress thermometer (National Comprehensive Cancer Network, 2003).

Standards for bereavement care

Bereavement care is an essential component of palliative care service delivery; however, there is little evidence-based guidance for health professionals and others providing this support. Bereavement Support Standards for Specialist Palliative Care Services have been developed by the Centre for Palliative Care in Melbourne, Australia (Hall et al., 2012). The bereavement support standards were developed to assist palliative care services in providing systematic and evidence-based bereavement support. The standards were developed based on a review of international evidence of the impact of bereavement and bereavement interventions, a survey, consultancy with key stakeholders, and an expert advisory group (Hall et al., 2012). The key principles underpinning the standards are that, in order for bereavement support to be delivered in a targeted manner, screening and assessment of risks and needs are recommended. The bereaved person's own resources and capacity should be taken into consideration. A range of bereavement screening tools that aim to identify family carers' risk of complicated grief are available for use prior to the death of the patient as well as after the loss. The recommended bereavement support is divided into two types of strategies: universal and specialist support. Universal strategies, which target all bereaved people, include participation in bereavement information sessions and opportunities to review and reflect on the experience of loss, or activity-based programs such as walking, meditation, music, and art groups. Specialist bereavement support strategies include bereavement counseling and psychotherapy using evidence-based interventions such as cognitive behavioral therapy for complicated grief (Boelen, de Keijser, van den Hout, & van den Bout, 2007; Kissane et al., 2006), complicated grief treatment (Shear, Frank, Houck, & Reynolds., 2005), and meaning reconstruction approaches (Allen et al., 2014; Breitbart et al., 2012; Chochinov et al., 2011; Lo et al., 2014).

We are aware of other models, such as the La Caixa model in Spain, and the Domus model in Denmark mentioned earlier in the chapter, and recommendations on psychosocial care, including recent recommendations from WHO (2016). In all cases, readers are advised to be aware of local directives and national guidelines, as they are most likely to be specifically adapted to their countries' socioeconomic, cultural, and political healthcare environment.

Models for psychological interventions

When the nature and severity of distress are assessed, the appropriate intervention by the relevant professionals can be discussed and applied by the multidisciplinary team. A range of different psychological therapies have been suggested as common in palliative care. However, it is important to note that there is limited evidence concerning the effectiveness of these approaches in palliative care services. The *Oxford Textbook of Palliative Care* (Cathcart, 2010) mentions goal-setting, problem-solving, behavioral strategies, relaxation and hypnosis, cognitive behavioral therapy, and other types of counseling and psychotherapy. A range of psychotherapeutic approaches is applied in palliative care settings, but psychotherapy with existential aspects has been shown to have some effect, some of which are described in this book (chapters one, four, and five). These include Dignity Therapy (Chochinov et al., 2011; Chochinov, 2012), Individual Meaning-Centered Psychotherapy (Breitbart et al., 2012), Managing Cancer and Living Meaningfully (Lo et al., 2014), and narrative reminiscence and creative activity interventions (Allen, Hilgeman, Ege, Shuster, & Burgio, 2008; Allen et al., 2014).

Psychosocial and psychological interventions in palliative care are characterized by many different types of interventions but few have undergone rigorous testing. Although psychological interventions in palliative care might use the evidence-base of modern psychology, few traditional interventions have been tested in a palliative care setting. To our knowledge, no meta-analysis of the efficacy of psychological interventions applied to patients in palliative care exists, and we are aware of only one Cochrane review on interventions supporting informal caregivers of patients in the terminal phase (Candy, Jones, Drake, Leurent, & King, 2011). The Cochrane review concludes that there is low-quality evidence that interventions directly supporting the caregiver significantly reduce psychological distress in the short term. However, the interventions were carried out by many different professionals, some without specific training in mental health, and did not distinguish support from psychological or psychotherapeutic interventions. This might partially be due to the challenges of distinguishing roles in palliative care but also challenges with research based on manualized and structured psychological interventions for patients near the end of life. Still, there are a range of interventions that have shown effectiveness, and we describe clinical guidelines on the management of depression in patients in palliative care and provide a systematic review of interventions for caregivers to patients in palliative care. First, the range and scope of interventions are described.

Psychosocial and psychotherapeutic interventions are primarily linked to the theoretical assumptions underpinning them (e.g., psychodynamic, narrative, or behavioral approaches) but they will also be influenced by the setting they take place in, such as the patient's home, a palliative ward in a large hospital, or a specialist unit like a hospice. Psychologists might direct their efforts to improve care at the level of the individual, groups, the entire family, staff groups, or at an organizational level. The choice of psychological intervention will also depend on the nature and severity of the person's psychological distress and preferences, his or her previous history with psychological problems, the availability of social support, and disease prognosis (Kasl-Godley, King, & Quill, 2014; Nydegger, 2008). In addition to the specific psychotherapeutic approaches, providing psychological support and treatment to patients with life-limiting illness is characterized by some salient and unique aspects. Sessions sometimes take place in the patient's own home and cannot follow the structure of typical psychotherapeutic planning. For instance, sessions rarely follow the typical 50-minute outpatient model, treatment course can be short, and structured sessions are made impossible by lack of time, limited resources, fatigue, and diminished cognitive flexibility in patients with advanced disease (Kasl-Godley et al., 2014). The potential for strong emotional responses and countertransference dynamics is imminent, and it can sometimes be necessary to tackle complex psychological issues and familial conflicts rapidly without the necessary time to uncover the entire problem. Psychotherapeutic sessions therefore need to be accommodated to the patients' medical status, with fatigue being a major limiting factor.

A clinical guideline on the management of depression

A clinical guideline on the management of depression in palliative care has been published by the European Palliative Care Research Collaborative (Rayner, Higginson, Price, & Hotopf, 2010). Evidence of treatment of depression in patients in palliative care is scarce, but this clinical guideline concludes that there is little ground to suggest that a radically different approach than the usually suggested treatment for depression is required. However, some of the modifications and considerations mentioned above are relevant and the patient's diagnosis, symptoms, prognosis, and life expectancy as well as the patients' treatment preferences should be considered in treatment planning. Mild symptoms of depression are not uncommon for patients with an incurable disease, and good palliative care is indicated with symptom control, good communication, and facilitation of effective social support. If depression is moderate to severe, commencement of antidepressants and psychotherapy is warranted, alongside management of suicide risk. Cognitive behavioral therapy is the most widely used and evaluated psychological therapy and may be appropriate in some cases. Problem Solving Therapy is short and focused and its brevity and simple strategies has made it a good choice for patients with life-limiting disease (D'Zurilla & Nezu, 2010). Interpersonal Therapy, couples therapy, group therapy, and mindfulness-based therapy have also been shown to be beneficial for patients with advanced disease, but the evidence base is limited (Mehnert, 2015). Creative therapies such

Policy and practice on psychosocial care   163

as music and art therapy have also been shown to promote pain control, relaxation, and even emotional expression (Rayner et al., 2010). In sum, the clinical guideline on the management of depression in palliative care constitutes a standardized and evidence-based foundation for provision of psychological support and treatment in palliative care. The question is whether it is possible also to extrapolate and adjust guidelines and best practice models on management of anxiety, PTSD, and adjustment disorders for application in palliative care (Kasl-Godley et al., 2014).

Psychosocial interventions for family carers of palliative care patients

Hudson and colleagues carried out a systematic review of psychosocial interventions for family carers of palliative care patients (Hudson et al., 2010). They included 14 studies with interventions targeting improvements in psychosocial support in caregivers to patients in palliative care. Interventions included psychoeducation, psychosocial support, carer coping, symptom management, sleep promotion, family meetings, and bereavement support. According to Hudson et al (2010), psychoeducational programs demonstrated significant, favorable effect on caregivers' perceptions of positive elements in their role and preparedness for death, and family meeting interventions reduced unmet needs (Hudson et al., 2010). A brief behavioral sleep intervention showed improvements in sleep quality and depressive symptoms, and supportive interventions showed improved quality of life and reduced perceived burden of care tasks (Hudson et al., 2010). The review showed that the empirical basis for discerning the types of strategies that help family caregivers has improved over the last decade, but there are still significant improvements to be made.

Development of core curricula in psychology

Core curricula in psychology regarding palliative care have been described in an expert paper from the EAPC called *Guidance on the Postgraduate Education of Psychologists in Palliative Care* (Jünger & Payne, 2011). The guidance aims to indicate the requirements for specialist training for psychologists working in palliative care contexts to ensure a uniform and evidence-based standard of clinical practice. The goal of the core curriculum is also to improve psychologists' profile and skills as well as their ability to meet the demands of their role and improve the quality of their professional performance (Jünger & Payne, 2011). The basis of the core curriculum is the assumption that psychologists who are working in the clinical area of palliative care have the appropriate education and experience in working with patients and families, and that the national requirements and curriculum for psychology studies and palliative care delivery should be taken into account.

The general goals and learning objectives of the suggested syllabus comprise history, definition and philosophy of palliative care, symptomatology, and psychological aspects of the dying patient, caregiving, and bereavement. Knowledge of the delivery of services in palliative care and the evidence base of psychological care are key elements in the list of competencies. Issues regarding research in palliative care and psychology, ethics, politics, organization, and strategy are also specific learning objectives (Jünger & Payne, 2011).

Last but not least, an important step in the postgraduate education of psychologists in palliative care is a formal recognition or even certification of psychologists who have undergone specialized training. To date, there is no formal certification for psychologists in specialized palliative care settings. In Europe, the European Certificate of Psychology (EuroPsy), is a qualification standard recommended by the European Federation of Psychologists' Association (www.efpa.eu/europsy). A formal certification has advantages because it could provide a framework for a formal standardization and recognition of psychological care within palliative care, which might also transcend the differences in tasks and roles from country to country. However, it may also represent a potential barrier to greater access to mental health services by limiting the availability of accredited professionals, especially in resource poor regions.

Goals and challenges

As palliative care continues to develop, psychosocial care faces a number of goals and challenges in intervention and support models, research, competency development, and policy making. There are considerable gaps in knowledge regarding the professional profile of psychologists in the field of palliative care and their role and function are still under construction. The spectrum of tasks, roles, and competencies of psychologists need to be more clearly outlined at a country level in the future, with an eye toward global concordance in order to secure unified standards. Therefore, a central challenge is to delineate unique core competencies and agree on an unambiguous definition of the role of the psychologist that differs from that of other professionals and is valued for its contribution, supported by policies, and acknowledged within the palliative care team.

Future interventions need to look at care programs and service delivery to enhance clinical practice and increase availability of psychosocial care. Changes that are likely to have an impact upon psychosocial services include the early integration of palliative care, with referrals anticipated for those patients living with chronic advanced conditions, rather than just those facing the imminent end of life. In many countries, aging populations are presenting with multiple comorbidities and frailty, requiring sensitive new approaches to supporting those dying in late old age (Gott & Ingleton, 2011). Specific psychotherapies still need to be developed for palliative care settings taking the unique characteristics of providing psychotherapy to dying persons into consideration. The methods are more likely to be effective if they are targeted and focus on accurate knowledge of the distress and the distinctive characteristics of the situation

Policy and practice on psychosocial care 165

of a dying person and family relationships. However, more research is needed to demonstrate the scientific basis and the benefit of psychological interventions in palliative care provided by diverse professionals such as nurses.

The methods and effects of therapies need to be tested rigorously to provide information on more optimal support and treatments. There are still significant improvements to be made in terms of developing interventions for patients with advanced disease who have depression, anxiety, PTSD, and adjustment disorders, as well as their families and caregivers. Standardized assessment tools concerning psychosocial distress and risk factors for use in a palliative population are in short supply, as are assessment tools for early identification of caregivers in need of support or at risk of adverse bereavement outcomes.

In addition to supporting patients and families, psychologists have an important contribution to make in facilitating the emotional labor of interdisciplinary teams and in providing opportunities for debriefing after challenging or difficult events. The ability to offer conflict resolution and insights into team dynamics also promotes healthy and sustainable working environments. Finally, psychologists have a potentially significant contribution to make at organizational and strategic management levels, with the ability to generate, synthesize, and interpret scientific evidence. In terms of policy development, equity in access to psychosocial care needs to be improved, as do assessment practices and standards of care.

Revisiting the case example

If we turn our attention back towards the introductory case example, Paul and Shirley are in distress. A systematic assessment of emotional distress and psychological needs initially by a specialist palliative care nurse or a general practitioner would make this apparent and ensure that their psychosocial needs are not overlooked. If their psychological needs require more than simple information provision, they could be referred to a social worker or clinical psychologist with specialist training and skills in palliative care. This might lead to appropriate interventions for both Paul, in managing the demands of caregiving, and for Shirley, in facing the existential distress of dying. Organizational policies and evidence-based support models and an integrated interdisciplinary approach between primary care, other specialist providers, and hospice care teams could secure them help for their suffering that is holistic during their end-of-life care. Kasl-Godley and colleagues state that

> the field of palliative care offers unparalleled opportunities to change lives for the better. . . . By helping seriously ill patients and their families find connection and healing in the midst of medical suffering, we ourselves are privileged to find deeper meaning in our own lives through these powerful and inspiring human encounters.
>
> (2014, p. 372)

Conclusions

This chapter defines and describes the provision of psychosocial care and psychological interventions in palliative care and outlines the policy and practice of psychosocial interventions in palliative care by presenting selected theories, models, reviews, and guidelines. The contribution of clinical psychology and core curricula are outlined. The development of psychosocial care in palliative medicine and psycho-oncology has greatly increased our knowledge of the assessment and management of psychosocial challenges in patients and families in palliative care. The nature and characteristics of psychosocial issues in patients and families in palliative care are unique, as are the techniques and interventions. Finally, fostering an environment of acceptance, recognition, and support for psychosocial problems is key to delivering high-quality care. Methods used in other populations are only partially applicable, and there are still gaps in knowledge as well as a number of goals and challenges to be achieved within this field. Clinical guidelines and standards are underway but still in their infancy. However, review of the achievements within psychosocial care in palliative care leaves little doubt about the meaningfulness and relevance of psychosocial care for patients and families faced with life-limiting illness.

Notes

1 The case study demonstrates an example from the United Kingdom, where there are often many services which may not be well integrated. All services are provided free at the point of care to the patient but service funding may include: general practitioner, community nurse, hospital (NHS); Marie Curie Cancer Care offers a night sitting nursing service at home, Hospice provides a specialist palliative care home nursing (Charities).
2 This model is used in England and Wales. In the UK, patient care is provided free of charge at the point of service delivery. Funding for mental health specialists will depend upon their employer: the majority will be employed by the NHS (government funded), a small minority by hospices (80% of hospices are charities funded by a mixture of public donation and some level of NHS contracts).

References

Allen, R. S., Harris, G. M., Burgio, L. D., Azuero, C. B., Miller, L. A., Shin, H., . . . Parmelee, P. (2014). Can senior volunteers deliver reminiscence and creative activity interventions? Results of the Legacy Intervention Family Enactment randomized controlled trial. *Journal of Pain and Symptom Management, 48*(4), 590–601.

Allen, R. S., Hilgeman, M. M., Ege, M. A., Shuster, J. L., Jr., & Burgio, L. D. (2008). Legacy activities as interventions approaching the end of life. *Journal of Palliative Medicine, 11*(7), 1029–1038.

American Psychological Association. (2005). *The role of psychology in end-of-life decisions and quality of care.* Retrieved from www.apa.org/research/action/end.aspx

Boelen, P. A., de Keijser, J., van den Hout, M. A., & van den Bout, J. (2007). Treatment of complicated grief: A comparison between cognitive-behavioral therapy and supportive counseling. *Journal of Consulting and Clinical Psychology, 75*(2), 277–284.

Breitbart, W., Poppito, S., Rosenfeld, B., Vickers, A. J., Li, Y., Abbey, J., & Cassileth, B. R. (2012). Pilot randomized controlled trial of individual meaning-centered psychotherapy for patients with advanced cancer. *Journal of Clinical Oncology, 30*, 1304–1309.

Candy, B., Jones, L., Drake, R., Leurent, B., & King, M. (2011). Interventions for supporting informal caregivers to patients in the terminal phase of disease. *Cochrane Database of Systematic Reviews, 6*. doi:10.1002/14651858.CD007617.pub2

Cathcart, F. (2010). Role of clinical psychology. In N. I. Cherny, M. Fallon, S. Kaasa, R. K. Portenoy, & D. C. Currow (Eds.), *Oxford textbook of palliative medicine* (4th ed.). New York, NY: Oxford University Press.

Chochinov, H. M. (2012). *Dignity therapy: Final words for final days.* New York, USA: Oxford University Press.

Chochinov, H. M., Kristjanson, L. J., Breitbart, W., McClement, S., Hack, T. F., Hassard, T., & Harlos, M. (2011). Effect of dignity therapy on distress and end-of-life experience in terminally ill patients: A randomised controlled trial. *The Lancet Oncology, 12*, 753–762.

Clinical standards: Specialist palliative care. (2002). Edinburgh: Clinical Standards Board for Scotland.

Department of Health and Children. (2001). *Report on national advisory committee on palliative care.* Dublin, Ireland: Department of Health and Children.

D'Zurilla T. J., & Nezu, A. M. (2010). Problem-solving therapy. In K. S. Dobson (Ed.), *Handbook of cognitive-behavioral therapies* (3rd ed.). New York, NY: The Guildford Press.

Field, D. (2000). *What do we mean by "psychosocial"? A discussion paper on use of the concept within palliative care.* The National Council for Palliative Care. Retrieved from www.worldcat.org/title/what-do-we-mean-by-psychosocial-a-discussion-paper-on-use-of-the-concept-within-palliative-care/oclc/500350399

Gamondi, C., Larkin, P., & Payne, S. (2013). Core competencies in palliative care: An EAPC white paper on palliative care education–part 1. *European Journal of Palliative Care, 20*, 86–91.

Gao, W., Bennett, M. I., Stark, D., Murray, S., & Higginson, I. J. (2010). Psychological distress in cancer survivorship to end of life care: Prevalence, associated factors and clinical implications. *European Journal of Cancer, 46*, 2036–2044.

Gómez-Batiste, X., Buisan, M., González, M. P., Velasco, D., de Pascual, V., Espinosa, J., . . . Breitbart, W. (2011). The "La Caixa" Foundation and WHO Collaborating Center Spanish National Program for enhancing psychosocial and spiritual palliative care for patients with advanced diseases and their families. *Palliative and Supportive Care, 9*, 239–249.

Gott, M., & Ingleton, C. (Eds.). (2011). *Living with ageing and dying: Palliative and end of life care for older people.* Oxford: Oxford University Press.

Grant, L., & Kalus, C. (2010). A survey of applied psychologists in specialist palliative care: Settings, roles and approaches. *Clinical Psychology Forum, 208*, 33–37.

Hall, C., Hudson, P., & Boughey, A. (2012). *Bereavement support standards for specialist palliative care services.* Melbourne: Department of Health, State Government of Victoria.

Haugen, D. F., Nauck, F., & Caraceni, A. (2015). The core team and the extended team. In N. I. Cherny, M. Fallon, S. Kaasa, R. K. Portenoy, & D. C. Currow (Eds.), *Oxford textbook of palliative medicine.* New York, NY: Oxford University Press.

Hudson, P., Trauer, T., Graham, S., Grande, G., Ewing, G., Payne, S., . . . Thomas, K. (2010). A systematic review of instruments related to family caregivers of palliative care patients. *Palliative Medicine, 24*, 656–668.

Hughes, S., Firth, P., & Oliviere, D. (2014). Core competencies for palliative care social work in Europe: An EAPC white paper–part 1. *European Journal of Palliative Care, 21*, 300–305.

Hughes, S., Firth, P., & Oliviere, D. (2015). Core competencies for palliative care social work in Europe: An EAPC white paper–part 2. *European Journal of Palliative Care, 22*, 38–44.

Jünger, S., Eggenberger, E., Greenwood, A., & Payne, S. (2010). Psychologists in palliative care in Europe: A discipline "under construction": Abstracts of the 6th Research Congress of the European Association for Palliative Care. *Palliative Medicine, 24*, 212–213.

Jünger, S., & Payne, S. (2011). Guidance on the postgraduate education for psychologists involved in palliative care. *European Journal of Palliative Care, 18*, 238–252.

Kalus, C., Beloff, H., Brennan, J., McWilliams, E., Payne, S., Royan, L., & Russel, P. (2008). *The role of psychology in end of life care: A report published by the professional practice board of the British Psychological Society.* Leicester: The British Psychological Society.

Kasl-Godley, J. E., King, D. A., & Quill, T. E. (2014). Opportunities for psychologists in palliative care: Working with patients and families across the disease continuum. *American Psychologist, 69*, 364–376.

Kissane, D. W., McKenzie, M., Bloch, S., Moskowitz, C., McKenzie, D. P., & O'Neill, I. (2006). Family focused grief therapy: A randomized controlled trial in palliative care and bereavement. *American Journal of Psychiatry, 163*, 1208–1218.

Lacasta Reverte, M. A., Rocafort Gil, J., Blanco Toro, L., Timoneo Limonero, J., Garcia, I., & Gomez Batista, X. (2008). Intervención psicológica en Cuidados Paliativos. Análisis de los servicios prestados en España. *Medicina Palliativa, 15*, 39–44.

Lloyd Williams, M. (Ed.). (2008). *Psychosocial issues in palliative care* (2nd ed.). Oxford: Oxford University Press.

Lo, C., Hales, S., Jung, J., Chiu, A., Panday, T., Rydall, A., . . . Rodin, G. (2014). Managing Cancer and Living Meaningfully (CALM): Phase 2 trial of a brief individual psychotherapy for patients with advanced cancer. *Palliative Medicine, 28*, 234–242.

Mehnert, A. (2015). Clinical psychology in palliative care. In N. I. Cherny, M. Fallon, S. Kaasa, R. K. Portenoy, & D. C. Currow (Eds.), *Oxford textbook of palliative medicine* (5th ed.). New York, NY: Oxford University Press.

National Comprehensive Cancer Network. (2003). Distress management clinical practice guidelines in oncology. *Journal of the National Comprehensive Cancer Network, 1*, 344–374.

National Institute for Health and Clinical Excellence. (2004). *Improving supportive and palliative care for adults with cancer.* London: NICE.

National Recommendations for Palliative Care. (2011). *Danish health authorities [Anbefalinger til palliative indsats, Sundhedsstyrelsen].* Copenhagen, Denmark. Retrieved from www.sst.dk/~/media/3B57BB8B65014D73B47A7023546B4A62.ashx

Nydegger, R. (2008). Psychologists and hospice: Where we are and where we can be. *Professional Psychology: Research and Practice, 39*, 459–463.

Parkes, C. M. (2000). Hospice: A psychiatric perspective. In H. M. Chochinov & W. Breitbart (Eds.), *Handbook of psychiatry in palliative medicine.* New York, NY: Oxford University Press.

Payne, S., & Haines, R. (2002). The contribution of psychologists to specialist palliative care. *International Journal of Palliative Nursing, 8*, 401–406.

Rayner, L., Higginson, I. J., Price, A., & Hotopf, M. (2010). *The management of depression in palliative care: European clinical guidelines.* London: Department of Palliative Care, Policy & Rehabilitation/European Palliative Care Research Collaborative. Retrieved from www.epcrc.org

Shear, K., Frank, E., Houck, P. R., & Reynolds, C. F. (2005). Treatment of complicated grief: A randomized controlled Trial. *JAMA, 293*, 2601–2608.

Vodermaier, A., Linden, W., & Siu, C. (2009). Screening for emotional distress in cancer patients: A systematic review of assessment instruments. *Journal of the National Cancer Institute, 101*, 1464–1488.

Von Heyman-Horan, A., Puggaard, L. B., Nissen, K. G., Benthien, K. S., Bidstrup, P., Coyne, J., . . . Guldin, M. (2016). Dyadic psychological intervention for patients with cancer and caregivers in home-based specialized palliative care: The Domus model. *Palliative and Supportive Care*, 1–9. doi:10.1017/S1478951517000141

WHO. (2016). *Planning and implementing palliative care services: A guide for programme managers.* Geneva: World Health Organisation. Retrieved from www.who.int/cancer/publications/cancer_control_palliative/en/ [Last retrieved online 12–3–2016]

Chapter 8

Synthesis and the future of end-of-life care

Brian D. Carpenter, Morgan K. Eichorst, Hillary R. Dorman, and Rebecca S. Allen

Core themes and needs in the evidence base across chapters

As in our companion volume, Table 8.1 presents a brief review of the information provided in the chapters within this book. As stated in Chapter 1 of both volumes, the editors asked that each of the writing teams include in their work certain material: 1) a review of behavioural interventions, 2) an evaluation of the strength of the evidence base, 3) identification of gaps within the knowledge base, 4) coverage of cultural and diversity issues, 5) consideration of ethical issues, 6) practice implications, and 7) at least one case example with questions illustrating salient issues. Certain core themes are evident across chapters in this text, as was true in our companion volume.

Each of the authorship teams makes clear and concise recommendations for practice that consider the wishes of the patient within the context of a given treatment site or illness context. Ethical considerations of the balance between patient autonomy and provider beneficent responsibility, and between provider beneficent responsibility and nonmaleficence, and considerations of justice permeate the chapters. A limiting factor that continues to pervade the establishment and implementation of effective behavioural mental health and wellness interventions in palliative and end-of-life care concerns reimbursement issues and the economic context of these services in healthcare systems globally. Within the United States, interprofessional palliative care provision that embraces behavioural and psychosocial care is the norm within the Veterans Affairs medical system but is rarely available in community healthcare. In the next section, we consider the cost effectiveness of palliative and end-of-life care as well as the economic context underlying healthcare systems.

Policy and the economic context of palliative and end-of-life care

Research supports the cost effectiveness of palliative and end-of-life care (May et al., 2016; Sahlen, Bowmen, & Bränströmm, 2016; Smith, Brick, O'Hara, & Normand, 2014), yet economic and policy barriers exist in the implementation

Table 8.1 Core themes in evidence base supporting behavioural interventions in palliative and end-of-life care

Chapter	Topic	Themes
2	HIV/AIDS	• Historic perspective on treatment of HIV/AIDS and discussion of its current status as a chronic disease. • Individuals with HIV/AIDS living longer. • Access to care as it relates to economic advantage and disadvantage (Deep South). • Urban-rural access to care issues. • Cultural issues (e.g., stigma). • Access to antivirals in the US and various countries in Africa. • Recommendations for elements of interventions within this disease context. • Case examples are two interviews with providers in the Deep South of the US, one in an urban university hospital setting and one in the Alabama Black Belt.
3	Severe Mental Illness	• People with SMI are vulnerable to more complicated illness trajectories, multiple comorbidities, and early mortality. • Individual, social, and institutional factors are prominent barriers to receiving adequate care. • Outside of depression and anxiety, there is very little evidence of the effectiveness of palliative care interventions. • Professionals with mental health expertise have much to share with palliative care providers.
4	Dementia	• Good bit of evidence based in the UK that dementia care is essentially palliative. • Emphasis on quality of end-of-life care for individuals with dementia through pain and other symptom assessment. • Ample evidence for the effectiveness of end-of-life interventions based on surveys with European Association of Palliative Care (EAPC) providers. • The role of caregivers for individual with dementia in end-of-life care. • Patient-centered care through systematic culture change within organizations. • To create and maintain sustained quality improvement, not only do staff need education and training but all levels of staff need leaders and collaborators to drive this change.

(*Continued*)

Table 8.1 (Continued)

Chapter	Topic	Themes
5	Ethics	• Patient autonomy, provider beneficent responsibility, and provider nonmaleficence can be in tension in end-of-life contexts. • Roles of physicians, psychiatry, psychology, nursing. • Impact of health literacy and palliative care literacy. • Medical aid in dying. • Interventions include educational interventions for providers. • Potential inclusion of family members in interprofessional team meetings.
6	Bereavement	• Clinical perspectives regarding bereavement practices in different populations (chapter written by providers). • There is little evidence-based guidance for health professionals and others providing bereavement support. • Diversity among subpopulations of the US.
7	Policy	• Role of psychologists in interprofessional or interdisciplinary teams across Europe with some information about Australia. • Varying levels of involvement of mental health professionals (NICE model). • Focus a good bit on the role of psychologists in interprofessional teams across Europe. Case examples primarily from Denmark and the UK, the location of the authors. Also cover programs in Spain. European Association of Palliative Care (EAPC) survey results list six roles of psychologists across countries. • No information on reimbursement or the role of palliative care within various healthcare systems as this would be a book in itself. • The underlying idea of the NICE model has been incorporated into clinical guidelines, including the evidence-based standards for bereavement care in Australia. Recommends that psychosocial and supportive care be provided in a targeted way and that people's strengths and resilience should be included in the assessment.

The future of end-of-life care 173

of palliative care worldwide. One such perceived barrier may be concerns about the costs of interprofessional palliative and end-of-life care, resulting in greater staffing needs and questions about reimbursement of each member of the inter-professional team (Kasl-Godley, King, & Quill, 2014). It is imperative for behavioural and mental health and wellness treatments to be patient-centered and of high quality; thus, questions about staffing costs may arise.

Smith and colleagues (2014) conducted a comprehensive literature review on direct costs and cost effectiveness of palliative care over the period from 2002 to 2011. These authors developed 31 quality indicators for rating research studies and examined international evidence of cost savings. Forty-six studies met inclusion criteria, and these studies consisted of randomized controlled trials, cohort studies, and case studies. It is notable that 31 of the studies were based in the United States, with other studies occurring in Europe, Canada, and Taiwan. Although studies varied widely in type and quality, palliative care was frequently found to be less costly relative to comparators. In most instances, this cost savings was statistically significant.

More specific examples of palliative care cost effectiveness research include May and colleagues (2016), who examined the impact of palliative care consultation on hospital costs for adults with advanced cancer and comorbidities, excluding dementia. Cancer is frequently the disease context in which palliative care cost savings analyses are conducted; however, this study is unique in addressing how cost savings might be impacted by physical and mental comorbidities near the end of life. These authors found that cost savings were greater when hospitalized patients had more comorbidities and when palliative care consultations happened earlier during the hospitalization. While important, these findings need to be extended by examining dementia as a comorbid condition. Chapter 4 of this book addresses palliative and end-of-life care within the context of dementia.

Not all palliative and end-of-life care is hospital based, as is clearly evident throughout the chapters contained in this book. Therefore, it is important to address potential cost savings of palliative care delivered in outpatient clinics or at home. A group of researchers in Sweden (Sahlen et al., 2016) examined potential cost savings among heart failure patients who were randomized to receive either palliative home care, care within a heart failure clinic, or care within the hospital. In addition to a significant cost reduction observed in palliative home care, heart failure patients assigned to this condition gained 0.25 quality-adjusted life years. Thus, the preponderance of evidence across studies is that, even if patient-centered palliative care may be more staff-intensive, concerns about cost outlay for greater staffing are outweighed by improved physical and emotional health outcomes among patients.

Given these demonstrated cost savings, why then is not palliative and end-of-life care the first-line healthcare delivery system globally? In the United States, Medicare and Medicaid are the two largest insurers, and although Medicare contains the hospice benefit, Medicare does not cover all of an older or disabled person's healthcare needs near the end of life (Norris, 2015). Profit seeking by for-profit organizations that provide palliative and end-of-life care has been identified as a major problem, as providers may be incentivized to spend less than they receive from Medicare and Medicaid (Ludwig, 2017). Ludwig reports concerns that, under a single-payer system, there would be a political incentive to require private hospice and palliative care providers to be more transparent in their financial affairs in order to receive public funds. Hence, in the United States, where a true and universal single payer healthcare system does not exist, even clear evidence of cost savings within palliative and end-of-life care may not overcome policy and political barriers for implementation.

These policy and economic barriers result in significant health disparities in palliative and end-of-life care, presenting ethical issues with regard to distributive justice, or the equitable distribution of resources (Chapter 5). For example, Medicare reimburses rural hospices at a lower rate because the hospice wage index does not account for longer travel times to homes in rural areas that result in higher costs of care for in-home service delivery (Lynch, 2013). Geographic disparities in hospice and palliative care may be exacerbated by racial/ethnic healthcare disparities, and relatively higher median household income is associated with increased availability of hospice services (Hardy et al., 2011; Silveira, Connor, Goold, McMahon, & Feudtner, 2011). People with adequate income are more likely to die in hospice care than those with lower income. It is possible that these disparities may be reduced and eventually eliminated by engaging rural service providers in dialogue to guide development of programs for remote service provision. Small rural hospitals that initiate palliative care programs save money (Cassel, Webb-Wright, Holmes, Lyckholm, & Smith, 2010). Cassel and colleagues found that hospital costs at a 76-bed rural nonprofit hospital were reduced by 25% after palliative care consultation services were initiated, and quality of care was not compromised.

The evidence presented here, and elsewhere in this volume, makes clear two messages. First, there are myriad benefits (e.g., reduced healthcare costs, effective symptom alleviation) to palliative and end-of-life behavioural interventions, for individuals, their families, providers, and possibly society as a whole. However, it is clear that there are significant barriers to implementing such shifts in the current paradigms of care. And those barriers operate at several levels: misconceptions among patients and care partners, lack of information among providers, and biases within policies. These realities lay out a clear path for the future of the field. What is needed is the will to follow that path.

Future directions

Forecasting the future of anything is a risky undertaking, particularly in the case of palliative care, given how rapidly it is developing and changing. Nonetheless, there is some value in considering what may lie ahead for the field, if only to suggest areas that currently need – and will continue to need – the attention of scholars and practitioners.

The likely future for palliative care

One trend already underway is a **broadening of the reach and scope of palliative care and hospice services**. A perennial challenge has been getting these services to patients earlier in the course of serious illness, and palliative care consultations and referrals to hospice continue to be provided later than is ideal (Kozlov, Carpenter, Thorsten, Heiland, & Agarwal, 2015; National Hospice and Palliative Care Organization, 2017). In fact, the median length of stay for hospice decedents was 17 days in 2015 and has remained relatively stable over the last ten years (Medicare Payment Advisory Commission, 2017). Some progress has been made in this regard, but services continue to be underutilized relative to their potential benefit and cost savings. Running parallel to earlier adoption are efforts to integrate palliative care in additional practice settings, such as primary care (McCormick, Chai, & Meier, 2012; Murray & Osman, 2012). The broadening application of palliative care is also evident in the expansion of the scope of service, as in the case of recent projects that have relaxed the definition of hospice eligibility and allowed patients to pursue curative treatments that might have been off limits in more traditional models. These demonstration projects have been conducted by several insurance carriers, and a similar model was written into the Affordable Care Act in the United States (Section 2302: Concurrent Care for Children). Finally, palliative care has challenged itself, as a field, to adopt a more expansive view of its role and potential contribution, as in calls for palliative care to embrace a public health mindset (Conway, 2008; Dempers & Gott, 2017).

These trends offer several opportunities for novel contributions. For example, theories and methods from the behavioural and social sciences could be useful resources to enhance awareness and promote uptake of palliative care and hospice services. Cognitive, social, and personality research within psychology could help us understand how people appraise personal risk and susceptibility, evaluate and act on the salience of their symptoms, and accept or reject messages from healthcare providers about service and treatment recommendations. For instance, the Health Action Process Approach (Schwarzer, Lippke, & Luszczynska, 2011) is one framework to understand the components of behaviour change, and this model has been applied specifically to people with serious chronic illness. In another area, research findings from the learning sciences could be applied to the development of effective methods for educating patients and providers. Likewise, basic research on attention, memory, reasoning, and judgement could be applied to the decision-making required of patients weighing treatment options, choosing surrogates, and clarifying goals of care. Similar cognitive processes are obviously at work when clinicians make prognostic formulations, treatment recommendations, and even decisions about when to seek a palliative care consultation and offer referrals to hospice. In sum, behavioural theories have much to add to how care for people with serious illness is enacted.

A second trend involves the likely **expanding role of technology** in the provision of palliative care and hospice services. Already we have seen technology applied to patient monitoring of sleep, activity level, and self-reported pain, among other symptoms (e.g., Patel, Park, Bonato, Chan, & Rodgers, 2012; Theile, Klaas, Troster, & Guckenberger, 2017), and telehealth has become more accessible for patient assessment and monitoring (de Jongh, Gurol-Urganci, Vodopivec-Jamsek, Car, & Atun, 2012; Guo, Cann, McClement, Thompson, & Chochinov, 2017). Innovative work by Wittenberg-Lyles and colleagues (2010) has demonstrated the benefits of team and family care coordination meetings conducted virtually, enabling involvement in care planning when time and distance might have otherwise posed substantial barriers. Social media platforms and virtual communities have been used in the context of some diseases (e.g., www.caringbridge.org/), to build networks for information and support, and these resources could be employed more strategically and their impact evaluated more systematically. Emerging technologies also offer the potential to deliver psychosocial services in a more efficient and accessible manner. Digitally based interventions delivered via smartphone or tablet, such as apps for relaxation or mindfulness, offer the promise of wider scale dissemination. Another example may be in the application of virtual reality technology, which is already used in some psychological interventions for anxiety but may also have applications for other symptoms. In addition to their potential therapeutic applications, these technologies often have embedded data gathering features that might simplify research. Promising though these innovations may be, it is imperative to consider issues of justice and the equitable access for *all* near the end of life, without prejudice based on personal or environmental characteristics.

Here, too, the behavioural and social sciences have expertise that could be utilized to enhance the expanding role of technology in palliative care. There is an opportunity to apply psychological theories and practices in developing efficient, psychometrically sound assessment strategies that rely on technology. In addition, behavioural expertise in communication, interpersonal dynamics, and healthcare communication is relevant as digitally delivered interventions expand. Finally, behavioural knowledge of human-machine interaction and human factors design could be useful as technologies are placed in the hands of patients and their care partners. With their knowledge of conducting intervention trials, evaluating efficacy and effectiveness, and developing community partnerships for these efforts, behavioural scientists are well positioned to make important contributions.

A third trend already emerging as important (and only likely to become more so) is the necessity of **demonstrating the clinical and financial impact** of palliative and end-of-life care services. The Triple Aim of healthcare reform is to improve the experience of care (quality and satisfaction), improve population health, and reduce per capita healthcare costs through greater integration of care (Berwick, Nolan, & Whittington, 2008). An extended version of this model – the Quadruple Aim – adds practitioner well-being as a priority (Bodenheimer & Sinsky, 2014; Sikka, Morath, & Leape, 2015). In order to accomplish these goals, of course, we must reach some consensus on the specific ways palliative and hospice care contribute to these aims, operationalize these contributions, and implement a systematic strategy by which they are evaluated, across care settings, types of patients, and other clinical and contextual attributes. Several initiatives are aligned with this goal.

For example, in the United States, the National Palliative Care Registry, a joint project by the Center to Advance Palliative Care and the National Palliative Care Research Center, provides guidance for member programs to help them evaluate their services (Dy et al., 2015). Four categories of data are recommended: operational data (e.g., volume and type of referrals), clinical data (e.g., pain and symptom control), customer data (e.g., satisfaction), and financial data (e.g., cost per day). Although the registry currently focuses on broad metrics related to service provision, it does hold the potential to include an expanded set of measures focused on psychosocial outcomes. One collection of such instruments has been gathered by the Palliative Care Research Cooperative Group, which maintains an instrument library and extensive description of the applicability of over 150 instruments selected based on a thorough literature review and analysis. Within efforts like these, behavioural and social scientists have the expertise needed to develop and evaluate psychometrically sound, culturally sensitive tools to assess constructs such as quality, satisfaction, and well-being.

A final important trend on the horizon is the ongoing evolution of **medical aid in dying** (MAID) policy and practice. Setting aside for the moment the complex ethical issues involved, in recent years there has been a gradual expansion of MAID, at least in the United States, as public opinion has grown more supportive and as legislative advocacy efforts have intensified (Gallup, 2016). Even among the U.S. states where MAID is currently legal, however, there is substantial variability in application, and no consensus has yet emerged on many key issues, including those with psychological implications. For example, legislation in every state requires that people requesting MAID be evaluated by a specialist (e.g., psychologist, psychiatrist) when there is concern about the individual's capacity to understand the choice they are making. However, despite valuable initial efforts (e.g., Hudson et al., 2006; Johnson, Cramer, Gardner, & Nobles, 2015; Werth, Benjamin, & Farrenkopf, 2000), there is neither a general consensus nor established practice guidelines that address 1) how physicians who have received a request for MAID should determine whether capacity is a concern and thus refer people for further evaluation, and 2) how mental health professionals should conduct such an evaluation, when a request for assistance in dying has unique clinical elements not seen in other capacity evaluation contexts.

With some exceptions, the research literature is scant on how to differentiate the sadness and a wish for a hastened death that might be expected when a person is near the end of life from clinical depression and suicidal ideation (Balaguer et al., 2016; O'Mahony et al., 2005). Requests for aid in dying are likely fueled by a complex set of personal, interpersonal, and situational factors (Smith, Harvath, Goy, & Ganzini, 2015), distinct in important ways from suicidal ideation and behaviour (Fiske, Smith, & Price, 2015). Likewise, there are more questions than answers about how to treat individuals whose psychological condition might disqualify them for MAID. For example, when a mental health specialist believes that a depressive disorder is clouding the judgement of an individual requesting MAID, how is that disorder best treated in an individual who may not have much time to live? And is the ultimate treatment goal to improve their mental health so that they can "rationally" request MAID? Beyond their role in evaluating and treating individuals who request MAID, behavioural health specialists also possess knowledge and skills that could be helpful to others involved in the practice. These include providers who receive requests for MAID, patients who make the request, and family members, both before and after MAID is implemented.

The wished-for future of palliative care

The trends mentioned above reflect the current evolution of palliative care and the likely direction that the field will grow in the years ahead. In this final section, we take one step further and share what we *hope* will happen for the field. These aspirations fall into three broad areas.

First, as mentioned in Chapter 1, there is a clear need to **improve public awareness** of palliative and hospice care and knowledge about how those services can benefit patients and families. Recent survey data reveal that despite the improved penetration of palliative care and hospice services throughout the United States (Morrison & Meier, 2015), knowledge among laypeople and even other healthcare professionals remains fragmented (Cagle et al., 2016; Kozlov, McDarby, Reid, & Carpenter, 2017; Shalev et al., 2017). A lack of knowledge about palliative care (or limited palliative care literacy; see Chapter 5) may be a significant obstacle to uptake, and educational efforts could help more people see the benefits of accessing palliative care services. Behavioural scientists may be helpful in this area, by developing educational programs that remedy misconceptions and address hesitation about the service. Furthermore, patient coaching interventions (see Carpenter & McDarby in *Perspectives on Behavioural Interventions in Palliative and End-of-Life Care*) could be used to empower patients and family members to inquire proactively about palliative care services and advocate for their availability.

A second aspiration for palliative care is for **more deep and broad interprofessional collaboration that integrates behavioural health providers** more routinely. To begin, within the behavioural health professions themselves it is important to articulate a set of core competencies about what psychologists, psychiatrists, and other professionals with behavioural and mental health training should know in order to work in this area. Such core competencies are essential for training and a clear definition of scope of practice. One effort in this area began in 2009, when the European Association for Palliative Care (EAPC) created a Task Force on Education for Psychologists in Palliative Care, which

The future of end-of-life care 179

began to formulate a scope of practice for psychologists working in the field (see Chapters 4 and 7). At the conclusion of its work in 2011, the Task Force published its Guidance on Postgraduate Education for Psychologists involved in Palliative Care (Junger & Payne, 2011), which provides input on curriculum development for postgraduate training for psychologists involved in palliative care, including details on target populations, core competencies, and key areas of practice. A parallel effort in Ireland has resulted in a set of discipline-specific competencies for psychologists working in palliative care (Palliative Care Competence Framework Steering Group, 2014). This competency framework covers six domains, including basic principles of palliative care; communication; optimizing comfort and quality of life; care planning and collaborative practice; loss, grief, and bereavement; and professional and ethical practice. The competencies are also structured to describe knowledge and skills that are expected of all psychologists, more specific competencies expected of psychologists who work more routinely with people with life-limiting conditions, and discipline-specific competencies for psychologists who work primarily in palliative care. The United States lags in this effort, although an informal set of competencies was articulated in a seminal article by Kasl-Godley, King, and Quill (2014).

A related challenge lies in articulating exactly what the aforementioned competencies are to colleagues in other disciplines. At least in the United States, palliative and hospice care is populated by a fairly standard team of professionals, most often consisting of a physician, nurse, social worker, and chaplain, with occasional ancillary services provided by other clinical disciplines. (One exception is in the VA healthcare system, where psychologists are required members of each palliative care team.) Before psychologists will be invited to participate in end-of-life care, other providers need to know – and likely be shown – how a psychologist's involvement could be helpful; that is, what is the unique knowledge and skill a psychologist has that could complement the services provided by other disciplines when caring for someone with serious illness. Behavioural health providers need to articulate more effectively what contribution they can make, acknowledging that there are areas of practice overlap with other disciplines on the team. At the same time, behavioural and mental health practitioners could be more proactive in promoting the services that can benefit patients and family members, such as specialized assessment and treatment of psychological distress, and their expertise in supporting other providers, such as offering insight into team dynamics and assisting with program evaluation and research.

Overall, behavioural and mental health providers need to be better and more consistently integrated across the care continuum. Behavioural and mental health symptoms should be included as key outcomes in end-of-life care. And other outcomes with obvious psychological foundations (e.g., quality of life, quality of death, existential distress) require more systematic, empirically grounded clarification.

A third and final aspiration is for an **expanded evidence base** that can guide behavioural and mental health practice in this area. For instance, the field needs updated and comprehensive data on the prevalence and incidence of psychological issues that arise when living with serious illness. Similarly, we need to determine whether constructs such as depression and anxiety, resilience and meaning making, have unique elements in the context of life-limiting illness that might alter approaches for assessment. Assessment tools are needed that are psychometrically sound in this group of patients and normed for key subgroups.

There are similar needs in terms of intervention and treatment. Systematic research programs are essential for developing evidence-based interventions for key symptoms (e.g., agitation, insomnia) and care processes (e.g., diagnostic/prognostic communication, goals of care discussions, bereavement support). One admirable example of this is the work by Chochinov and colleagues (2013) to develop a model of therapeutic effectiveness and evaluate their Dignity Therapy treatment (see *Perspectives on Behavioural Interventions in Palliative and End-of-Life Care*). Once well established, treatments need to be tailored for distinct patient groups, based on characteristics such as age, social identities, health literacy, and disease. Finally, in order to broaden access to services, interventions are needed that can be delivered by a range of professionals, via flexible modes. In the case of depression and anxiety, for instance, it may be effective to adopt a stepped care approach: teach nursing staff to administer brief interventions for relatively mild symptoms, train non-palliative care specialty mental health providers to deliver treatments for more moderate symptoms, and expand access to behavioural and mental health practitioners with specialty training and competence in end-of-life care.

In conclusion, as this chapter and both of our edited books have made clear, there is much work to be done. Behavioural and mental health needs are a critical facet of high-quality care for people with serious illness. Indeed, any contemporary definition of palliative care cites the importance of psychological and social factors. In order to address that need, behavioural and mental health practices (and providers) are essential. The challenge ahead – and the opportunity – is to make that care more systematic and more accessible for the benefit of patients and their care partners.

References

Balaguer, A., Monforte-Royo, C., Porta-Sales, J., Alonso-Babarro, A., Altisent, R., Aradilla-Herrero, A., et al. (2016). An international consensus definition of the wish to hasten death and its related factors. *PloS ONE, 11*(1), e0146184. doi:10.1371/journal.pone.0146184

Berwick, D. M., Nolan, T. W., & Whittington, J. (2008). The triple aim: Care, health, and cost. *Health Affairs, 27*(3), 759–769. doi:10.1377/hlthaff.27.3.759

Bodenheimer, T., & Sinsky, C. (2014). From triple to quadruple aim: Care of the patient requires care of the provider. *The Annals of Family Medicine, 12*, 573–576. http://dx.doi.org/10.1370/afm.1713

Cagle, J. G., Van Dussen, D. J., Culler, K. L., Carrion, I., Hong, S., Guralnik, J., & Zimmerman, S. (2016). Knowledge about hospice: Exploring misconceptions, attitudes,

The future of end-of-life care 181

and preferences for care. *American Journal of Hospice and Palliative Medicine, 33*, 27–33. doi:10.1177/1049909114546885

Cassel, J. B., Webb-Wright, J., Holmes, J., Lyckholm, L., & Smith, T. J. (2010). Clinical and financial impact of a palliative care program at a small rural hospital. *Journal of Palliative Medicine, 13*(11), 1339–1343.

Chochinov, H. M., McClement, S. E., Hack, T. F., McKeen, N. A., Rach, A. M., Gagnon, P., . . . Taylor-Brown, J. (2013). Health care provider communication: An empirical model of therapeutic effectiveness. *Cancer, 119*, 1706–1713. doi:10.1002/cncr.27949

Conway, S. (2008). Public health and palliative care: Principles into practice? *Critical Public Health, 18*, 405–415.

de Jongh, T., Gurol-Urganci, I., Vodopivec-Jamsek, V., Car, J., & Atun, R. (2012). Mobile phone messaging for facilitating self-management of long-term illness. *Cochrane Database of Systematic Reviews, 12*. Art. No.: CD007459. doi:10.1002/14651858.CD007459.pub2

Dempers, C., & Gott, M. (2017). Which public health approach to palliative care? An integrative literature review. *Progress in Palliative Care, 25*.

Dy, S.M., Kiley K. B., Ast, K., Lupu, D., Norton, S. A., McMillan, S. C., . . . Casarett, D. J. (2015). Measuring what matters: Top-ranked quality indicators for hospice and palliative care from the American Academy of Hospice and Palliative Medicine and Hospice and Palliative Nurses Association. Journal of Pain and Symptom Management, 49, 773–781.

Fiske, A., Smith, M. D., & Price, E. C. (2015). Suicidal behavior in older adults. In P. A. Lichtenberg & B. T. Mast (Eds.), *APA handbook of clinical geropsychology* (pp. 145–172). Washington, DC: American Psychological Association.

Gallup. (2016). *Euthanasia still acceptable to solid majority in U.S.* Retrieved from www.gallup.com/poll/193082/euthanasia-acceptable-solid-majority.aspx

Guo, Q., Cann, B., McClements, S., Thompson, G., & Chochinov, H. M. (2017). Keep in Touch (KIT): Feasibility of using internet-based communication and information technology in palliative care. *BMC Palliative Care, 16*, 29. doi:10.1186/s12904-017-0203-2

Hardy, D., Chan, W., Liu, C.-C., Cormier, J. N., Xia, R., Bruera, E., & Du, X. L. (2011). Racial disparities in the use of hospice services according to geographic residence and socioeconomic status in an elderly cohort with nonsmall cell lung cancer. *Cancer, 117*(7), 1506–1515.

Hudson, P. L., Schofield, P., Kelly, B., Hudson, R., Street, A., O'Connor, M., . . . Aranda, S. (2006). Responding to desire to die statements from patients with advanced disease: Recommendations for health professionals. *Palliative Medicine, 20*, 703–710. doi:10.1177/0269216306071814

Johnson, S. M., Cramer, R. J., Gardner, B. O., & Nobles, M. R. (2015). What patient and psychologist characteristics are important in competency for physician-assisted suicide evaluations? *Psychology, Public Policy, and Law, 21*, 420–431. doi:10.1037/law0000058

Junger, S., & Payne, S. (2011). Guidance on postgraduate education for psychologists involved in palliative care. *European Journal of Palliative Care, 18*, 238–252.

Kasl-Godley, J., King, D., & Quill, T. (2014). Opportunities for psychologists in palliative care: Working with patients and families across the disease continuum. *American Psychologist, 69*, 364–376. http://dx.doi.org/10.1037/a0036735

Kozlov, E., Carpenter, B. D., Thorsten, M., Heiland, M., & Agarwal, A. (2015). Timing of palliative care consultations and recommendations: Understanding the variability. *American Journal of Hospice and Palliative Medicine, 32*, 772–775. doi:10.1177/1049909114543322

Kozlov, E., McDarby, M., Reid, C., & Carpenter, B. D. (2017). Knowledge of palliative care among community-dwelling adults. *American Journal of Hospice and Palliative Medicine*, 1–5. doi:10.1177/1049909117725725

Ludwig, M. (2017). Single payer is the alternative to dying under austerity. *Health over Profit*, 1–6. http://healthoverprofit.org/2017/06/14/single-payer-is-the-alternative-to-dying-under-austerity/

Lynch, S. (2013). Hospice and palliative care access issues in rural areas. *American Journal of Hospice and Palliative Medicine, 30*(2), 172–177.

May, P., Garrido, M. M., Cassel, J. B., Kelley, A. S., Meier, D. E., Normand, C., . . . Morrison, R. S. (2016). Palliative care teams cost-saving effect is larger for cancer patients with higher numbers of comorbidities. *Health Affairs, 35*(1), 44–53.

McCormick, E., Chai, E., & Meier, D. E. (2012). Integrating palliative care into primary care. *Mount Sinai Journal of Medicine, 79*, 579–585.

Medicare Payment Advisory Commission. (2017, March). *Report to Congress: Medicare payment policy*. Retrieved from www.medpac.gov/docs/default-source/reports/mar17_medpac_ch12.pdf?sfvrsn=0

Morrison, S., & Meier, D. M. (2015). *America's care of serious illness: 2015 state-by-state report card on access to palliative care in our nation's hospitals*. New York: Center to Advance Palliative Care. Retrieved from https://reportcard.capc.org/wp-content/uploads/2015/08/CAPC-Report-Card-2015.pdf

Murray, S. A., & Osman, H. (2012). Primary palliative care: The potential of primary care physicians as providers of palliative care in the community in the Eastern Mediterranean region. *Eastern Mediterranean Health Journal, 18*, 178–183.

National Hospice and Palliative Care Organization. (2017, September). *NHPCO facts and figures: Hospice care in America*. Alexandria, VA: National Hospice and Palliative Care Organization.

Norris, M. (2015). Evolutions and revolutions in Medicare policy and reimbursement of geropsychology services. In P. A. Lichtenberg & B. T. Mast (Eds.), *APA handbook of clinical geropsychology* (Vol. 1, pp. 45–70). Washington, DC: American Psychological Association.

O'Mahony, S., Goulet, J., Kornblith, A., Abbatiello, G., Clarke, B., Kless-Siegel, S., . . . Payne, R. (2005). Desire for hastened death, cancer pain and depression: Report of a longitudinal observational study. *Journal of Pain and Symptom Management, 29*, 446–457. doi:10.1016/j.jpainsymman.2004.08.010

Palliative Care Competence Framework Steering Group. (2014). *Palliative care competence framework*. Dublin: Health Service Executive.

Patel, S., Park, H., Bonato, P., Chan, L., & Rodgers, M. (2012). A review of wearable sensors and systems with application in rehabilitation. *Journal of NeuroEngineering and Rehabilitation, 9*, 21. https://doi.org/10.1186/1743-0003-9-21

Sahlen, K.-G., Bowmen, K., & Bränströmm, M. (2016). A cost effectiveness study of person-centered integrated heart failure and palliative home care: Based on a randomized controlled trial. *Palliative Medicine, 30*(3), 296–302.

Schwarzer, R., Lippke, S., & Luszczynska, A. (2011). Mechanisms of health behavior change in persons with chronic illness or disability: The Health Action Process Approach (HAPA). *Rehabilitation Psychology, 56*, 161–170. doi:10.1037/a0024509

Shalev, A., Phongtankuel, V., Kozlov, E., Shen, M. J., Adelman, R. D., & Reid, M. C. (2017). Awareness and misperceptions of hospice and palliative care: A population-based survey study. *American Journal of Hospice and Palliative Medicine*, 1–9. doi:10.1177/1049909117715215

Sikka, R., Morath, J. M., & Leape, L. (2015). The Quadruple Aim: Care, health, cost and meaning in work. *BMJ Quality Safety, 24*, 608–610.

Silveira, M. J., Connor, S. R., Goold, S. D., McMahon, L. F., & Feudtner, C. (2011). Community supply of hospice: Does wealth play a role? *Journal of Pain and Symptom Management, 42*(1), 76–82.

Smith, K. A., Harvath, T. A., Goy, E. R., & Ganzini, L. (2015). Predictors of pursuit of physician-assisted death. *Journal of Pain and Symptom Management, 49*, 555–561.

Smith, S., Brick, A., O'Hara, S., & Normand, C. (2014). Evidence on the cost and cost-effectiveness of palliative care: A literature review. *Palliative Medicine, 28*(2), 130–150.

Theile, G., Klaas, V., Troster, G., & Guckenberger, M. (2017). mHealth technologies for palliative care patients at the interface of inpatient to outpatient care: Protocol feasibility study aiming to early predict deterioration of patient's health status. *JMIR Research Protocols, 6*, e142. doi:10.2196/resprot.7676

Werth, J. L., Benjamin, G. A., & Farrenkopf, T. (2000). Requests for physician-assisted death: Guidelines for assessing mental capacity and impaired judgement. *Psychology, Public Policy and the Law, 6*, 348–372. doi:10.1037/1076-8971.6.2.348

Wittenberg-Lyles, E., Parker Oliver, D., Demiris, G., & Baldwin, P. (2010). The ACTive intervention in hospice interdisciplinary team meetings: Exploring family caregiver and hospice team communication. *Journal of Computer Mediated Communication, 15*, 465–481. doi:10.1111/j.1083-6101.2010.01502.x

Index

acceptance and commitment therapy 41, 48; suffering 1–2, 8, 37, 43, 61, 68, 70–71, 91, 105–106, 144, 148–149, 152–155, 160, 165

Acquired Immunodeficiency Syndrome (AIDS) 3, 7–10, 13–17, 20–24, 26, 28, 119, 171

addiction 16, 19, 27, 33, 36–37

adherence: medication 7, 9–11, 13, 15–16, 32; treatment 8, 11, 13, 14, 15, 95–96

advance care planning 34, 60, 73–74, 93, 98–101, 108, 148

Africa 2–3, 11–12, 18, 20–22, 125, 136, 171

Alzheimer's disease 58–59, 61–62, 74–76, 78–79

antiretroviral therapies 7, 10, 28

anxiety/anxiety disorders 9, 16, 34–35, 41, 43–47, 49, 63, 78, 96, 121, 129, 149, 154–156, 158–159, 163, 165, 171, 176, 180

assessment 8–9, 13–14, 18, 34, 38, 41, 44, 61, 63–69, 76, 81, 91, 93, 112, 119, 153–157, 159–160, 165–166, 171–172, 176, 179–180

autonomy 20, 40, 70, 91, 94–96, 98, 100–101, 103, 105, 110, 123–124, 170, 172

beneficence 70, 92, 94–96, 98, 103

bereavement 3, 9, 12–13, 15, 22, 73, 77–78, 81, 91, 99, 119–128, 133–134, 136–137, 139–144, 148–149, 156–157, 159–160, 163–165, 172, 179–180; definition of 120; *vs.* grief and mourning 121; healthy 122; rituals of 125–126

biopsychosocial 2

cancer 8, 10, 15, 27, 33–47, 58–59, 61, 92, 100–101, 103, 119, 123, 140, 150–151, 153, 156–157, 159–161, 173

capacity/decision-making capacity 22, 36, 38, 42, 44–45, 70–74, 92–95, 100, 103, 105, 111, 160, 177

carer/caregiver 1, 9, 13–14, 18, 21–23, 33, 66–67, 70, 71–74, 76–78, 81, 92, 99, 109–110, 148, 156, 161, 163, 165, 171

chronic disease 11, 16, 27, 35, 171

Clinical Practice Guidelines for Quality Palliative Care (NCP) 108

Codes of Ethics 91, 108

cognitive behavioral therapy 15, 41, 145, 158, 160–162

comorbidity/multimorbidity 11, 35, 41, 69

cost effectiveness 170, 173–174

death with dignity *see* medical aid in dying

decision-making *see* capacity/decision-making capacity

delirium 71, 94, 155

dementia care 58–62, 76, 79–81, 171

depression 9, 12, 15–16, 27, 35, 39–41, 43–44, 77–78, 82, 119, 149, 154–155, 159, 161–163, 165, 171, 177, 180

desire for hastened death 43, 155, 177

dignity 41, 75, 157, 161, 180

discrimination 9, 11–12, 26, 28, 60, 127, 135

diversity 3, 7, 17–18, 23, 60, 81, 119–144, 170, 172

do-not-resuscitate orders 100, 124

Elder's life course approach 21, 25

environmental modifications 1, 48, 79, 176

ethical issues 2–3, 7, 20–21, 25, 38, 42, 60, 70–71, 73, 91–112, 119, 124, 170, 174, 177, 179

European Association for Palliative Care (EAPC) 58–61, 67, 69, 71, 74–75, 76–77,

186 Index

79, 108, 153–154, 157, 163, 171–172, 178; survey of European psychologists in palliative care 154
euthanasia *see* medical aid in dying

family 1, 8–9, 12–15, 17–19, 22–23, 27, 33, 37, 39–40, 42–43, 48, 60, 63, 65, 66, 70–74, 76–81, 91–95, 97–101, 103–104, 106, 109–112, 119–144, 148, 150, 152, 155–157, 159–160, 162–163, 165, 172, 176, 178–179

good death 92–93, 103

health literacy 11, 92, 96–98, 100–102, 104, 112, 172, 180
Hepatitis C 10, 16, 27
highly active antiretroviral therapies (HAARTs) 7–12, 13, 15–17, 21–22, 25, 28
Homegoing service 136
human immunodeficiency virus (HIV) 2–3, 7–28, 119, 171
hypnosis 161

implicit bias 26
interdisciplinary team *see* interprofessional team
interprofessional team 1–2, 4, 7, 11, 14–15, 17–18, 22, 27, 91, 93, 97, 106, 108–112, 149–150, 152, 154, 156, 165, 170, 172–173, 178
intersectionality/layering 12, 120

justice 20, 92, 95, 97, 110, 170, 174, 176

last rites 139–140
LGBT 127–128

medical aid in dying 43–44, 96, 172, 177
meditation 129, 160
Mental Capacity Act 70, 72–74
mindfulness 44–45, 48, 162, 176
mood disorders 39–40, 158

Namaste Care program 75–77, 80–81
National Institute for Clinical Excellence in England (NICE) 153; guidance on improving supportive and palliative care for adults with cancer 159; model of provision of psychological care within palliative care 157–159
National Palliative Care Registry 177

nirvana 129
nonmaleficence 20, 70, 92, 96, 110, 170, 172

opioids 67–68

pain 1, 7–11, 13, 15–16, 19–20, 27–28, 36–40, 43–45, 47–48, 61–81, 96, 105, 121–122, 124, 129, 144, 148, 154–155, 163, 171–172, 176–177; discomfort/distress/existential distress 11, 15, 19, 33, 40, 43, 47, 49, 50, 63, 65–67, 75–78, 99–100, 155–156, 158–162, 165, 179; management 8, 10, 16, 19, 36–37, 39, 119, 129
palliative care literacy 96–99, 101–102, 111, 172, 178
person-centred care/person-centred dementia care 58, 60–62, 79, 108
personhood 62, 71, 75
physician aid in dying *see* medical aid in dying
posttraumatic stress disorder (PTSD) 47–48
preferences, cultural diversity and 21, 71–72, 93, 110, 120, 123–124, 129
psychological distress 43, 47, 100, 149, 179; assessment of 159–160; interventions for 155–156, 158, 161–162

quality of life 1, 8, 11–14, 18, 23, 27, 37, 43, 58, 62, 70, 72, 74–75, 81, 91, 99–101, 148, 163, 179

reincarnation 128, 142, 144; Buddhist belief in 129; Hmong belief in 138; Sikh belief in 135
relaxation 44–45, 48, 77, 119, 161, 163, 176
resurrection 128, 142; Church of Jesus Christ of Latter-day Saints belief in 130; Islamic/Muslim belief in 133; Orthodox Judaism belief in 129
rural 12, 16, 20, 23–24, 26, 28, 49, 127, 171, 174

samsara (rebirth) 130
Saunders, Cicely 1, 61, 149
schizophrenia 33, 38–39
serious mental illness (SMI) 2–3, 32–50
shared decision making 60, 92, 94, 96–99, 103–104; by families 109–111; patient preference to not engage in 101
sitting shiva 134
socioemotional selectivity theory 3

spiritual/spirituality 1–2, 7–9, 14, 16, 18, 22, 27, 42, 47, 58, 60–61, 66, 91, 103, 121–122, 129–130, 141–143, 148–149, 156–157

strength and vulnerability integration model 3

stress processes 2–3, 13, 40, 46, 61, 71, 73, 76–79, 101, 143

stigma/stigmatization 8–9, 11–13, 19–20, 23–24, 26, 28, 33, 49, 74, 102, 127, 171

substance use disorders 11, 32, 35–37, 41–43, 45, 49

suicidal ideation 35–36, 38, 40–43, 104, 155, 162, 177–178

symptom management 16, 28, 35, 81, 109, 148–149, 156, 160, 163

Tai Chi 9

Task Force on Education for Psychologists in Palliative Care 178–179

technology 107, 175–176

therapeutic touch 75

'train the trainer' model 79